Robin Oben
3/28/08

OVERSIZE BOOK

INFLUENCE

INFLU

MARY-KATE OLSEN

EDITED BY
DEREK BLASBERG

UENCE

ASHLEY
OLSEN

DESIGNED BY

RODRIGO CORRAL

RAZORBILL · NEW YORK

Influence   NOV 0 5 2008

RAZORBILL

Published by the Penguin Group
Penguin Young Readers Group
345 Hudson Street, New York, New York 10014, U.S.A.
Penguin Group (USA) Inc., 375 Hudson Street, New York, New York 10014, U.S.A.
Penguin Group (Canada), 90 Eglinton Avenue East, Suite 700, Toronto, Ontario,
Canada M4P 2Y3 (a division of Pearson Penguin Canada Inc.)
Penguin Books Ltd, 80 Strand, London WC2R 0RL, England
Penguin Ireland, 25 St Stephen's Green, Dublin 2, Ireland (a division of Penguin
Books Ltd)
Penguin Group (Australia), 250 Camberwell Road, Camberwell, Victoria 3124,
Australia (a division of Pearson Australia Group Pty Ltd)
Penguin Books India Pvt Ltd, 11 Community Centre, Panchsheel Park,
New Delhi – 110 017, India
Penguin Group (NZ), 67 Apollo Drive, Rosedale, North Shore 0632, New Zealand
(a division of Pearson New Zealand Ltd.)

Penguin Books (South Africa) (Pty) Ltd, 24 Sturdee Avenue, Rosebank,
Johannesburg 2196, South Africa

Penguin Books Ltd, Registered Offices: 80 Strand, London WC2R 0RL, England

10 9 8 7 6 5 4 3 2 1

Library of Congress Cataloging-in-Publication Data is available

Manufactured in China

Dedicated
TO OUR FAMILY,
FRIENDS, AND THE PEOPLE
WHO HAVE INFLUENCED
US AND CONTINUE
TO INSPIRE US.

FOREWORD
· · · · · · · · · · · · · · · ·

The making of this book followed a simple routine: Mary-Kate and/or Ashley Olsen would pick me up and take me to a location where a scheduled interview would take place with a creative visionary. There may or may not be Starbucks waiting for me. En route, we would vacillate between excitement and nervousness over the impending interview, the thrill of meeting someone whose work the girls highly respected and getting the opportunity to pick that person's brain. We would predict what might happen: Would Karl Lagerfeld talk about his weight loss? (Yes.) Would Terry Richardson allow MK and Ashley to leave his studio without posing for his notorious lens? (No.) Is Diane von Furstenberg a feminine yet powerful force of nature? (Absolutely.) I would go over some sample topics of conversation, possible questions to ask, and facts about the designer or artist—often a waste of time to two prepared twenty-one-year-olds who had already read up on their subjects. Whether at a home, in the studio, or in a swanky restaurant, each of the twenty interviews was treated like a religious pilgrimage. We approached the creative visionaries with heads bowed, offering pleasantries, and then we'd follow these icons on verbal journeys, learning about their references and hopes, and reactions to the past and to the present.

As a writer who has conducted his fair share of interviews, I was impressed that two girls, so accustomed to being on one side of a recorder were so proficient at taking control of the other side. Ashley and Mary-Kate were genuinely excited about the people they were talking to; in some cases they were even starstruck. Because each person they spoke to encouraged them to chase their dreams—be it becoming an independent woman or hosting more dinner parties—their goal is to proliferate the ideals, thoughts, theories, and design processes of their interviewees with this book. I think we've succeeded.

I am indebted to Mary-Kate and Ashley Olsen—two self-educated, shrewdly careful, ferociously thoughtful, and sweetly endearing young women—for allowing me to particpate in this enriching literary voyage. (And for thinking to snap the Polaroids on the opposite page!) It was a joy bringing together friends and a group of people—from our generation and generations that are influencing ours—who are helping shape today's cultural landscape. The time I spent editing this book was exciting, informative, and enlightening. It was an influence I appreciated. And I hope you, the reader, have a similar experience.

—DEREK BLASBERG

CONTENTS

12
INTRODUCTION

14
PETER BEARD

20
ALEXANDRE DE BETAK

30
BOB COLACELLO

42
DAVID COLLINS

50
GEORGE CONDO

60
FRANCISCO COSTA

68
DIANE VON FURSTENBERG

76
JOHN GALLIANO

86
LAZARO HERNANDEZ & JACK McCOLLOUGH

96
LAUREN HUTTON

106

KARL LAGERFELD

120

PETER LINDBERGH

132

CHRISTIAN LOUBOUTIN

142

MARGHERITA MISSONI

150

ROBERT LEE MORRIS

198

JACK PIERSON

208

RICHARD PRINCE

220

TERRY RICHARDSON

234

GIAMBATTISTA VALLI

244

EVAN YURMAN

252

CONCLUSION

I photog
anythin
and poo
person
dried le
blood, l
pieces,
Mixing
animals
in the sa
beauty i
remind
New Yo
between
his wife
no secre
scene of
out with
Warhol,
lucky en
fashion
Beardia

2·29·08
DATE

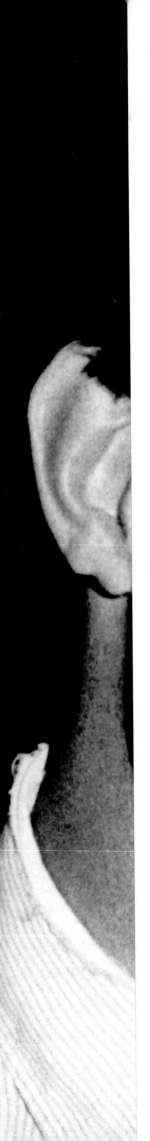

AO: Rumor has it that you were at Stella McCartney's show this morning.

PB: I know! I got up for it. It socked me back to life—now I've gone nearly two days with no sleep. I'm doing a very nice quiet project with Stella called "A Children's World"—African animals, African drawings on wallpaper, pajamas, curtains, pillowcases, stationary. So I wanted to meet her with all her kids—and they were all there.

AO: How did all that come about?

PB: It was a long process. Lots of ideas—all good. Best to leave it at that.

AO: Okay, let's start with the basics. How did you begin your career in the visual art world?

PB: I've always taken pictures. I've always had a camera. I've always thought of photography as life-thickening, life-enhancing, and something to hang onto. The camera is magic. It's my working memory. I wish I had one right now in fact. Anyway, I just stuck with that, collecting and accumulating one thing after another. By the way, I don't consider myself a photographer, but I do take pictures.

AO: What do you consider the difference between being a photographer and taking pictures?

PB: Well, I'm a collector, that's all—a parasite off subject matter. One thing I want to say before I forget it: everything I've learned is not from art school or photography school. No, I learned from people—like Richard Lindner, Josef Albers, Larry Rivers, Jonas Mekas, and most importantly (and most luckily) Francis Bacon, in his Reece Mews compost heap London world—and even Andy Warhol, and obviously from books and exhibitions.

AO: So how did you first start collecting?

PB: I'd say I started seriously (by luck), bumping into Richard Lindner at a Thanksgiving lunch in the east 80s, 1964. Do you know his work? He's an old master draftsman, very Germanic, very detailed, a natural teacher. He always said he knew too much. I have to say the best way to get started is through an authentic, individual, actual artist. He influenced me a lot in every way, and it helped me get started with a book, *The End of the Game* in 1965. I was in transit through London to or from Nairobi—I can't remember now—and somehow the artist Francis Bacon had gotten this book of mine. I was at one of his shows, going through the reception line, and embarrassingly introduced myself. He responded, "Whoa, Peter Beard!? *The End of the Game*?" And I just about dropped over because he'd seen it. So we had lots of meetings, and he took lots of things from the dead-elephant-die-off pictures and the general wildlife world, or what was left of it—the disappearing evolutionary realities of things in East Africa. I guess that's the best way to put it. I was just lucky to be in the fast-fading right place, the Pleistocene primitava. And I guess I was dependent on all the things around me.

AO: I think you told me that before— "a parasite in life."

PB: Exactly. That is more or less what photography is to me—skip the technicals.

AO: Speaking in terms of your fashion photography, do you consider yourself a parasite of the fashion world?

PB: No, not really, because I was never interested in the fashion part—the 'layered-look,' etc.

AO: But your take on it is so different from most of the other stuff out there. Why did you start taking fashion photos?

PB: I was in college—New Haven, Yale—and I thought, "God, there's a lot of beauty in that industry." I was just drawn to it as a way of meeting those extraordinary girls.

AO: I bet you just charmed the pants off of them.

PB: No, I was simply hanging in there gaping. I didn't care about those dresses; I cared about them.

AO: Well, something must have worked, as your work started popping up all over the magazines.

PB: When I was still in college, *Vogue* signed me under contract. I used to go from New Haven to New York to do sittings. That was my schooldays period with great subjects like Veruschka, Wilhelmina, Nena von Schlebrügge, Dorothea McGowan, Betsy Pickering, Erica Bower, Jean Shrimpton, Chirsta Fiedler, and that girl who married Ted Williams—it'll come to me in a minute—Dolores Wettach!

AO: Were you at Vogue when Diana Vreeland was there?

PB: Actually *before* with Jessica Daves and Priscilla Peck. But Diana Vreeland was tops. I was lucky to have experienced her stubborn individuality and the early period of real fashion and photography under Babs Simpson, Mary Kruming, and also Polly Mellon. Now I feel it's getting so, well, extreme, but one must say in the exceptional cases, extremely superior–evolution is working away in the urban world: Giorgio Sant'Angelo, Azzedine Alaia, John Galliano, and actually quite a few others. But I've been pretty far away.

AO: Okay, I'm going to switch gears for a second. Talk to me about the use of blood in your works. Is that your blood? That aspect of your work is slightly haunting.

PB: I don't use my own blood anymore. Of course I used to. That's all there was, but now I get it from restaurants, butchers like Schäller und Weber, or in Africa, where it's easy.

AO: Restaurants?! What kind of bottles do they come in?

PB: Well, right now in Cassis they're in water bottles. The other morning in a desperate thirst at about 5 a.m., I staggered into the kitchen and took a big swig out of one of those grape-juice-looking bottles in the icebox in the darkness of dawn—just a mouthful—and gagged it out in the knick of time. It looked so much like a cranberry or grape label. It was worse than it sounds because the older the blood gets, the better it is to work with. I'm doing the best blood things I've ever done now. It's slightly instinctive: you let the blood splatter on, let it half dry in its weird way, and then go to work with paper towels, followed by pen and ink.

AO: So what sort of animal does this blood come from?

PB: Oh I don't know. Pigs, crocs, whatever's in reach.

AO: When did you first say to yourself, "Blood would look great here"?

16

Special Delivery to Ashley
from Zarafeard & Peter(Beard) &

ZARA'S TALES &

@ new years 2005 ad NYC (too real jungle)

Perilous Escapades
in Equatorial
Africa

PETER BEARD

Hog Ranch | Nairobbery

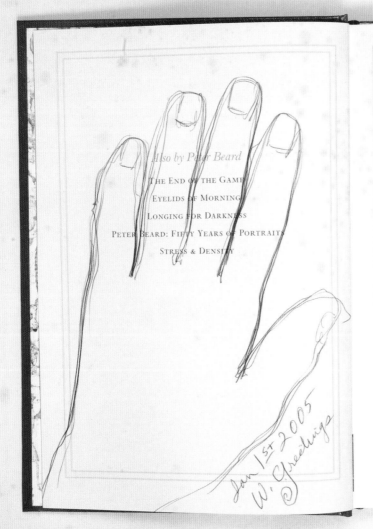

Also by Peter Beard

THE END OF THE GAME

EYELIDS OF MORNING

LONGING FOR DARKNESS

PETER BEARD: FIFTY YEARS OF PORTRAITS

STRESS & DENSITY

Jan 1st 2005
W. Greetings

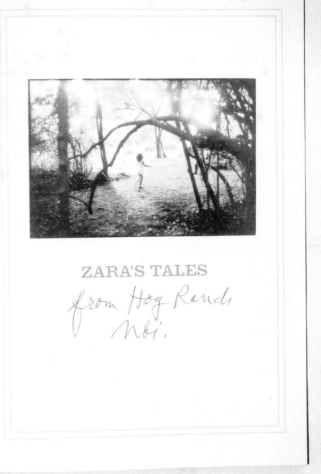

ZARA'S TALES

from Hog Ranch
Nbi.

PB: I used to do it a lot way back in school, being a bit of a scab picker. I had a good friend, Harry Deutsch, who gave me a great echoing Göethe quote: "Blut ist ein ganz Besonderer Saft." (Blood is a very magical juice.)

AO: Well, your friend was right. Your work is so beautiful.

PB: It's all a matter of how you blot it. It can be quite oriental—the figure-ground relationships. You've got to hold back and let it coagulate. It took me a while to figure that out. You have to control yourself. It usually looks pretty good when you first put it on, and then, eventually, you think, "Do I dare touch it?" Then when you hold back just long enough—before the blotting—and venture to go after it, it can be ten times better than ever. "Le hazard" is the greatest artist (Balzac).

AO: What are some of your memories of New York? Is the New York your daughter lives in different from the one you used to know?

PB: Well, there were organ-grinders and monkeys on the street, and the Third Avenue El (elevated train) made a lot of noise. There were trolley cars underneath with dressed-up-conductors: all that's gone. There were even open-at-the-top double-decker buses on Fifth Avenue. A ride cost a nickel.

Once upon a time there was a really rude conductor on the Third Avenue El. He was always getting into arguments and fights. One day, in a pushing match, an equally rude New Yorker fell over backwards and ended up under the trolley's wheel. Profusely bleeding, the passenger eventually died, and the conductor was convicted of manslaughter and sent to Sing Sing to be electrocuted. But strapped into the chair, shock after increasing shock, the poor guy stayed alive, and apparently there was this rule that if you could survive the first three or four shocks they had to let you go. You've heard about that right?

AO: No, I never have.

PB: Well, I think it was four or five times—they kept upping the voltage—and if you made it through, you were home free. So there were all these reporters in attendance, all gathered around . . .

AO: Wait, he lived through this?!?

PB: Well, let me finish. They all said to him, "It's amazing. You're the first person who's ever made it through

Zara's Tales by Peter Beard, Knopf 2004, from Ashley Olsen's collection.

every one of those heavy-duty shocks. How in the world did you do it?" And he answered, "*Well, I always was a poor conductor.*"

AO: God, I wish I was around for old New York.

PB: You missed it completely. But you know something, we've seen each other at some pretty other-worldly get-togethers, and things aren't as bad as they all say.

AO: True, but it's just very different.

PB: Yes, but now it's your time. I'm grateful every time I see you—both of you. I always see double after midnight, but in truth, you're great. Where did all those brains come from? I thought Hollywood was supposed to be *Dumbo* country?

AO: Oh yes, you're telling me. But we were born into Hollywood as it were. So funnily enough we learned how to navigate the terrain early and not care too much about it at all. It was just a job.

PB: I've never seen that show (*Full House*) or the other things you've done, so you'll have to catch me up. Some friends of mine were here yesterday. They knew all about you. You were their hero. Quite fantastic—not to mention that gang of motorcycle cameramen out there. What a horde! What a following!

AO: Between my sister and me, and I can tell you our lives are a much more interesting story than Full House.

PB: Well, you survived it beautifully.

AO: Yep, I somehow managed to come out on the other side. It's just a balance, making sure you're listening to the right people and getting out of town as much as possible—and staying true to yourself. How long are you in Paris?

PB: Paris is kind of like a contagious disease.

AO: It is—you never want to leave. It's one thing after another.

PB: I must confess after getting home at dawn and up again at 11:50 this morning to rush over here for our twelve o'clock appointment—hearing the church bells ringing across the street just as I came in at high noon—it's unbelievable; I am for once on time.

AO: Well, thank you for meeting me. I'm beginning to discover that food is one of the best catalysts for picking one's brains. Bob Colacello told my sister and me once that we have to start doing more dinner parties with more interesting people.

PB: That's how I met Bob Colacello. There used to be these weekly dinners at my cousin's room at the Algonquin Hotel almost every Thursday, 1971-72 (Suite 1205). And they were damn funny. Brigit Polk, Larry Rivers, Jonas Mekas, Andy Warhol, and Bob Colacello, the very night he first arrived in New York City from Florida, I think.

AO: I **wish I could have RSVP'd to that dinner party. You guys were all coming from that same . . .**

PB: . . . Creative-Play-Period. All video-taped, needless to say.

AO: You guys did something a little different. It's that sophisticated way of socializing that seems so special.

PB: Not to contradict, but we were way out of line all the time and working on one loony project after another—in my case escaping African primitava. Possibly, looking back, it may have been a better quality of life back then. Lately the importance of Warhol seems to add something to our goings-on.

AO: When did you marry your wife?

PB: December 22, 1986, on the edge of the cliff at Driftwood Cove (Montauk). You did meet her didn't you? She runs the whole show. I do just about nothing. By the way, I think you'd make an exceptionally efficient mother, Ashley. Maybe you should have a kid right now.

AO: Yes, sometimes I feel like a mother. I don't know what it is, but it's something I feel from time to time. I'm going to be a working mom for sure.

PB: You might want to observe Stella McCartney. She's literally a perfect mom—amazingly perfect.

AO: God that sounds disgusting!

PB: Well they're English so it's okay. With Americans it would probably be nauseating.

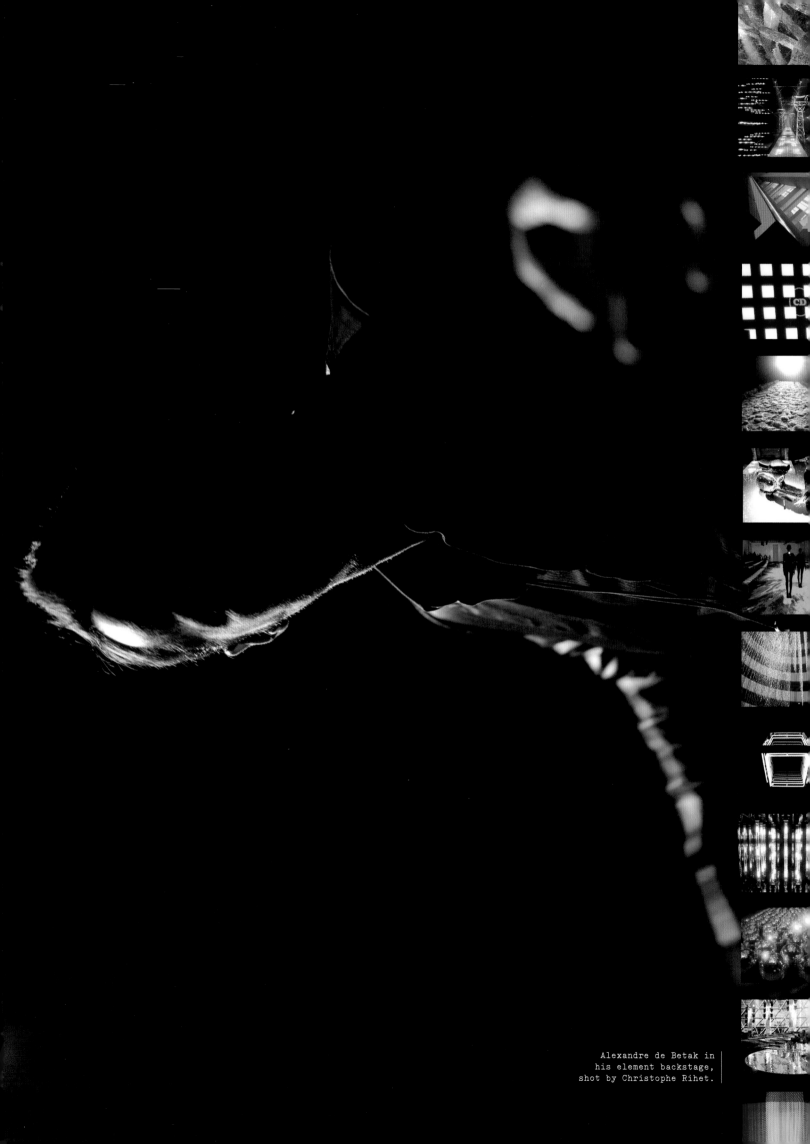

Alexandre de Betak in
his element backstage,
shot by Christophe Rihet.

The modern fashion industry revolves around a hectic, constantly shifting schedule: six official fashion weeks (two seasons in menswear, ready-to-wear, and couture throughout a single year) in over a dozen cities (the festivities in New York, Milan, Paris, and London have branched out to Los Angeles, São Paulo, Moscow, and Tokyo, among other cities), with as many as fifteen shows and presentations in a single day. A show lasts about thirteen minutes. That means a designer or fashion label has one fourth of one hour to sum up an entire season's thesis on a runway. Enter Alexandre de Betak, one of the industry's most renowned producers. He answers the long list of questions that must be asked before a fashion show: Is the lighting bright enough, the runway long enough, the music loud enough? Are there enough seats, and are the right people sitting where they're supposed to? And for his bigger clients, like Christian Dior and Victoria's Secret, the variables become even greater. While the clothes are the focus of the show, the production is paramount. And according to nearly everyone in the fashion industry, Alex has perfected the fashion event. He answers all the questions and pleases both the audience and the designer. I bumped into him in Paris, and though fashion week in that city is a most chaotic time for him—he does several shows, including John Galliano, Christian Dior, Hussein Chalayan, and Giambattista Valli—he set time aside for a chat with me at the Hôtel Costes.

3/1/08

DATE

HÔTEL COSTES IN PARIS

LOCATION

INTERVIEWED BY

мко: I wanted to be your intern for a while. I'm not kidding. I feel that creating different environments is an art in itself. And I think you do that really well.

AdB: Yes, I guess. More than that, more than the result itself of whatever you do, if you're creative, you apply it to anything you do.

мко: Where did you grow up?

AdB: I grew up in Paris. I left for New York about ten, twelve years ago, but I've basically come back here. Well, halfway. I've kept a foot in New York and a foot here.

мко: Were your parents creative people?

AdB: Not exactly. I grew up in the late '70s, with my mother and my grandparents—your typical Polish-Jewish grandparents—and an incredibly young mother who was kind of a bit out there. That probably helped, the balance of the two. My mother was a writer and a journalist, so she wasn't exactly creative, but she was surrounded by it. I think that creativity is not something you calculate. It sounds very pretentious to talk about it like that, but I ultimately think that if you're creative, you can apply it to millions of different things; it doesn't really matter what you ultimately do with it. And today's creativity, because of the pace people create for the ones who do anything, has to be multitalented and multitasked. Like, you have to do everything, not just fashion shows or clothes or photographs or films or whatever. Hopefully, if you have a point of view of your own, it can be applied to any story that needs to be told in an unusual way, and then it can be told through any method.

мко: Did you ever intern for someone? Like a set designer or an interior decorator?

AdB: No, actually, I never worked for anyone but myself. I started doing pictures when I was a kid, literally when I was really young.

мко: You were into photography?

AdB: Yes, photography. And when I was in school I was traveling and I was doing pictures for . . . you know Berlitz? The travel guides? I don't know how I fell into that, but I did. And so when I'd go on holidays, I'd take pictures, and I remember going to Chicago, Canada. I was completely passionate about taking pictures. And then I met a designer in the late '80s—and this was a trendy moment in Spain when Madrid just exploded—and that's how I started. First with pictures, and then I met a designer I really loved and I started doing her PR. I had no idea what I was doing, exactly.

мко: It's good experience, though.

AdB: Yes. I had no idea of anything. I can remember that I literally started in this business by going down to my grandmother's news agent and spending the day just writing the names at the top of the mastheads of every magazine. I would only take the first two names, and then the phone number at the bottom of the page. So it was like, "*Vogue,* Anna Wintour." And then I would just pick up the phone and call them. Literally. I had no clue. And the truth is that it worked on a couple of them. When I think back it's funny, because now I see the power and the influence these people have. A few came to my home. I remember I was living in a little studio on the ninth floor, and at the time the Italian *Vogue* editor-in-chief came out of the blue.

мко: And that's how you got started.

AdB: I never interned because I basically opened an office right away, first in my studio, then in a little apartment I turned into a pretty big office. And then after five years, I got really bored of doing PR.

мко: And then you started doing shows for the brands that you were representing?

AdB: Yes. My first shows were for the designer in Madrid, and then, here in Paris, I had my first big production for a store opening, which was really fun. And that was about fifteen years ago. That first production from the store opening was good—we did a fashion fun fair kind of thing. There were little stands with games—so funny—that were all fashion-based. Like normal games, but just based on fashion. Like you would have a little carousel with little girls wearing clothes—

мко: Instead of horses

AdB: Yes, exactly, and then the people watching the show were painted little balls, like we did Suzy [Menkes]'s hair, and Anna [Wintour]'s, and André [Leon Talley]'s. There was a circus scene and puppets for kids. It was really hysterical. And that's pretty much how I started doing what I do today.

мко: Do you always work with the same team?

AdB: Yes, I have a very steady team. And most of them have been with me for ten years.

мко: Have you ever done other things, perhaps a film or wedding?

AdB: No, I've never done films, but I've been asked a million times. The reason is that I wouldn't even know what position to have in a film. What's really great about doing something in fashion is that it's a very short moment, it's completely live, and you hardly have enough time to see, which is good and bad at the same time. It can be frustrating, but the pace is so crazy and the adrenaline is on the edge. Ultimately when you're in my position you pretty much control everything, so you're like the director, the producer, the set guy, the art director. A film set feels very diluted to me, because there're so many people. I would love to do film one day, though.

мко: Thinking of someone like Tim Burton and his films— he has his own singular vision.

AdB: I admire him a lot, to be honest. Wes Anderson is one of my favorite directors because his vision is incredibly clear. As a spectator, too, when you watch the movie you know exactly what the vision is. But on the other hand, when you put yourself in his shoes, the small subtleties must be so hard to delegate to other people. It's quite brilliant that he gets to it, because you know it takes so many people—to find a way to make other people understand your subtleties and then have them communicate it back. The luck of what I do is that it's the same on a much smaller scale—you end up doing it yourself, which makes it easier than to have so many people doing your subtleties.

Snapshots of several of Alex's projects, including Christian Dior, Donna Karan, and John Galliano fashion shows; large-scale charity benefits around the world.

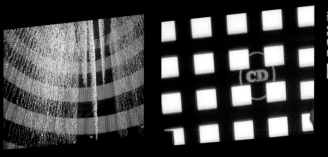
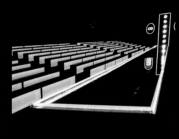

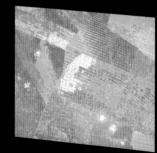

MKO: You're the director, in a way.

AdB: Yes, absolutely, but on such a smaller scale. So movies I haven't done yet. And weddings? I've never wanted to get into them, not even my own, right? I've never gotten married. I couldn't.

MKO: But I was thinking you could probably create the most beautiful spaces. I'm not planning on getting married either, but if I were ever to have a wedding I would want you to do it. I'm not great at communicating my vision—I think I use fragments instead of full sentences. Or when I try to explain a fabric and someone brings it back to me and it's wrong, I have to go pull a swatch from my curtain because they don't understand. But you probably have a team for that.

AdB: Yes, I have a brilliant team and you seem brilliant, and that makes your ideas come to life. But don't get me wrong—you'll still be pulling swatches off your curtains forever. That's great, because you're very hands-on with every part of the show, which is another great thing in comparison to other mediums like movies or theater.

MKO: Do you have a favorite show you've done? Can you remember all of them?

AdB: I do remember all of them, but no, I couldn't just pick one. That would be impossible. I've had a few most memorable ones, though.

MKO: For a good reason or a bad reason?

AdB: For good reasons and bad, but mostly good. I don't think I could have one favorite show, because one thing that is most brilliant about fashion is the pace of it. [The shows are] short-lived, but what's good about it is you do many of them, and it keeps you going all the time. I've done hundreds of shows in my life, so some stick in your head more than others. But what's really great is to keep going. I mean, the first Hussein Chalayan show I did was the story of chadors—basically we did something on the Muslim chador and we reversed the stage. I designed the stage so the chador was going up, and it was basically five girls, the first one in a full one, the second girl's came to about the knee, the third one came to about the waist and she was naked below, the fourth one came to here and she was completely naked, and finally there was only the mask left. And you can imagine the picture of a full chador to a completely naked girl, crudely. It was so moving.

MKO: Yes, it sounds like an unforgettable moment in fashion.

AdB: Yes. A moment. That was something I'll always remember. And then a lot of shows with John Galliano and Dior were quite amazing, like last summer's Dior couture show. And Victoria's Secret I've done for years.

MKO: Victoria's Secret is a big production.

AdB: You're not kidding. We had a PETA moment at one show— a couple of girls jumped on stage with a banner saying, "Giselle something" and started running behind Giselle. Giselle just started walking really fast down the runway with these girls running behind her. And Giselle walking so sexily and these girls with posters huffing behind her—it was hysterical. There are moments like that.

MKO: Has anything gone completely wrong?

AdB: Well, on that show in particular, it was very complicated. We had flying angels, the airplanes—it was in the New York Armory—that were meant to fly incredibly fast and very close to each other. It's all computerized and it's a sick program, so we spent days rehearsing, to make sure they didn't hit each other. But you didn't know, something could have gone wrong. The show was basically one big computer program, but when these PETA people intercepted we had to backtrack the program, which we had never done before. So not everything was starting at the same time— I didn't know what was going to happen. Nothing went wrong, but it could have been a disaster.

MKO: Do you ever have moments where you don't feel inspired? Where you have no idea where to start?

AdB: Oh yes, sure. It's like when people ask me why I'm not more stressed on the day of a show. Well, I have no reasons to stress that day—I stress massively all the days before. I basically get a brief, and then I'm supposed to create something out of the brief. Sometimes you're inspired, but other times you're not, and then I have to bring everything back to the designer or the client.

MKO: And that's what's stressful?

AdB: Yes, there's no formula, no way out of it. I think sometimes the only way out of it is to get really close to your deadline, and then you have no choice and you've got to work something out. Or it's the other way around, when you have an instant idea, and that one that formed in a second is the one you end up doing.

MKO: What's a brief like? What do they say to you?

AdB: There's not two the same. When I work for John Galliano, John sometime gives two words, like *sex* and *red,* or *danger* and *black.*

MKO: Does he show you the collection before?

AdB: This is way before that. Before we propose a venue, an idea, an environment—the collection's not even started. Especially for couture. In most cases they show me nothing when I get a brief. And then later down the road I see sketches. The clothes I see at the very end. When I started working for John Galliano we started doing more modern shows; they were more directed and the energy was concentrated and people could really, really understand John's ideas in a more modern setting. So for years the designs of mirrors, the designs of lights everywhere, and now we're changing it again. And for Hussein Chalayan I will take his words, pull from my inspirations as well—which can be anything, really—and it's processed so much that ultimately you never see anything left of it. It's got to be very clear in the way you receive it, even if it's not clear what the inspiration is, basically. But no, a brief means nothing. Sometimes I get nothing, and sometimes—and this can be even worse—you get way too much. They try and do it for you, laying every scene. They want a room like this, it should be like that, like that—and they go so far into the detail that you're lost. So it's a weird thing. In a way, the less the

More of Alex's projects, including several of his design projects, and fashion shows for Christian Dior, Hussein Chalayan, Jil Sander, and John Galliano.

better. The more trust and confidence you give them the better you'll be.

MKO: Do you ever stop? Do you ever take vacations?

AdB: Yes, I take vacations—but I never really stop, honestly. The mind never stops. I'm sure you understand. Actually, I take a lot of vacations compared to most Americans. It's the French side of me. You know, I take a full month in August like all French and Mediterranean people, but the truth is the mind never stops. And the fashion shows are one thing, but I also do events in the night world, and art—designing at restaurants and clubs and hotels and light installations and furniture.

MKO: You do furniture?

AdB: Yes. I do furniture as well. I do weird stuff. I did a disco Vespa. I do a lot of disco stuff, like a '60s Vespa but all turned into a disco ball, covered in thousands of mirrors.

MKO: Do you collect furniture?

AdB: I don't really collect—I don't like the word *collect*, to be honest.

MKO: Buy.

AdB: I do buy. Not furniture. I buy things that make light or move. I'm quite light-obsessed, I have to admit. So I buy a lot of lights, or light sculptures, or kinetic '70s sculpture.

MKO: I have to talk to you about stores to go to. I love furniture and sculpture. Or we should just go with you.

AdB: Ah, yes. But tomorrow I am going to ski in the south of France for a few days. My destinations are more predictable in a way than yours, because fashion is more planned. It used to be only New York, Milan, and Paris. Now it's that, plus Shanghai and Tokyo and Beijing and Florence and Venice and Rome and Mumbai and you name it. I mean, Moscow? It's quite crazy, actually. And then I'm going to Punta Cana for two days, well, for work, actually. I'm doing environmental stuff.

MKO: You mean green, environmental events?

AdB: Yes. I'm very interested in helping to reverse some of the damage.

MKO: Do you drive a Prius?

AdB: Ha! No, I don't drive a Prius. I drive a Smart car or a Vespa. I'm actually going to Punta Cana to have a brainstorm; the idea is to basically use people like us to try and help. What I want to do is to use our skills—and that world we're in—to make green glamorous.

MKO: Yes, I think you can make the green movement glamorous. That would be a great thing. I started using green lightbulbs, but the color is very harsh. I would rather use candles than that lightbulb.

AdB: I know what you mean. If it were a bad light, I wouldn't have been able to use it either. Light is very important to me.

MKO: Candles I love. The lighting is better. Or at least it's dimmer. Everything is better when dimmed!

AdB: Yes, I'm the same. I want to do an organic project here. America's quite ahead of us on this subject; in Europe some people consider environmental considerations as very kind of hippie, bohemian, granola-y—not very sexy. In America you already have a lot of people into it. Here, I want to help make it a little more glamorous and shiny and the opposite of what women think it is.

MKO: Well, that's great. Do you like doing the other projects more than production?

AdB: Well, yes and no. I love fashion. Love. But I can't take fashion every day of my life. However good it is, I need something more . . .

MKO: Fulfilling.

AdB: So in order to have something to turn to from the fashion world, you have to go to many other places and fulfill yourself. I enjoy everything that I do, but I also think I enjoy the mixture of the two in other worlds. I design installations and things, but there's always a sparkle and fashion in it. There's a bit of my fashion experience and background in everything that I do, and vice versa. I'm sure a hundred years ago the speed of information was obviously slower and not globalized; now the world is one big thing and everything is sped up. People get bored too quickly. It's sad, because we're jaded. Even if we didn't want to be, we'd still be jaded because of the speed at which we receive and get bored by information.

MKO: In your environment is there one thing you like to be surrounded by? Like in your home—is there something you feel you always need to be surrounded by?

AdB: Yes and no. Earlier in my life I would have said my books, but not today. I have thousands and thousands of books of inspiration, about installation art and design and fashion and whatever. And the truth is, I hardly ever have the time to dig into them now, because I can do it online wherever I am. The only tool I really need is a laptop and the other tool is a plane. I think ultimately, and this will sound very cheesy, the only thing I need to be is interested, in love, like everybody else. And my two little kids, too.

MKO: I met them yesterday, and they're so cute. I bet they're little troublemakers.

AdB: They are little troublemakers. It's funny, talking about kids— I think they're reaching such a pace of . . . of *life*. Which is great, it's like an addiction, probably the most addictive ever. But I wonder what the next generation of people like us will do—we probably have pushed it so far that they'll want everything to be slow. They'll want everything to be the exact opposite: fewer toys, fewer houses, fewer planes. I think they'll take a boat to get to New York, not the Concorde. They'll take a week to get there, take a train to China. But you know what, you always feel—because everybody knows about everything, which again wasn't the case in previous generations—we feel everything and we want to be everywhere. You can't hide, really.

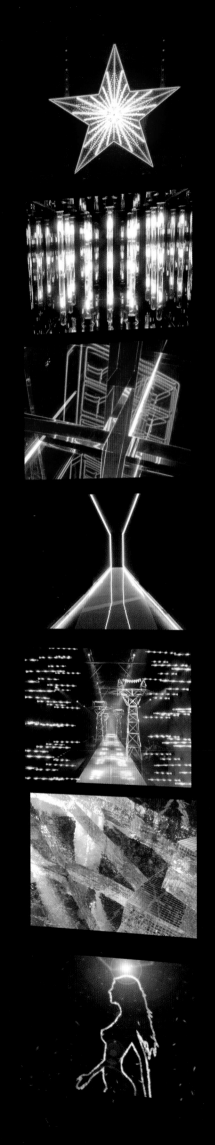

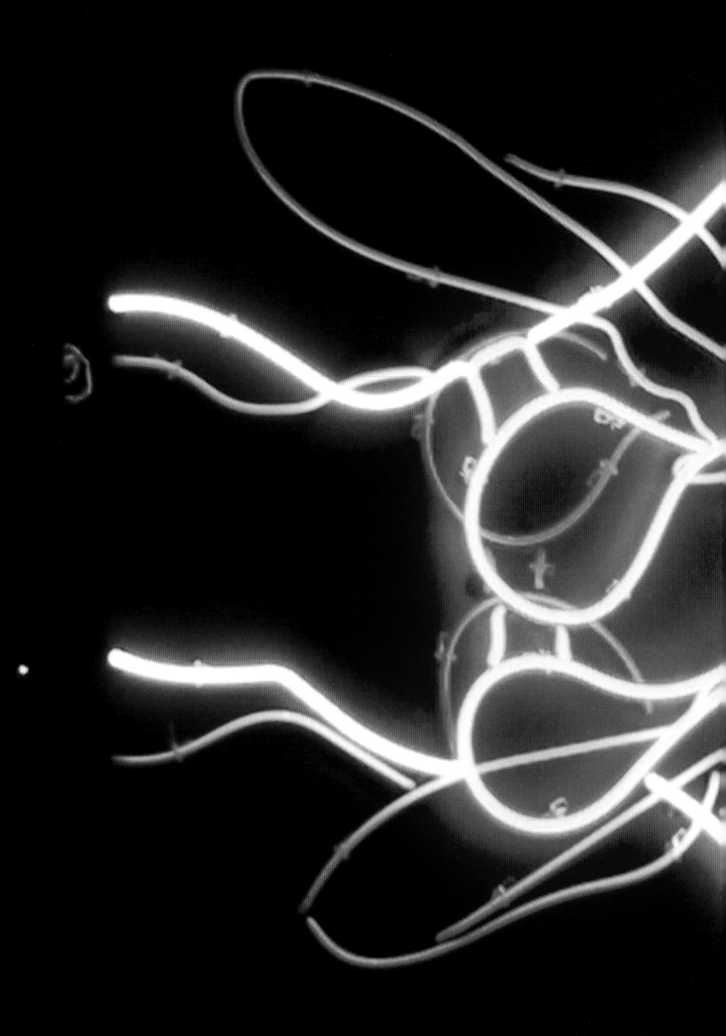

Bob Colacello was the editor of *Interview* magazine from 1971 until 1983, when he moved to *Vanity Fair*, and he has been a *Vanity Fair* special correspondent since 1993. He has profiled notables from Naomi Campbell to Ivana Trump to King Constantine of Greece. Aside from his literary prowess—which he has proven in both magazine and novel form—Bob is a living, breathing archive of a time that both of us reminisce about often, when society queens had Andy Warhol and Jean-Michel Basquiat over for catered lunches, when Liza Minelli danced on Halston's kitchen table, when Studio 54 was pumping with electro tunes and scantily clad beauties. He's a gregarious man, who, when we cold-called him to talk about his life and career, invited us to his Upper East Side apartment to look at his walls of Warhol prints and personal photos from the days of the Factory, when he was Warhol's right-hand man, coconspirator, and confidant. We sat in his quaint living room—with snapshots of Carolina Herrera on one table and pictures of the progeny of European royalty on another—and talked about parties and posses gone by. He was an inspiration to us; he reminded us of the creative pursuits the world has to offer. He told us to have our own dinner parties, to look at art seriously and ignore the tabloids, and to build our own Factory of creative, productive minds. And he's right.

2/3/08   NEW YORK CITY
DATE   LOCATION   INTERVIEWED BY

MKO: Where does your story begin, Bob?

AO: And start from the very beginning.

BC: I went to Georgetown's School of Foreign Service in 1965, and I thought I wanted to be a diplomat, until I got caught up in the whole late-'60s countercultural movement. That's when I became totally fascinated with film, especially the European films—Pasolini and Bertolucci, and Godard, Truffaut, Resnais, all the French and Italians. But I also loved Andy Warhol's *Chelsea Girls,* which came to Washington, D.C., in 1967. There was one art theater, and it played for weeks and weeks. I saw it about five times. Anyway, I decided I wanted to become a filmmaker, so when I graduated Georgetown I went to Columbia University's graduate school to study film history and filmmaking. The film criticism professor was named Andrew Sarris, who in those days was the critic for the *Village Voice,* which was like *the* paper back then. We had to review a film a week as homework, and he would publish some of the reviews in the *Voice* if they were any good. He published a review I wrote of Andy Warhol's *Trash,* which I said was a masterpiece along the lines of *Our Lady of the Flowers,* that it was very Catholic in the Mary Magdalene sense of Catholicism by which anybody could be redeemed. I wrote that Andy was redeeming these junkies and transvestites and hustlers—the next thing I knew, I got a phone call from Paul Morrissey, who directed the film. He said that Andy had read my review and they loved it. He asked, "How did you know we were all Catholics at the Factory?" And then he said Andy wanted to meet me, that they had just started a magazine called *Interview,* and maybe I could write for it. I was living with my parents at that time, so I hung up and said to my mother and father—we were having dinner around the kitchen table—"You won't believe this: Andy Warhol wants to meet me."

AO: Were they excited?

BC: No, my father was like, "That creep! The one who makes those X-rated movies?" But of course the next day I couldn't wait to get out of class and take the subway down from Columbia to Union Square. So I started doing some reviews for them.

MKO: Within the first year?

BC: Well, the magazine started in 1969. When I began, they had this strange guy as editor named Soren Agenoux—he thought he was an ingénue but he was actually a forty-five-year-old hippie with a little ponytail. This Factory—the second of Warhol's four Factories—was on the sixth floor of 33 Union Square West, but *Interview* had this tiny closet of an office on the tenth floor. One day I went up there to hand in an assignment and it was all locked up, so I went down to the sixth floor and Andy was sitting beyond this little foyer. (There was a steel bulletproof door, because that's where Andy had been shot, and there was a little window you could look through.) Andy was sitting at the reception desk, and when I pressed the bell, he buzzed me in. He said, "Oh, hi. Oh, we had to fire Soren and you should talk to Paul, Paul wants to talk to you." So I went to talk to Paul Morrissey, and he told me that Soren was fired, "We think you should be editor." I was still at Columbia and hadn't edited anything. He said, "Oh, it's really easy. You go to this hippie magazine, and they do all the layouts. And then you go to this printer in Chinatown." But I was like, "What do you put in the magazine?" He said, "We'll pay you forty dollars a week. It's a part-time job; you can still go to Columbia, and I'm sure they'll give you credits for working for us." I thought about it and came back the next day with a new deal: fifty dollars a week, and Glenn O'Brien, who had gone to school with me at Georgetown and Columbia, could be my assistant at forty dollars a week, with Glenn's wife, Judy, as our first intern. They agreed and we were a staff of three.

MKO: What was *Interview* like then?

BC: We printed five thousand copies every other month, give or take, at this terrible printer in Chinatown where I'd be shouting, "Less ink! Less ink!" We'd give them out for free at places like the Museum of Modern Art, and we had about three hundred, four hundred subscribers. It was like learning on the job—but that was the great thing about Andy. He loved taking young people and putting them to work, and it was very clever on his part, because it didn't cost him much, and things were more creative because we really didn't know what we were doing. We had guidance from Andy and Paul Morrissey and Fred Hughes, but the bosses basically let us do our thing. We kind of just invented things that seemed so startling at the time, like Art Deco type—nobody had seen Art Deco type, but Andy was into collecting Art Deco, so we did Art Deco type! And then every other magazine copied it. Soon after I was hired, Andy told me that they were going to Europe for the Venice Film Festival, and I thought, "Oh great, now we don't have anyone to ask a question to." But on his way out Paul handed me this brown paper envelope and said, "Just put one of these photos on every page." They were all stills from Rita Hayworth movies in the '40s, but the magazine was full of reviews of avant-garde European movies. You have to listen to the boss, though, so we put a Rita Hayworth photo—from *Gilda* and all—on every page. I remember everyone said, "Oh my God, this is like a revolution in magazines—the photos don't go with the stories. How brilliant!" We did an Elvis Presley special issue soon after, which was very popular because nostalgia was not yet a big deal in those days. That whole nostalgic movement of watching old Hollywood movies and collecting old Hollywood stills—none of that really existed yet. But then as the seventies went on, more and more people got into Art Deco and '50s furniture and the whole thing. To use your word, we had this huge influence, even though we were so tiny. All the editors at *Vogue* and *Bazaar* and *Time* and *Newsweek*—they all thought if Andy's onto something, they should watch it too.

AO: What was it like at the Factory? Tell me about the scene.

BC: I got there after Andy was shot. He was shot in 1968 by Valerie Solanas, so it was very different than it had been in the '60s, because Andy was frightened. If he saw a homeless person he would cross the street or duck into a shop. Valerie Solanas got three years in a mental institution, and when she got out she actually started calling for Andy. We'd hang up. Then Joe Dallesandro, who was like the Factory bodyguard between starring in the movies, would rush Andy downstairs, we'd get him in a taxi, and Andy would go home. When I started there, they were making *Women in Revolt* with Holly Woodlawn, Candy Darling, and Jackie Curtis. Candy was like the very well-behaved transvestite who wanted to marry someone rich and live on Park Avenue, but Holly and Jackie were both a little crazy. Holly would show up at the Factory and start screaming at Andy and Paul that they were making a fortune

A snapshot of Bob in Venice
when he was the editor
of *Interview*.
PHOTOGRAPH © BOB COLACELLO.

off her. They used to pay the *superstars* like twenty-five or fifty dollars a day to shoot these movies, and then those stars would read in the paper that *Trash* took in three million and they'd be all upset. But Andy was trying very hard then to turn it into a business, to take it to the next step, in a way. He hadn't been painting for several years. In 1965, when conceptual art was really ascendant, Andy decided he was going to announce painting was dead. After he was shot he really didn't have the energy to paint much, and he started doing commissioned portraits because they were easy to do. They were small, rich people would commission him, and it was a way to make quite a lot of money to finance *Interview* and the movies.

AO: So this Factory was tamer?

BC: Pat Hackett, Vincent Freemont, Jed Johnson, Glenn O'Brien, myself—we were all from more middle-class backgrounds, we all went to college. So Andy would say sometimes, "Oh, you kids are so boring, you're not creative like the speed freaks," and we'd be like, "Well, then, hire the speed freaks again." Little by little, of course, by hanging around the Factory we all became crazier, shall we say. But it was a very creative place because Andy's whole motto was: Make it different, make it modern, make it new—and do it cheaply. When you didn't have a whole lot of money to spend, you had to go out and discover new photographers. Every Wednesday was portfolio day, and any photographer could come up and show their work to the art director and the managing editor. This was a little later in the '70s. Bruce Weber, David Seidner, Robert Mapplethorpe, Christopher Makos—*Interview* was the first magazine that really published their work, or started working with them early in their careers.

MKO: How did all these people come into Andy's life? How did the team at *Interview* get so many of that era's people involved?

BC: In 1975 we moved to 860 Broadway, which was much bigger. The chairman of the company that had been there before had built himself this beautiful wood-paneled office, which we used as our dining room. We used to have a mix of people over for lunch; basically, the idea was to sell portraits and sell ads for *Interview* but to disguise it as a social situation. Andy liked to have people around, so we would have, like, invited you two if you were in town. The two of you would have loved it. We'd invite models, young artists, socialites, but there was always the "victim." That was the person whose portrait we were trying to get, or the advertiser we were hoping would give us a twelve-month contract. I bet they gave us ads sometimes just so they could be sure they'd be invited to lunch again. The lunches would go on until four or five in the afternoon, and Andy would wander off into the back room, where he had his studio, where he would paint when he started painting again. He became very prolific again in the mid-'70s. He did the Mao series, the Hammer and Sickles, the Drag Queens, the Skulls. We didn't take it that seriously: Oh, Andy's churning out more paintings.

MKO: But you were more of a fan of his movies than his artwork?

BC: I liked his art before I ever met him. He was painting stuff as a kid growing up in the suburbs that I was interested in: Elvis, Marilyn. He was painting the stuff that young people were interested in. Pop Art. I think he broadened the audience for art in general.

AO: How do you think it's changed—the art scene, the art world?

BC: Back then, in the Middle Ages, the art world was a pretty small scene. You pretty much knew everybody. There were a certain number of artists, and there were a much smaller number of collectors; it was like a village almost. And then you'd go to Germany, or Italy, and there was a bit of a scene there. But really, you were totally centered in New York. Now it's this huge thing. I think young people are probably more interested in art today than in movies or music. Going to art fairs is the thing to do. There was nothing like Miami Art Basel before—fifty thousand people showing up. And there wasn't as much of a connection between the fashion world and the art world. Andy really pioneered that, because he came out of the fashion world. He was really criticized by the art world for hanging out with Halston and Calvin and Diane von Furstenberg and Yves Saint Laurent and Karl Lagerfeld. The critics thought this was proof that Andy had never really left the fashion world, and that he was still a kind of illustrator. And then when he started doing society portraits, people said he was totally frivolous. Jasper Johns and Lichtenstein and Rauschenberg, they were nice to Andy—well, Johns wasn't so nice—but they all thought Andy was like,

Bob clowning around with
Andy Warhol and Paul Weiss
PHOTOGRAPH BY PAUL
WEISS FROM THE "AMERICAN
BEAUTIES SERIES"

"Oh, sweet little Andy, he's always going to clubs and fashion shows." No other artist went to fashion shows in the '70s. That's why I think *Interview* was so influential in a way, because it was the first magazine to put art with fashion and music and politics. We always thought *People* magazine was an outgrowth of *Interview,* and certainly *W* was. The art world now is so commercial and the amount of money involved—it's ridiculous. A Warhol portrait was $25,000, which seemed like a lot of money at the time, but now a commissioned portrait will go for $2 million.

MKO: Every time I look at my auction books I get sick to my stomach for that very reason!

BC: So do you both collect?

AO: She collects more than I do.

BC: Who do you collect?

MKO: Warhol, Basquiat, Araki, Thomas Ruff, Helmut Newton . . .

BC: I remember when we put Jodie Foster on the cover of *Interview*—she was about twelve or something—and she was collecting prints already. Andy thought that was so great that someone so young would already be collecting, and that it was so smart.

AO: There are a lot of good ways to invest your money, but art is a great one. If you know what you're doing, that is.

MKO: And what a great thing to be surrounded by.

AO: Do you think that fashion and art are related? You'd mentioned the blending of art and fashion in Warhol's time, and that the fashion industry wasn't exactly celebrated by the art world then. Is it okay now for artists, like Richard Prince and Murakami, who did projects with Louis Vuitton and Levi's, to do fashion projects? Are they delegitimized?

BC: Now I think people understand it. First of all, fashion is taken more seriously and seen as more creative than it used to be. People used to go the couture and worship Balenciaga—that was always seen as creative—but the general public was dismissive. And certainly intellectuals were dismissive. Now it's almost like you don't even have a high culture any more. It's almost like everything's popular culture and fashion's part of popular culture and it's all okay.

MKO: So has fashion lost some of its glamour? Some of its excitement and romance?

BC: I don't think fashion is as glamorous— that's why I think kids are more into art. I hadn't been to a couture show in seven or eight years, and then [*Vanity Fair* editor] Graydon Carter asked me to go last January. I went to Dior, which was an incredible production: It was a Japanese kabuki collection and it was incredible just in the way it was lit, the way it was staged; it was like theater. And then Chanel. Karl is so clever; he's the only one who actually makes clothes you could see people nineteen to ninety actually wearing. But what struck me was the lack of these wonderful ladies. The couture world used to be very small, and the front row at Saint Laurent or Chanel would be filled with a very particular type of sophisticated woman—Marie-Hélène de Rothschild, Sao Schlumberger, and so on. Each one of these women had their own style, and they bought the clothes instead of borrowing them. Now it is like—no offense—so-called celebrities and tons of press. It is no longer like the couture, which was a small, exclusive little world. Andy used to go because it was a great place to get portrait commissions. And then when I got to *Vanity Fair,* I convinced Tina Brown to let me

go because it was a great place to get all the gossip and come up with stories to write. But that's changed; at the risk of sounding like an old person, everything's gotten too big. It's like traveling. You don't want to be an elitist, but it was so nice when not that many people traveled. And I don't know, everything's so accessible. I don't even e-mail, but now people are texting while you're at dinner. I guess it's great in a way.

AO: It's great but it's awful.

BC: I mean, I don't really want to watch movies or listen to music on my cell phone when I'm out to dinner. I don't need to have my radio and VCR traveling with me. I don't know if this is really a good thing. We've been going in this direction for so long—that's what Andy foresaw when he said in the future everybody will be famous for fifteen minutes. The total media takeover of the world. We've become a society in which we spend so much time looking at ourselves and entertaining ourselves that we don't really produce very much anymore. After airplanes, our number two American export is entertainment. I don't know if this is really healthy for a society.

AO: Well, look at our society. It's really hard not to think that if we were focusing on the right things, and everything wasn't so accessible, then there would be a little bit more balance.

BC: And I think everything gets dumbed down to appeal to the masses. Diana Vreeland used to go over *Interview* with me every month; she had been fired at *Vogue* just about when we started *Interview*, so she had all this editorial energy and no place to put it. She would say, "What's this horrible photo? You call that photography?" I would say, "Diana, people like that sort of thing." And she would say, "How many times have I told you—your job as editor is not to give people what they want. It's to give people what they don't know they want yet!"

MKO: **She was a genius.**

BC: Well, there are not many people doing that in any of the creative areas. Real creativity is being true to yourself and getting people to go with you. That's influence. But today everything is from the bottom up because it's so unfashionable and politically incorrect to say that you actually believe in quality, or that you believe some ideas are superior to others. *Elitism* has become a bad word, and I think it can be bad if it's just inherited. But if elitism is based on accomplishment and creativity and productivity, then I think it's a good thing. A lot of colleges don't have requirements, they don't have grades, because someone's feelings will be hurt if they get a B instead of an A. Well, we used to work really hard to get A's, and certainly my generation did a lot of partying, but still, as a student, you took your studying seriously.

MKO: **Did you maintain your work ethic when you graduated and started working for Andy Warhol?**

BC: I don't consider myself a typical journalist; editing *Interview* was like editing the school newspaper—we ran the tape back, basically. People could say what they wanted, and we wouldn't slant it in any way. Andy would have me sit in on most of his interviews, and I saw how dumb and intrusive and obnoxious many reporters could be. I mean, the first question they would ask was, "Are you gay?" Or, "Are you a millionaire?" And then he would have his stock answers: "Oh gee, sex is so much work," or, pointing down to his paint-splattered cowboy boots, "Well, look at my shoes." Why didn't they ask that question at the end of the interview, once they've relaxed him and become friendly? Or find a nicer way to bring it up—like, say, "You're

one of the first filmmakers to really make films about homosexuality. Why is that?"

AO: **It's all about exploitation. But in a way I'm happy to know that there was an element of that back then, too. Because today, that's such a major part of our news organizations.**

BC: It's sensationalism. People say that's what sells, but again, I believe that if you give people something more interesting, they will respond to it. I mostly profile well-known, successful people. I don't do movie people so much, because they're so controlled by their public relations people that you really can't get to the human being, and that's what my job is. What I like to do is take a name and make it into a human being, so that the reader can come away having a feeling for what that person is like. That involves a lot of research. You do have to spend time with the person. That doesn't mean it's a puff piece, but that doesn't mean it's a hatchet job either. There are some people who deserve hatchet pieces, but most don't. Most of us have our pluses and minuses and we've had ups and downs in our lives. And if there's a scandal, you have to address it and ask those questions. But as my grandmother always used to say, "It's not so much what you say, it's the way you say it." I just think for the most part that the press just wants to attack and get that counterattack, and it all becomes . . . Well, you guys know what that's like.

MKO: **Oh yes, we're familiar with that concept.**

BC: I had dinner with a friend in California before I met you guys, and she was saying that the two of you are among the very few celebrities that have a style of your own, and an influence. But when you look at Britney Spears and Paris Hilton, the way they dress and the influence that it has on young girls . . . If I had a teenage daughter, I think I'd be going crazy.

AO: **Well, it's really scary to think about having kids. I love kids—I know I'm young, but I want kids more than anything—but that's in the back of my mind. How do you protect someone from the visuals of it? Just the visuals. You don't even really need to read anything. It's horrifying.**

BC: And with computers, with the Internet, they could be in their rooms looking at anything. I mean, when I was young,

just to buy a porn magazine was a major production. Where to hide it when you got home? I think that, in a way, we're looking at the fall of the Roman Empire.

MKO: **It's all very depressing in a way. And at times all you want to do is stay inside, do nothing, hide from the world and some of these realities. But then again, that's not exactly practical.**

BC: I agree. One of the worst things I think you can do is isolate yourself. What was great about Andy, as opposed to Jasper Johns, was that he was out there. He would walk down the street with *Interview*s under his arm and hand them to people; he was in constant contact. He'd go to clubs, he'd travel, he went to dinners, he didn't judge. He didn't put down rich people, he didn't put down poor people. He was interested in it all. I think that's why his art, more than that of any of his contemporaries, has retained its power. That's because he really did capture his time. I think that when you're isolated—whether as an artist, a politician, a tycoon—things fall apart. It's so important to have a variety of opinions, to see a mixture of people. That's where so much creative stuff happens. I always say it's easy to hate a name, but it's very hard to hate a person. I mean, I could hate Barbara Streisand, but probably if we sat down next to each other at dinner we'd find something in common. I'm very critical of the press, but I think it's important to cultivate the press. That's why Andy was so clever. He got so much negative press and I'd say, "I want to write a letter to the editor of *Time* magazine—how could they say that?" And Andy would say, "I got ten pages and ten color photos—we should invite them to lunch!" And he would do this time and time again—invite the people who'd attacked him to lunch. And they'd have such a good time, they'd feel so guilty they would neutralize.

AO: **Do you think that some of these trends will go away, like the paparazzi or the salacious stories?**

BC: Well, it's gotten so ugly now. I don't really know how you guys do it.

AO: **Well, we can't really go anywhere. I don't want to feel like I'm constantly in hiding, but I'd much rather stay at home than get a picture of me out somewhere. I think the way we handle it makes us a lot different than a lot**

The Metropolitan Museum of Art

SPECIAL CONSULTANT   August 9th, 1973

Dear Bob,

I think your piece about Josephine Baker is really very, very
good.

I think the spread looks marvellous.

I think the whole thing comes off.

I really think my language is something which could do with a
little bit of grammar but I guess that's me and you can always
just say "Well, that's the way she talks as she comes from
Brooklyn"!!   However, I was very pleased that you asked me
and I was very pleased to do anything for you boys and for
Josephine Baker.   We all agree that she is totally unappreciated _in_ U.S.

I have to say that I think the whole paper looks so well this week.
Every single article is interesting.   It is far and away the best
reading on the newstand and everyone who takes it, such as Lee
Radziwill, agrees.

a bit

I will see you soon, though I am going abroad next week, so it may
not be for ~~some time~~.   In the meantime, all my very best wishes.
You are an extremely good writer.

                              Diana
                              Diana Vreeland

Mr. R. Colacello
33 Union Square West. N.Y 10003

OPPOSITE PAGE, CLOCKWISE FROM TOP:
Calvin Klein with then-wife Kelly and Bianca Jagger;
Diane von Furstenberg; a picture Bob took of Old Hollywood
actress Paulette Goddard and Truman Capote: PHOTOGRAPH ©
BOB COLACELLO; Bob with camera: PHOTOGRAPH © NICHOLAS
VREELAND; with Nancy Reagan at a White House function.

THIS PAGE, CLOCKWISE FROM TOP:
Jean-Michel Basquiat; John Stockwell, Calvin Klein, and
Andy Warhol; Bianca Jagger and Halston: PHOTOGRAPH ©
BOB COLACELLO; Truman Capote with his *Interview* cover;
Basquiat, Tina Chow, and Andy.

of people. I think others still try to live their lives, or act out against it, which is inevitable. We just know that it is what it is, and you can't change it. You can only change what you do for yourself, and how you live your life.

BC: The privacy laws in France are very strict.

MKO: I love France. I love Paris. I'd like to live there at some point in my life. Not only do I think they're not as consumed with celebrity culture—and attacking people in the public eye—there is so much more culture in that city.

AO: That's what we want this book to be, something that is filled with interesting things about the art world and fashion. I'd like to think that this book is inspiring people to read about or focus on other things than just the oversaturated, scandal-driving media.

BC: One thing I think is important is to get young people to not only read contemporary stuff, but also the classics. You almost have to force yourself to do it today, because I don't think you get it so much in school the way we used to. That's the only way to know where we come from or how we got here as a culture. Today people break the rules without even knowing what the rules are. Someone like Andy knew art history forwards and backwards. When he was in Pittsburgh in the public schools, in fifth grade each principal of each school picked two children who showed some talent in art, and they were enrolled in the special Saturday program at the Carnegie Museum of Art. So Andy was able to break the rules like Picasso did because they both knew what they were rebelling against. Today kids are just rebelling, but in this aimless way.

MKO: That's what our parents were like. We have a big family, and we'd all go together, which I can now look back and appreciate. They cared about us respecting our elders, and they gave us a moral code and a set of values and manners.

BC: Yes, exactly. I had a point in my life where things were getting out of control. Something saved me that was within me. Thank God. It is so easy just to get distracted and swallowed up. I was the most obnoxious twenty-three-year-old in New York. A year after working for Andy, I was

flying off to Paris all the time to have lunch with Yves Saint Laurent. At twenty-three, I was the worst name-dropper. My friends were all, like, "Bob's so full of himself." You do get caught up in it. It's hard to keep your perspective. Fame has become our highest value. I think people want fame more than anything, even if it means doing anything to get it.

MKO: That's funny, because I would never wish it upon anyone. Not even my worst enemy.

BC: Well, I think if celebrity meant you were celebrated for your achievements, for your work, that would be a good thing. But it's become about everything else.

AO: It's become a word with a negative connotation.

BC: It didn't used to be like that. Somebody who makes a great movie or paints a great painting is put on the same level as someone who distributes a porn video of themselves and their boyfriend. For young people, that's very confusing, because the media doesn't discriminate. It doesn't say, "This isn't fame, this is infamy." Now kids are saying, "Why should I spend five years writing a novel or ten years making myself a really good artist when I could just appear in public naked and I'll get on the front page of the *New York Post*?"

MKO: What do you think Andy would think of all of this?

BC: Andy would love it, in a way. Andy would probably be dating Paris Hilton, but I think he would kind of love it to death. "Oh, gee, how great it all is." That was his technique for just kind of destroying something. He was so subtle. He'd say something was so—"Oh, gee, it's so great"—but in a way you'd know he wasn't serious. I think he has turned out to be a prophet; he really predicted it, anticipated it—in some ways he contributed to it. Like everything, there's an upside and a downside. We have to say this: Andy was very voyeuristic. He was not that happy as a person. Andy wanted to be a beauty and he wasn't a beauty; he worshipped beauty and he wanted to be surrounded by beautiful people. He sort of saw the beauty in people, but because he was unhappy in that regard—Jed Johnson was his boyfriend for years, but he couldn't believe that someone like Jed would love him—he became overly involved with everybody's private lives. The first year I

was there Andy would be tape-recording me in a taxicab going uptown, and I would stupidly just say anything. He would ask me, "Who went home with who last?" And then it would get back to me that Andy said I had said this. And then I realized this was not a good way to behave, of course, but if you let him, that's what he would do. He was funny because you'd go to some really conservative dinner party, and Andy would ask the hostess, "Is your husband good in bed? How big is your husband?" Some of them would really think this was funny and they'd play along with it, and others would be like, "I'm never inviting him back again." And he tape-recorded it all! He'd try to slip the tape recorder under the centerpiece, in the middle of the table, and the hostess would say, "Please turn that off."

MKO: I don't think many people entertain at home anymore. I love to do it—I do it all the time—but I get the impression that it's not as common.

BC: I'd much rather go to somebody's house than a restaurant. For people who have nice places and can afford to have people, it's almost wrong not to entertain. I think it's so nice to introduce people you'd like to get to know to each other. That whole idea of mixing people. Andy did that so well; so did Mrs. Vreeland. She would have all young people to dinner, seven kids all in their twenties and herself in her seventies. If she knew a friend's grandson or granddaughter was getting out of college and was interested in music, then she'd have Mick Jagger. I think it's a shame that people don't mix as much, and that everyone is in these sort of categories now, thanks to identity politics. The great thing about Studio 54 was it wasn't gay and it wasn't straight. It was everything. It was uptown and downtown. You'd see UN diplomats and you'd see transvestites all together. People danced in groups, they danced alone, they danced two girls, they danced two boys. There was a freedom to that. Now everything's an uptown black lesbian bar, or a downtown Chinese gay bar. That's what was so great about Andy—he would never become a part of any of these causes. The gay movement would get very angry with him because they felt he wasn't taking a stand, but he was in his movies. Why should he go on TV and talk about, "Yeah, I'm gay, I lust after young boys." If a straight guy did that, we'd all think it was tacky. You're on TV talking about how many good women you've slept with? That seems like common sense to me.

MKO: Do you ever think there'll be another Factory? A group of people working together and producing in the same space?

BC: Well, I wish there would be. You girls should have a Factory.

MKO: I love bringing together a random crowd of interesting people—and I love it even more when that happens unintentionally.

BC: It's worthwhile to host those types of parties, yes; it's really hard work to get it all together: the food, the staff, the lighting, the music, the people. But if you go out of your way to bring people together that wouldn't ordinarily get together, it can be really exciting. Malcolm Forbes used to constantly entertain, constantly take people on trips, and he would throw people together. He would have Fran Lebowitz with the ex-king and queen of Bulgaria, Margaret Thatcher's son, some big CEO and professional balloonists—and everyone would have this great time. Then again, it was easier for us: We never had to worry about somebody taking a picture with their cell phones.

AO: Or that a picture of a high status person sitting on a couch smoking a cigarette would even be worth anything.

BC: *Vanity Fair* doesn't pay for anything, but I always forget that actually there's this whole part of the press that pays for things. I guess you get to the point where you feel like you may as well sell your wedding to a magazine since . . . they're going to try to invade it anyway.

AO: That's the worst part for me. What kind of options are those? Sell your pictures to a tabloid, or expect to be eavesdropped on?

BC: I know, it's really bleak now.

AO: It's really unconscionable.

BC: But I think that by speaking out against it, doing this book, taking a stand, I think you have to make the point for the public to listen. Yes, the press is at fault, but certain celebrities or people who call themselves celebrities are also at fault. Nobody wants to stand up and say Paris Hilton is terrible. But somebody should. It's funny, because Andy and I would be

having a fight right now, because he would say Paris Hilton should be on the cover, and I would be like, "We're not putting her on the cover." I can't believe we even put her on the cover of *Vanity Fair*. And it was one of our worst sellers.

MKO: My sister and I are busy; we make work and our careers a priority.

BC: Andy really believed in work, and I think work will save everybody. Great old people like Diana Vreeland or Eleanor Lambert, who was about 101 years old and still doing PR—they're the greatest people because they still have an interest in life. And I think the sooner you can figure out something you like to do and get into it the better. You two have been working from a very young age, but I'm sure it is work that keeps you sane. It gives you a sense of responsibility, of accomplishment. What's that saying? "A busy mind is a happy mind." We all have problems in life, but if you have all this time to just focus on the problems, they're going to get bigger and bigger. But if you can say, "Okay, look, I have to do all this stuff today. I have to put this aside now," your mind can change gears.

AO: I agree. Keeping busy can keep things in perspective. That's why I think it's important to work.

BC: Exactly. Kids always used to say, "Well, I want to be a photographer but I don't have the right camera," and Andy would tell them to just go buy a cheap one in a thrift shop and start taking pictures. "Oh, I want to be a painter but I don't have a studio." —Well, go paint in my bathroom. Just do it. Just do it! Andy would say it in

a gentle way, but he didn't really have any patience for people who said things and didn't back them up. That's why he liked Basquiat. He was this kid from the street who was making this work. Andy thought that was cool, that was amazing. You had to take him seriously because he just was doing it. In his way I think Andy really did try to help Basquiat get off drugs and everything, but who knows how you do that?

AO: You seem to have a fond, gracious memory of working with Andy. What made you stop working with him, then?

BC: I was really lucky, but at a certain point you realize you can't hang around a genius forever, and I do believe that Andy was a genius. Part of being a genius is taking everything from everyone around you; I helped Andy write his *Philosophy* book, and I remember Fran Lebowitz told me that it was the stupidest thing I ever did. She said that my sense of humor was now Andy's sense of humor, and if I wrote a book like that people would say I was copying him. So at a certain point you have to get away. On the other hand, it was a privilege, and I learned so much from being around Andy.

AO: Hearing about him, about that era and about your experiences, motivates me to try and do something different.

MKO: Me too.

BC: But you're both so young. And you've already done a lot.

AO: Yes, we have. But I feel like our childhoods and what we've done in the past are just laying the groundwork for our future.

LIZA MINNELLI

March 15, 1978

Dear Bob,

Thank you for the black glasses. I adore them!

Much love to you,

Liza

lb/LMH

A thank you note from Liza Minnelli.

David Collins
in London.

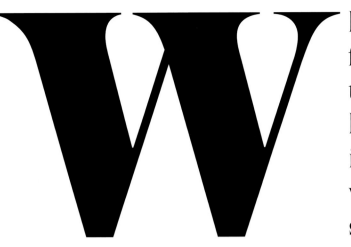

While we were in Paris for fashion week, a good friend told me that if this book had anything to do with interiors or fashion or art we would be remiss not to speak to the interior architect David Collins. She added that he has done fabulous houses, like Madonna's and Tom Ford's, and other spaces that my sister and I love, like the Wolseley and the Blue Bar in London. As chance would have it, as my friend was saying this, she looked across the courtyard of the Hôtel Costes, where we were having lunch, and David was there. *And* it just happened to be his birthday. It seemed too right—especially when he blushed as a surprise birthday cake we had ordered for him arrived. As it turned out, our friend was right. David—who was born in Ireland, lives in London, and works wherever a project may take him—is one of the foremost architects and designers working in those fields today. The following day, when he agreed to meet us for lunch and have a chat about his life and career—again in the Costes—he told us about his emotional connection with his work. I admire fashion and art, but when I interviewed David I discovered a newfound respect for my interiors, too. I have David to thank for that.

3/2/08
DATE

HOTEL COSTES IN PARIS
LOCATION

INTERVIEWED BY

Early in our chat, David said blue was his favorite color. He proved that with the Blue Bar, Berkeley Hotel, London.

Detail shot of the Blue Bar's interior.

MKO: Where did you grow up?

DC: I grew up in Dublin. I became an architect on the grounds that I wanted to go into fashion design, but my parents would have had apoplexy if I said I was going to become a designer. And I wanted to become a musician, too, but my parents would have had an apoplexy over that as well. Nowadays I think parents would probably push me on the stage, but back when I was young it was simple: music out, fashion out.

MKO: What does that leave? I can't think of anything else! Ha!

DC: So I thought, Well, I'll do architecture because I hated Latin, which was a class I could skip because of my school schedule. That's the only reason I did architecture. I went to college when I was sixteen, and it went very well. I've never lived or done anything but that.

MKO: Did you go to school in Dublin?

DC: Yes, and then I went to London for a short time. I worked as an architect for a little while but then I decided, "Okay, I'm going to write a book." So I wrote the first chapter of this book and gave up my job—too bad the book had no plot, no beginning, middle, or end. But then the week after I had given up my job, this friend of mine said he wanted me to design his house; he asked if I could do interior design. I said, "Yes, sure." I'd never even read a copy of *Homes & Gardens*—nothing!—but I thought I would give it a try.

MKO: Were you inspired by spaces when you were younger?

DC: I was inspired by color. I used to sleep in a blue bedroom, and I still sleep in a blue bedroom.

MKO: A dark blue?

DC: Pale blue. Sky blue. I'm very consistent with my colors. All of my clothes are blue—not deliberately. It's not as if I set out to buy blue clothes. It's just, if I buy something else that's a different color, I end up never wearing it, and it goes to my brother.

MKO: But colors have always been important to you, even if you didn't realize it.

DC: Yes, I was very inspired by color. Blue really inspired me. Growing up in Dublin you're near the sea, so I imagine that's where I got my obsession with blue and green. The other thing I was really inspired by was all these amazing green tweeds that were made in those days, like green-blue heather tweeds. You know what, I think you should bring them back again. They were very in fashion in those days.

MKO: Maybe I will. Funnily enough, I'm very inspired by green right now. I want to do a print-on-print green in a room in my house, almost like *Great Expectations*, full of different patterns and possibly a floral.

DC: The other thing that inspired me growing up was *Gone with the Wind*. Or rather, the way it was written: back to front. It's one of my favorite books in the whole world. I've read it three or four times in my life, and I could read it again tomorrow. It's a really well-written book, and as a designer I think the interesting thing about that book is that it was written backwards.

MKO: From the end.

DC: It has twenty-six chapters or something, and the author wrote them backwards. That's why it's such a good ending. I think that's why most things have such foul endings. So I have this design idea—

MKO: I never knew that. If I'd known that, I think I would have approached creative writing classes differently!

DC: Yes, you have to know the ending; how you got there is the story—because there are so many things that are a series of accidental happenings. That's why, when I'm approaching a design project, I've got to try to figure out what it's going to feel like in the end. I need to think about the ending first. You don't always know what it's going to look like totally, but you have to think of what it's going to feel like at the end.

MKO: Architecture and design are almost like storytelling.

DC: That's right. I studied architecture for six years, plus a bunch of postgrad, and so to me, to understand this, I have to be quite emotional and nostalgic in what I do. I'm not the most creative designer around, or the most talented or imaginative or far-reaching, but I think I'm very emotional. In my whole life, everything is all or nothing—and obsessively romantic. I'm very interested in how things feel, how it would feel if you were there and you were lying in a chair looking up at the ceiling, and how it would smell and how the flowers would look and things like that. I don't like fussy things; I like simple things.

MKO: How would you describe your design aesthetic, then? Would you call yourself modern?

DC: That's tough. Now what is modern is nostalgic. The idea of something that's contemporary now is nostalgic—we're so surrounded by fear and uncertainty about the future, so we look to the past. When I was a kid I realized that. My friend had a book called *I Remember the Future,* which was written sometime back in the '50s or '40s, when they were imagining skyscrapers and people living in buildings. This idea, that you would never have to leave the building because there'd be little shops downstairs, all sounded so amazing. Then, of course, the future turned out to be flawed because humans got in the way. But from that point of view, I think what is contemporary now is a sense of new things and technology teaching us that everything new is very disposable.

MKO: Are you referring to technology as a whole, or our society's obsession with gadgets and newfangled toys?

DC: What do you do with your Samsung phone or your iPod touch or whatever? There's a moment when all this is new. Then all of this technology makes us very insecure, because people get very obsessive with them—the way that in the nineteenth and eighteenth centuries, they might have become obsessed with these little cameo brooches that they would treasure and wear around their necks.

MKO: There is a store down the street here— they always have the next new things. But when you go back—

DC: They're gone when you go back, and replaced with something newer and better. And you lose about fifteen minutes to something new.

MKO: Which is not like color.

DC: When I think of the word *green,* I think of texture. Green in particular can change based on its consistency. Green cotton? Boring. Green silk? Okay. Green satin can be very beautiful. Green velvet? Beautiful! Green is an interesting color— you can wear green and green and green and green together—and it's all fine. And you can use black with green, and it's fine as well.

мко: Yes. I found this vintage wallpaper that was this beautiful, worn black with a washed floral pattern but with the green in it, which would have been overwhelming in this particular room.

dc: It's a very strong thing: color! I would say the thing that inspires me most is color. I don't respond very well to black for superstitious reasons. I see that you're wearing rosary beads around your neck, so I associate black with the Bible, prayer books, rosary beads, weeping.

мко: Yes, but I usually wear something else with it to keep it religiously neutral. Aesthetically, though, I think a cross is beautiful.

dc: I was given one of those red strings once.

мко: The Kabbalah strings?

dc: Yes, and I couldn't wear it because it was red.

мко: Ha! Do you tend to stay away from that color?

dc: It just really irritated me that there was something around my wrist—and it was red. To be honest, I couldn't care less about being struck by lightning. You bring that stuff on yourself if you believe in it.

мко: I understand where you're coming from.

dc: I honestly think that if you're so superstitious about wearing anything around you, then you're going to be very affected by it. I have two girlfriends who, when we were in college, got a job at a really well-known fashion magazine. They were responsible for the horoscopes. They used to mess up all the months just for a laugh. They'd put the Taurus reading under the Gemini sign, and things like that.

мко: I read my horoscope occasionally, but not in fashion magazines, mind you. Changing the topic, do you do any set decorating?

dc: Well, some of the things I've done I suppose are a little bit like set designs! Some things that you might have seen are the Wolseley restaurant and the Berkeley Hotel, both in London.

мко: That makes sense with your obsession with the color blue. I love the Blue Bar in the Berkeley Hotel.

dc: When you come to London you should give us a call. Come around for a drink. My apartment is not very grand, but I think it's very relaxing. It's very indulgent. It's one bedroom but indulgent.

мко: I would love to see your place. Do you have a favorite room?

dc: Oh, it's my dining room. Ha. Sometimes I feel guilty—there are so many other things going on in the world, and what I do might be the most ridiculous job. But I try to do something useful with my time as well. Anyway, I've had my dining room walls upholstered in silk, in pale green silk, and the silk walls are then also embroidered with trees.

Detail of the curtains David had dip-dyed and embroidered for his home in London.

I wasn't sure if the color would really look hideous, kind of like a tattoo parlor, so I was very limited in what I'd let them do with the embroidery. It might be a bit too subtle, and it has a dyed feel to it too, like a dip dye phasing into a fainter color. Miuccia Prada did that one season, and I was really taken by it, which is quite simple—it's just a simple dip dye. So the silk is dip-dyed, which was complicated to do, but so beautiful in its simplicity. As somebody once said, "Simple isn't easy."

MKO: Are you inspired by fashion a lot like that? Like you were by Miuccia Prada's dye jobs at Prada? Where do you find your inspiration?

DC: I'm inspired by certain fashion things. Definitely Miuccia Prada. Her big ideas are so kind of incomprehensible many times. They're very intellectual and, to be honest, I have no idea what she's talking about. But she's right, nonetheless. I'll tell you one thing that really inspired me about her. I'm in Milan, fashion capital of the world, blah blah blah, and one night she had a very small party at her apartment. I had arrived there with—hideously embarrassing—two friends. I didn't know how small it was, and I was so embarrassed that I had brought two friends that I thought the ground would open up and swallow me. Anyway, the apartment was in a very mature, intellectual part of Milan, kind of like office buildings and the like. You can imagine that every one of these tall, faceless, seven-story buildings, all of which were identical, were all psychiatrists' offices and medical facilities. Anyway, we went through this gateway to a courtyard, and at the end of the courtyard was a small house. You walked in the house and down a long corridor into an enormous room like this, and the room was decorated with furniture that could have come out of a dentist's office or a doctor's office from the 1950s or '60s. They even had green linen tablecloths and books everywhere. Books, bookcases everywhere. I walked in and all the people were standing around, very conformist, and talking about intellectual things. At one side of the apartment, a big room, there was a long, narrow opening, which I entered. I looked out and it was a veranda entirely lined with books on one side and on the other with glass—an enormous glass wall that had, essentially, this apartment's floral arrangement. But it wasn't a vase or something. The outside of this apartment, this very austere apartment in the middle of Milan, was a lawn of about ten thousand daffodils. It was breathtaking. And apparently she changes them throughout the year so it's always something new—always a new arrangement.

MKO: She is a genius. She knows exactly what she's doing and how to do it, but always maintains her own visually pleasing aesthetic.

DC: She does something that's subversive, but she manages to do it on a commercial level.

David's living room
in his home in London.

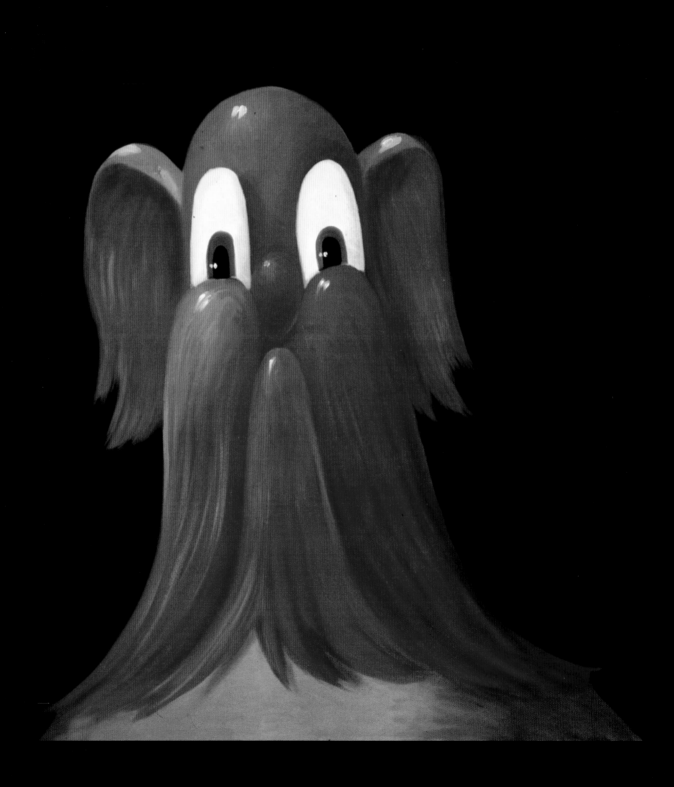

We visited George Condo at his apartment and studio in New York City, and it was obvious from first glance that it was an artist's space. Wet canvases were stacked against the wall, some finished and some still in progress, and paint was splattered everywhere. Like a genius wizard in the middle of his creative playpen, there was George himself. The paintings we discussed, including *God 2007* (on page 59), the one he was working on at the time, summed up many of the characteristics that have come to define his work. Full of references to cubism, modernism, surrealism, and popular culture, his pieces are almost like dreams: Some of them incite fear, and some of them incite laughter. In fact, most of them are both frightening and ridiculous! His humor comes out in his work, and so does his cynicism. Born in New Hampshire, George studied art history and music theory in college, and then spent some time in Paris, whiling away his days copying the works of Old World masters in the Louvre. Later, when he moved to New York, he blended that classicism with his own quirkiness. After a tour of his place and his current work, we sat down and talked. George was only our second interview ever (we hadn't perfected our technique just yet)—but we walked out of his house thinking he was an inspiring guy to talk to.

10/29/07   NEW YORK CITY

DATE   LOCATION   INTERVIEWED BY

MKO: **Should we start at the beginning?**

AO: **Who inspired you?**

GC: As a painter?

AO: **Sure, were you painting at a young age?**

GC: My older brother and I both tried out for Little League, so of course I wanted to be on the team more than anything else. I swung the bat and I didn't hit the ball; I couldn't possibly get into being a baseball person, so my mother said, "Well, why don't you do something you really like? We'll put you in painting classes since you're really good at drawing"—so I went and started painting at around eight or nine, and then I just kept doing it all the time. By the time I was about fourteen or fifteen I felt like I was a painter, so then when it came time to go to college—I was also into music, playing classical music—I was torn between whether I should go to study music or study art. So basically after two years of studying music and art history I moved to New York City.

MKO: **Did you study psychology? Your paintings seem to have a sociological undertone.**

GC: I always read books and found it interesting to educate myself on those subjects, like philosophy and psychology. In a lot of ways what's nice about being a painter is that you can encompass all of those things in art somehow—all great paintings lead to numerous different sorts of studies, like politics, psychology, sociology, humanities. So, yeah, that was the beginning.

MKO: **That's a good beginning.**

GC: It's a super-early beginning—starting from Little League.

AO: **How do you go from one series to the next?**

GC: Things sort of appear on the canvas. You start out doing something like a landscape or something simple, like a portrait of your kid, and one of these characters pops up on the screen. Somehow the series are dictated by the characters that have popped in on the canvases. And they seem to arrive in their own time, at their own will, and sometimes they appear again later in my work.

AO: **Are you influenced by average people?**

GC: Yeah. I think so.

MKO: **How old are your children?**

GC: They want to see you.

AO: **How old are they?**

GC: Seventeen and twelve.

MKO: **Cool.**

GC: But they want to come over and get money anyway, because they're going Halloween shopping.

MKO: **I went to a good Halloween party the other night.**

GC: You already had a Halloween party? The thirty-first isn't for days.

MKO: **Yeah, it's crazy in New York. Everyone is just waiting for a party and an excuse to wear something ridiculous. I went as a Japanese bondage girl. Do you know the artist Araki?**

GC: Yeah.

MKO: **I took a cue from some of his pictures. I wore a kimono and wrapped myself in rope.**

AO: **I was a little vampire girl in a Victorian dress; I had bloody handprints all over me, a big black bow in my hair, and these little black ballet flats.**

GC: I've used costumes in my art before, when I dress up my models. [*Pointing to a painting*] You see, that's God over there, and I'll show you the giant painting I did of a nun and a priest—they're insane.

AO: **I love your couples—**

GC: I feel like you walk into their life—they're always right there in your living room.

MKO: **Tell me about teaching. You've taught at Harvard and at Columbia, right?**

GC: I like teaching. I did one semester at Harvard; at Columbia I did a lecture series. I like it, but at the end of the day it was a drag to have to be on schedule. The greatest thing about it, obviously, was that the students at Harvard were super cool and they're actually very, very smart kids. Some of them weren't necessarily just art majors. I had one girl who was from MIT who was an architect, and a doctor, and they were really good painters.

MKO: **Was there a moment in your career when you felt established?**

GC: Well, there were a bunch of moments. One was a long time ago in California. I had never sold anything in America—I call California another country, I guess—

AO: **It's its own world.**

GC: Yeah. Just by accident I said it again.

AO: **It's like a bubble.**

GC: Yeah. It's bizarre out there.

MKO: **The older I get the weirder I think it is.**

GC: Anyway, I went to Los Angeles—I was working at Warhol's Factory for a while—

AO: **How was that?**

GC: That was great.

MKO: **When?**

GC: Like, '81. It was one of the first jobs I had in Manhattan as an actual job, so I did that for like nine months. I met this girl who was an actress and she was in a few of the Warhol movies—she was like, I don't know, fifteen years older than I was. Her name was Susan Tyrrell. She was in *Bad* and she was in *Cry-Baby* with Johnny Depp—

MKO: **Really? I just saw that movie.**

GC: Yeah, she played his mother or something like that. Anyway, she was a riot, and she got this TV show and she said, "You should get out of there, get out of New York, come over to LA." I'd never been there so I went, and I stayed there for six, eight months, and I did paintings all the time. This one guy bought a painting and I couldn't believe it. He paid like $220 or something.

AO: **What was the painting? Do you remember what it was of?**

GC: I think it was called *The Adoration of the Sacred Cow*. I did two paintings after I went to the de Young Museum in San Francisco; they had these two Tiepolo paintings. I came back and I did the first fake Old Master paintings in LA and this one guy bought one. And I couldn't believe it; it was great. After that a couple of other paintings sold and then my paintings started selling—but that was really the first one I ever sold.

AO: **What was your first series?**

GC: The first series of paintings were the ones that had jewels and gold and my name written in jewels in the clouds—things like that, sort of semi-surrealistic Old Master painting.

MKO: **I love your self-portrait with the bubbles.**

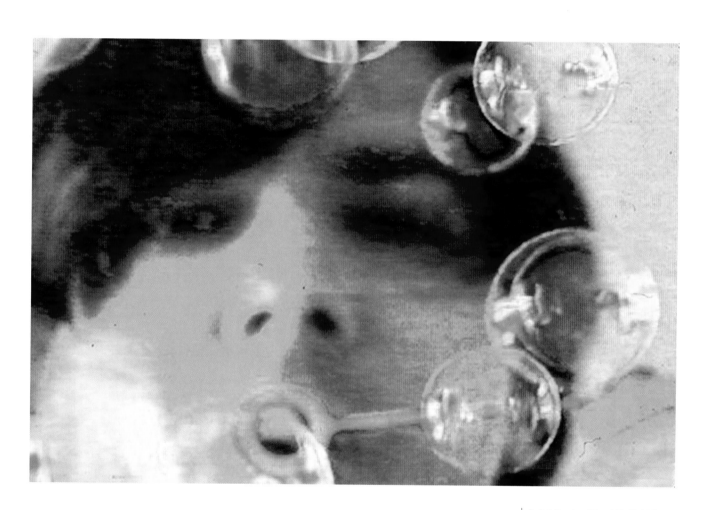

Self-Portrait with Bubbles,
1999, silk screen on paper,
40 x 50 inches. COPYRIGHT
© 1999 BY GEORGE CONDO,
REPRINTED WITH PERMISSION
OF THE WYLIE AGENCY, INC.

Batman and Bunny, 2005, oil
on canvas, 32 x 28 inches.
PHOTO CREDIT: LARRY LAMAY.
COPYRIGHT © 2005 BY GEORGE
CONDO, REPRINTED WITH
PERMISSION OF THE WYLIE
AGENCY, INC.

Visitation, 2004, colored
pencil on paper, 26 x 19
inches. PHOTO CREDIT:
LARRY LAMAY. COPYRIGHT ©
2004 BY GEORGE CONDO,
REPRINTED WITH PERMISSION
OF THE WYLIE AGENCY, INC.

GC: Those came after I did this movie with John McNaughton, *Condo Painting*. I took film stills and I made silk screens out of them. And I did a whole series of the TV characters. But I've never shown them in New York. Actually, that's not true. I showed three or four with Sandra Gering and that was it, and then Pace showed them in LA, and then that's the last. I think Bruno Bischofberger showed them in Zurich and there was *McHale's Navy* and *The Beverly Hillbillies* and—

AO: *Lassie*?

GC: Yeah, I did *Lassie*. I did *The Beverly Hillbillies, Lassie, Gunsmoke*—yeah, they were really cool paintings. I saw one the other day that I did called *Get Dumb*. It was the guy from *Get Smart* overlaid on top of Gilligan's Island. All of a sudden Granny's face from *The Hillbillies* was sort of peeking out from the cracks and it's great. I wish I had a few of those around.

AO: **Everything definitely has a sense of humor behind it.**

GC: When I did the lecture at Columbia we got to the point where we were trying to make determinations on how you could say if something's good or not. And I said, "I think something's only truly good if it's totally believable." All of those characters like Andy Griffith—they're just so "them" that you can't imagine "them" in any other way. That's when you realize that they're great works of art, these characters that they created somehow. And so I realized that the characters in your paintings have to be just as believable somehow as real life. If it's not believable then it's not quality. And in my paintings, if it's good, they become people who actually talk to me, in a way. And I talk to them too. Like that one over there against the wall; I paint 'em and then I turn 'em around, you know, against a wall. That's how I work.

AO: **It must be hard to stare at your work.**

GC: It's not even that. I just want them to be completely dry, and then be able to go in and just work a little bit more on it. But if I look at it the whole day long I won't work on a new painting.

MKO: [*Pointing to the crucifix on the following page*] **How did that one come about?**

GC: Well, I wanted to do this religious series. That's what I'm kind of thinking of now. Like the priest and then a big crucifixion piece. I did Jesus and the two thieves. This one I'm still working on, the Saint Jerome. I think this is going to be good.

AO: **I love how everything has such a humor. It's really dark but you look at it and you smile. It just makes me laugh and it makes me happy in a dark sort of way.**

GC: I have to paint God. I was going to go with the same Halloween costume. I love Halloween—God coming from a Halloween costume.

MKO: **Trick-or-treat!**

AO: **Let's talk about your sculptures. What's your artistic process with those? I love the faces.**

GC: Thanks. I worked with them with clay and then sent them to the foundry. They come back with a wax mold or a plaster and then I work the plaster a little bit. And then I send them back to be cast.

AO: **The faces look exactly like the people in your paintings.**

GC: I used to do sculpture like every ten years or so. I did some in 1990—those were the first ones I ever made—and then I didn't do any again for another ten years. The next time I did them was in 2002—no, in '01, when 9/11 happened. When 9/11 happened it was so weird; I was working in sculpture at that time and I was working in clay and I was literally thinking of this book of Nietzsche's, *The Birth of Tragedy*. It's all about Apollo and Dionysus, so as I was sculpting these heads I was thinking of them in terms of these Greek gods and heroes. And then 9/11 happened and it was all about uncovering people in the rubble and the heroes, and I was uncovering these faces in clay while they were sort of trying to uncover people. It was so bizarre. I had a studio in Soho, so it wasn't that far away from it all—I think something about that really gets into the work. In some way or another.

AO: **Well, you pick people apart but you also—what is it? Like the roles people play in real life.**

GC: Paintings will be called like *The Schoolteacher* or *The Nun* or *The Truck Driver* or *The Gas Station Attendant* or *The Kmart Girl* and then just thinking of the number of different people that I've done that are sort of a "type," or a "role," like the cashier, and a lot of times the extreme pressure, social pressure—it's more like a portrait of their interior than their exterior. You know what I mean?

MKO: **Of course.**

GC: I feel like it's the expression of what they feel like, under the pressure that the world imposes. I think you see it.

MKO: **Isn't your whole process based on memory or—?**

GC: To paint somehow from memory, yes. You know how some artists like working from photography, and they spend more time copying photographs and trying to individualize them? I like to work from my imagination and I think to do that you have to be able to remember the way things look in a painting. If somebody looks for that version of Saint Jerome somewhere they'll never find it because it's just a memory of all of those paintings. You can figure out how to paint without a model. I like working from dummies. But I'm not that into working from models anymore. Occasionally I did and at the end of the day I just spend all my time trying to look if I've pleased the models themselves.

AO: **When you really just want to bring out their inner beauty, right?**

MKO: **And you don't want to be offensive.**

GC: Yeah.

MKO: **Do you sketch your paintings first?**

GC: Yes, absolutely. I'll be sitting here at this desk and I'll have a sketchbook like this and I'll think of fifty different ways to paint—I'll do a lot of different versions of what the painting could be, so I have to redraw the whole thing, think of an idea, see what it looks like on a drawing.

AO: **And maybe you'll throw in a Batman or Spider-Man, right?**

GC: Yeah. I like superheroes.

MKO: **When did that come into your work?**

GC: I did Batman and then the Playboy Bunny a couple of years ago. I guess I suddenly realized that these characters had just invaded the psyche of these other imaginary people.

AO: **I like that Batman and the Playboy Bunny sitting next to each other.**

GC: [*To his daughters, who have just entered the room*] Girls, come in! And meet Mary-Kate and Ashley. Look at my new painting of God. And that's Saint Jerome.

Jesus, 2007, oil on
canvas, 86 x 86 inches.
PHOTO CREDIT: LARRY
LAMAY. COPYRIGHT © 2007
BY GEORGE CONDO, REPRINTED
WITH PERMISSION OF THE
WYLIE AGENCY, INC.

God, 2007, oil on canvas, 92 x 78 inches. PHOTO CREDIT: LARRY LAMAY. © 2007 BY GEORGE CONDO, REPRINTED WITH PERMISSION OF THE WYLIE AGENCY, INC.

If anyone has taught me a valuable lesson in what it means to be beautiful since I first moved to New York, it's my friend Francisco Costa. As creative director of Calvin Klein's women's collection for the past five years, Francisco drives home a clear message with his designs that applies to so many aspects of my life: Less is more. He breaks complicated ideas down to their bare bones—and always with stunning results. When I turned eighteen and began to understand my own stylistic choices, Francisco took over the reins at Calvin Klein Collection, so I think it's safe to say that he and I are kindred fashion spirits. I've been wearing his designs to everything from casual dinners with friends to art openings ever since. The man understands tailoring. One of my favorite pieces is a long T-shirt dress that wraps around your body like tissue paper. Maybe it's the fact that he is a native of sunny Brazil or has previously worked with designers as diverse as Oscar de la Renta and Tom Ford, but Francisco manages to execute the most simple of designs in the most creative ways. He imbues his one-of-a-kind pieces with a rare warmth that's much like his own sweet and passionate personality. But while he's on the minimalist track now, who knows what's next for him? There's always a surprise with Francisco. And it's as simple as that.

2·15·08   CK HEADQUARTERS, NY
DATE   LOCATION

AO
INTERVIEWED BY

AO: Did you ever think you would be doing anything else with your life other than being a fashion designer?

FC: No, I really didn't. I mean I painted, I did a lot of artsy things, but fashion was just natural—I never questioned it. Am I going to be a fashion designer? That was never a question.

AO: Was your love of clothes instilled in you at an early age?

FC: I grew up in a very small town: two thousand people and the only business in town was my mother's business, which was selling textiles and fabrics, and later clothing. Growing up, it was very natural that my brothers and sisters and I would work for her after school. As kids we did everything.

AO: Did you help her? I hope you were a good son.

FC: Oh, yes, absolutely. Our lives were really functioning around the business and my mother's fantastic and inspiring work ethic; she was quite entrepreneurial. A real leader, and very creative, too. She could just cut a pattern—just take scissors and a paper and cut the pattern; it was something quite insane. I never understood that. I was very inspired growing up in this small town in Brazil. I think we provided so many jobs to the whole town that everyone kind of knew us, and we knew everybody. It's tiny—nothing fancy, just a tiny town in the middle of nowhere.

AO: When did you decide that you wanted to move to the U.S.?

FC: In 1985. I was already living in Rio and I had just finished school for production and manufacturing. And then I came here. My mom had passed away, and I felt less connected to Brazil. So I came here. And I didn't speak any English. Not a word of English. I went and I looked for a school, which led me to Hunter College. I found it merely by chance. I could have gone anywhere but I walked in there. I registered because I wanted to learn English and there was a program for foreign students where you could actually go to class and get your visa. But fashion was definitely the most important thing in my life, and learning English was secondary.

AO: Did you have any formal fashion training?

FC: Well, I took all the money I had and registered at Hunter only later to find out that in order to get the visa, I had to go back to Brazil. It was just one of those impulses, and I had already given all my money to the school. Anyway, I went back to Brazil and told my father that I had to go back, that I had to study. And when I got back to the States, that's when my life really started. I began taking English classes in the morning, and then fashion classes at night at the Fashion Institute of Technology. There, I won a scholarship, which made my life so much easier. That's how it all started. And it's been fashion ever since.

AO: That takes drive, though. To wake up every day just to work your ass off, not knowing where it's going to take you because you have all these different obstacles in front of you.

FC: Yes, but you can't question those things. I would never question anything—like, who cares? There's always tomorrow. One door closes, two doors open.

AO: Have you always had that attitude?

FC: Always.

AO: I think that the concept of what work really means has become an issue today for my generation. Personally, I work my ass off. But a lot of people my age don't necessarily have that attitude.

FC: It's all about the work.

AO: Bob Colacello told me once that work was the one thing Andy Warhol believed in. Get up and do it. That's why he gave so many young people and young artists so many opportunities, because people would be questioning what they wanted to do with their lives. They'd ask, "Do I want to be an artist? Or do I want to be a photographer?" And Andy would say, "Just pick up a camera," or, "Come work for me, come start writing, come work." You actually have to work to get it done.

FC: It's true. It's interesting that you're saying that. I think that it is very important. We've had many interns, and oftentimes, everybody gets so excited without understanding the whole process.

AO: They just want the rewards of working hard, but not the labor of it. Work is not a philosophy of life

Calvin Klein
Collection,
Spring 2007.

like it used to be. **Work hard, enjoy life, and be open to anything—because then everything will come. It's a continuous process.**

FC: And a smart mind can transition that into their designs, into their work. I actually think that the aesthetics that I grew up around, and I'm talking about fashion here, were actually very simple. We had a Gap kind of style—we had the basics. Brazilian culture—apart from when you're in Rio during Carnival—it's not very far from the Calvin Klein aesthetic. It's all about the elements and the simplicity of the elements, the basics. Considering all the places that I've worked at, from Oscar [de la Renta] to Gucci [with Tom Ford], I was able to get so much more leverage to see a different way, and take a unique approach to what I could do for Calvin.

AO: **I think that's so interesting that you are designing under the name of a man that is still alive.**

FC: I respect what Calvin did very much, but I couldn't design what Calvin did himself.

AO: **No. It's doing what you want to do in the mind-set of the house's simplicity and how you choose to reinterpret it.**

FC: Sure. But it's very challenging. You have to offer the magic. Otherwise the clothes just become soulless. And I really don't think people today want soulless stuff—they want some sort of fulfillment, some sort of interest. Be interested. Be interesting. So being here [at Calvin Klein] is always an environmental experience that leads you to one type of thing. Everything is so sparse, so white, so precise. Calvin is so great, and he has accomplished so much—that's why it all holds itself together so strongly, like nobody else, like no other company. And we're all

a part of this little company that he created, and all very happy that we're here, that we're doing this and still getting inspired by his legacy.

AO: **Is it hard because he sold his company to a giant corporation? What I mean is, is it hard to be as free as you need to be as a designer? I don't know if there's a group of people you have to please or how that works.**

FC: No. I've been very lucky and I've done everything I wanted. That might change, but I don't know. And I think that the greatest thing is that there was an enormous response from the marketplace, from the press, so that's substantiated the transition.

AO: **Right. You walk the line between being very respectful and still very creative.**

FC: In other words, it's also inspiring for me to be able to be in this position and to have boundaries. It's all an exercise. Respecting boundaries. And I think that restraint is the most exciting thing. That for me is fascinating. It's so different. Anybody can do anything. But it's the creativity; the challenge is to go the route that you can't—

AO: **Yes, exactly. Part of being creative is breaking it down to what the basics should be of that particular creative element.**

FC: Yes, it's really cool.

AO: **Wait, how long have you been at the helm of Calvin Klein's women's Collection?**

FC: This is my fifth year. Can you believe that?

AO: **That's crazy.**

FC: It is crazy.

AO: **Calvin Klein is one of the biggest, most recogniz-**

MAY 6, 2004
New York Minute premiere, Los Angeles.

MAY 12, 2004
New York Minute premiere at Tribeca Film Festival, New York.

SEPT. 13, 2004
Calvin Klein Collection, Spring 2005, runway.

FEB. 17, 2005
American Museum of Natural History Winter Ball.

MAR. 19, 2005
Accessories Council Excellence (ACE) Awards.

able names in fashion and you're one of the driving forces!

FC: I think we have made our contribution. I think we have brought great awareness to the brand, but it's a combination, too. It's all about timing.

AO: You know, when you started at Calvin Klein Collection, that's when my involvement with the fashion world began. That's when I first started attending fashion shows.

FC: And now look at you. You have your own line now.

AO: It's amazing thinking about how much you've influenced me and the passion you've brought to my life. You've really taught me that something can be just so aesthetically beautiful but utterly simple at the same time. It's really influenced how I live my life every day, and how I dress, and what I do. You definitely inspire my own line.

FC: You always look gorgeous in my designs.

AO: So tell me, how do you do it? You have your whole life ahead of you. Is it really just one day at a time?

FC: Well, you have goals, so it's really not one day at a time. The goals are what you dream of: ideals, the perfect thing. You set up those challenges, and then you take it day by day. And then you realize those things in an honest, peaceful way without stepping on anybody else's toes.

AO: I'm always on the lookout for your latest ideas and the new twists to each collection.

FC: What about you? How are you doing?

AO: I'm good. I'm twenty-one and I'm trying to run The Row. I'm learning as I go because I've never done any of this before. It's all new to me. So it's just a huge learning process. I don't read any magazines.

I really just try to stay in my world and figure out what I want, what makes me happy. I've got to trust my instincts. I really try to block out all the media and all the press, magazines, everything. At the end of the day I'm with myself, and I feel like that's the way I've been able to move forward. Block out the nasty things. And there can be a lot of them! [*Laughs*] Apart from my friends like you whose shows I go to, I try not to go to too many shows, or else my focus kind of wanders off into places where other people are going.

FC: But in fashion that makes sense. It's very easy to be influenced.

AO: I really believe that an individual looks best in jeans and a T-shirt, or a black dress or a white dress, or something beautiful with a simple silhouette or whatever it may be. But at the end of the day it comes down to the person and who they are.

FC: You can't forget there's glamour to it. I have seven tuxedos, and jeans and T-shirts—but I don't ever see myself in a suit. Never! I never dress like this. So then I think it's kind of sexy to go to dinner in a tuxedo. It's like a ritual. It's fun. I think for a man or a woman the ritual of going out, putting on perfume—

AO: The idea of putting on makeup, and the lipstick, and the perfume, and the dress, and the heels.

FC: It's amazing.

AO: It feels sexy.

FC: I think it's very sexy. That's fashion. It's women in style, women who dress impeccably for that one occasion. It's so wonderful that women are able to do that.

AO: And trust me, it makes women feel good.

SEPT. 15, 2006

Calvin Klein Collection, Spring 2006, runway.

SEPT. 15, 2006

Calvin Klein Collection, Spring 2006, post-show dinner.

FEB. 9, 2006

Calvin Klein Collection, Fall 2006, post-show dinner.

NOV. 16, 2006

Teen Vogue party.

NOV. 15, 2007

CFDA/*Vogue* 7th on Sale.

NOV. 28, 2007

Calvin Klein hosts the opening of the New Museum.

Feel like a woman,
Wear a dress!

Diane Von Furstenberg

When we left Diane von Furstenberg's office in the Meatpacking District of New York City—housed in a building her empire built—one thing she told us in our interview resonated. She called herself Diane the Hunter. We are drawn to strong women, and Diane's tales of following her own path since she was a young woman living with her Holocaust survivor mother in Belgium are an inspiration to us. This hunter always pursued what she wanted, whether it was a life with her children in New York, an identity as a powerful icon of femininity, or a role as the head of a fashion empire based on simple, modern dresses. She met Prince Egon von Furstenberg when she was studying economics at the University of Geneva. They had two children. In 1970, Diane's jersey wrap dresses became a phenomenon and she was catapulted to the top of the fashion world. (Her designs and growing dominance landed her on the cover of *Newsweek* when she was just twenty-eight.) She took a hiatus from her company in the '80s, but a decade later she regained control of her eponymous label, infused it with renewed vigor, and expanded into accessories and cosmetics. In 2006, Diane was elected president of the Council of Fashion Designers of America. We were her dates to the 2008 Metropolitan Museum of Art Costume Institute gala, and we codesigned our dresses with her. After a fitting, we sat down to talk about her life.

4/17/'08   NEW YORK CITY

DATE   LOCATION   INTERVIEWED BY

DvF: So we're supposed to talk about the people and things that inspire you, right?

MKO: Yes, exactly. We didn't want to this to be a book *about* us; we wanted to focus on the others that we think are influential. People like you.

DvF: What sign are you?

MKO: Gemini.

AO: Born on Friday the thirteenth.

DvF: No.

MKO: Yes; I think I took one personality and she took the other.

DvF: That's amazing. But you really love each other.

AO: It's a connection and love that we can't describe.

DvF: Talk to me about the book.

AO: It's about influence, about the artists and image makers who we think have had an impact on our cultural landscape. And, in a way, we want to help educate our generation, and the generations before and after us, if they read this, about what other people have done with their lives to become influential.

MKO: Exactly. You're a complex woman who has built and maintained a huge company from a very young age, while raising a family. I admire you for your hard work and independence. We want to hear your story.

DvF: Okay, I was born in Belgium. The thing that is special about my birth, and that at the end I now realize really explains everything, is that I am my mother's revenge. When my mother was twenty-one she was a prisoner of war in Germany, and she went to a concentration camp, and she stayed for fourteen months. When she came back she weighed forty-nine pounds and the doctors said she couldn't have children for many, many years; she had gained some weight and was close to being normal after six months, but the doctor still said it wasn't time. And two years later I was born. So in many ways I realize that I am my mother's revenge, you know? She always said that she didn't die so that I could be born. I was a miracle at birth. I think that explains much of my character. What also explains me is that, as a child, she never told me that people could be evil, or stuff like that. The only thing she told me was that fear is not an option—and the other thing is that you have to be your best friend. And very early on I was lucky

to become my very best friend. That gave me so much strength: No matter what happens—the ups, the downs, the this, the that—I'm always with me. And I have a great relationship with me. And I think that's probably my best thing: the relationship I have with myself.

AO: When did that come to you?

DvF: I had it pretty early on, but even when you're frustrated and you feel unattractive and whatever all those negative emotions are that we all have—nevertheless, I always had a good relationship with myself. I always counted on me and I always ended up being with me. And as far as my career—I didn't know what I wanted to do, but I always knew the woman I wanted to be. Now I sound like the American infomercial or something. . . .

MKO: No, no!

AO: We're intrigued! Go on.

DvF: But it's true, it's true. I always knew the woman I wanted to be—I knew I wanted to be a woman who was independent, a woman who was in the driving seat, a woman who didn't need for the man to decide. So I could sleep with anybody and I didn't care if they called the next day. Let them worry if I call, you know? And that is really what I wanted more than anything. I didn't know where I was going to end up, but I knew the feeling of the woman I wanted to become. Fashion was an accident, kind of, I was an intern for this man who had a big factory in Italy, and he had a crush on me. I was learning from him, even though I didn't know I was learning. Now I know that I learned about printing and about fabric and about fit—all from him. But I didn't really know that at the time.

MKO: Where was this?

DvF: In Italy. But meanwhile I had met Egon—Egon von Furstenberg, who was a very attractive, good-looking young prince. I met him when I was eighteen, and he was nineteen. We went out together when we were at school; then he went to America and I went to work for this guy in the factory. He came back and we kept in touch, so to speak. When he came back we became engaged. Even though he gave me a ring I didn't really take it very seriously, but we had an engagement, and that very night I wanted to feel sexy—so I said to him, "I'll make you a son." It was really

more to be sexy than anything else, as I was a very young girl. But sure enough, I got pregnant with Alexander, and I was really upset because I thought, Oh my God, this is the worst scenario. I wanted to be this independent woman and now I'm getting married and I'm pregnant. At the time this was not what I wanted.

AO: How old were you?

DvF: Twenty-one. And this was a time when things were different. Abortions were not as controversial then; we didn't have AIDS, you know. So Egon was in India and I sent him a telegram saying that I had a baby and I didn't think I should keep it. Instead he tells me, "No, no, no, we are getting married." I thought, Oh my God. I couldn't believe it. Here I wanted to be this independent woman—

MKO: You told him over telegram?

DvF: Yes! But I had told him in code. I said I was going to deal with it, and he said no, and that we were going to get married. This was exactly what I didn't want: I'm marrying this attractive, good-looking, rich *prince*—so it really looks like I've put myself in this situation on purpose, like I got myself pregnant to get married. So I go to this man in Italy who I was working with and said to him, "Listen, I'm getting married and I'm going to move to New York so it's really important that I make a few clothes in your factory and try to sell them in America."

AO: And that's how it started.

DvF: Yes, that's how I started. And then I came to America and I had [my son] Alexander, and three months later I became pregnant with [my daughter] Tatiana. It was a whole different life: I was married, going out, living the life, and starting this company that became successful *very* early. At twenty-eight I was on the cover of *Newsweek* [*see right*]. I think it was too much for my husband, so we separated. That's it.

AO: Did you come straight to New York?

DvF: Yeah, I was living in New York. I was basically doing nothing until I got married, and then I had two kids. I started to work—and I did everything. And then from that moment I didn't stop. That's basically my story.

MKO: What was your first design? Or what were the first pieces that you produced?

DvF: A shirtdress. A little jersey shirtdress.

· *NEWSWEEK* Magazine (March 1976). COURTESY OF THE FRANCESCO SCAVULLO FOUNDATION AND SEAN BYRNES.

March 22, 1976 / 75 cents

Newsweek

Rags & Riches

Dress Designer Diane von Fürstenberg

Interview

march

$1/00
35p U

AO: **Was it *the* wrap dress?**

DvF: No, the wrap came afterwards. There was one little wrap top, which then turned out to be a dress, and then became my iconic piece. But [before that] it was all about the fabric, the jersey; at the time I came to America and there was Halston and Giorgio Sant'Angelo and all of those people, and so I was inspired by that movement. But I made clothes that were kind of proper and weren't very expensive. Later it became—I became a brand before I knew it. I branched out into all these different products—I went into cosmetics and made that a success—and then I sold everything and moved to Paris. By then my children were teenagers and I was in love with a writer—I sold everything, and then the company completely disintegrated without me. It became nothing. And then I started to see young girls wearing the old clothes from the vintage shops, from when I was at the company, so I started everything up again. That was ten years ago.

AO: **So you've never had any sort of downfall?**

DvF: Oh yes. I've had many downfalls. Of course. The end of the company the first time, I've had cancer, other things. I've had plenty of downfalls.

AO: **But how did you figure everything out along the way? How did you get people involved and how did you pick your team?**

DvF: At first I had men, which was always the wrong thing. I just assumed that a man in a suit was the right thing for a company. That's not true. No men anymore—everybody's a woman here practically. I made many mistakes along the way, but I've always rearranged it. Something is bad, then I say, "Okay, this is it, I have to deal with it." And then you rearrange it and you see the right thing to do.

MKO: **You've learned to trust your instincts.**

AO: **How do you design from season to season?**

DvF: You know, it's always a little bit of the same in the sense that I am inspired by women and I design to inspire them. I love women. I mean, I love men too, but I respect women so much. I think women are so strong, so interesting, so resilient, all of that. I was lucky because I became the woman I wanted to be, through fashion.

And therefore while I was becoming that woman I was giving other women the tools to be the women they wanted to be. That's what turns me on.

AO: **Me too.**

DvF: That's what I like. I know how to do that at this point. I've had a long life, and I've had lots of boyfriends, and lots of whatever—I've had everything I wanted to have, actually. You know, I can say that now. I have wonderful kids. Great grandkids.

MKO: **Is there anything else you want to accomplish?**

DvF: Sure. I have a vision of where I want to be in this whole thing and it's definitely on its way. I want to be more involved with organizations that empower women. That's what interests me. That's really what interests me.

AO: **Is that why you're working more closely with the CFDA [Council of Fashion Designers of America]? You're the president—talk about an empowered woman!**

DvF: The CFDA asked me to do that and at first I didn't want to do it, but I am very good at getting people together—and I speak all the languages, so I can deal with the French, the Italians, and so on. I simplify things, you know? I have learned how to have it all, and in order to have it all, you've got to work for it. It's not given to you.

MKO: **We know about working hard for things. I take pride in our work ethic.**

DvF: Yes, you've got to work for it—but to be able to have it all you have to give back, because giving back is part of what you get. It's a privilege to give. And to share. This is the second time I've developed this company, and now I'm everybody's mother. The president of my company —I could be her mother! I could be everybody's mother! So it's nice, you know? I'm enjoying the aging process, I really am. There's a lot of advantage about aging, too.

AO: **I love aging too.**

DvF: Yeah, but you love aging when you're twenty, and I'm sixty. It's a bit different.

AO: **I know, but there's some security each year that goes by in my twenties. Like you, we've been working since a young age, and we've experienced some successes. But each year that goes by give me more confidence.**

MKO: **When did you move [into this building]?**

DvF: I built this building. This was a butcher's. I completely created this entire building. I used to be on Twelfth Street. When I started this company again I bought this little carriage house on Twelfth Street and then I decided I would sleep there, because my real home is in Connecticut.

AO: **Oh, okay. How often do you go home then?**

DvF: On the weekends. But when I'm in New York I sleep here, above the office. It's divine. Wait until you see it.

AO: **You have some amazing furniture in this office. Who are some of your favorite furniture designers?**

DvF: I like the twentieth century. [*Pointing first to a table in her office, and then some zebra chairs*] So Michael Graves did this; these I bought in the flea shop—it's a combination. [*Now pointing to her desks*] These are from Norland in the '70s, this is Gibbons. I like bold things.

MKO: **[*Pointing toward DvF's Warhol portraits*] You have quite a collection of artwork in your office, too.**

DvF: [*Pointing to two pictures*] That's my daughter and that's my mother.

MKO: **I recognize the picture of your mom from Bob Colacello's book. Isn't that the same one?**

AO: **He's in the book as well. We had a great conversation with him.**

DvF: He's sweet.

AO: **He was telling us about *Interview* magazine when you were on the cover [*see opposite page*], and the story behind it.**

DvF: When I was on that cover—that was in '77. I have curly hair. But I used to iron my hair; I always had my hair really, really straight. I took this cover picture with a friend of mine and it was late at night and after we did the picture he said, "Okay, now wet your hair." I said I didn't want to, that my hair was curly and I had just straightened it and if I got it wet it would curl. He said, "Precisely. We've already done the shoot so let's do it." And then I saw myself on the cover and from that moment on I left my hair curly.

MKO: **Were you a part of the Warhol scene?**

DvF: I was here in the '70s. And to some degree I was in that scene; I always saw

Andy and he came to all my parties—and I gave a lot of parties. But I wasn't really one of his acolytes.

AO: Bob was telling us how it was a little bit more interesting for younger people in the fashion industry—or New York in general—during that time because there were so many dinner parties. It was really about bringing everyone together, so there were a lot more opportunities. That sense of communication is gone.

DvF: Well, it's different. Now it's all about photographs and celebrities and photo ops and it's so, it's so—I don't know. Let's just say it was much more genuine then.

MKO: How were you able to find balance in your life? Between work and socializing and family—

DvF: But I enjoy my work. I love my kids. I have a great life, I travel, I have a house, I go on the boat, I hike, I do yoga.

AO: And when you were younger?

DvF: When I was younger it was a little tougher. See, I had all the boyfriends—

MKO: They can take up a lot of time!

DvF: Ha, and they were all I was after. I was a hunter. I loved cute guys. Diane the Hunter. I was a hunter—but now I don't have to do that anymore.

MKO: Is there anyone who influences you today?

DvF: Today? I don't know. My mother's the person who influenced me the most, and other than that, my children influence me a lot. We're very, very close. We speak five times a day. I'm just really close to my kids. They're my best friends. Because they always were with me and they were always around. Otherwise, women in general. The strength of women always fascinates me.

MKO: I look up to you so much. I'm such a fan of what you've done, what you've accomplished and the person you are. I hope to be able to be where you are one day.

DvF: Yes, but you're doing well. And you care, and you pay attention, and you have each other.

MKO: That's probably our strength. It's the collaboration. We balance each other out.

DvF: I was talking to my friend who has a twin, and it's something to cherish.

AO: It's a connection you can't really explain. It's kind of beyond any sort of relationship—you don't know it unless you're in it.

MKO: I don't know what else to ask. There are so many things that I want to learn from you, from boys to design to art to furniture.

DvF: Life is about giving, you know? That's a lesson I can give. It's a luxury to give. And even if people take advantage of you a little bit, it's okay. And you have to learn not to get into something that you don't understand. You have to be careful whom you give money or your time to. You should always understand. You're totally capable of understanding everything.

MKO: Yes. We don't do anything if we don't understand it.

DvF: But you're different. You've worked your entire lives, right?

MKO: Since we were six months old.

AO: So our earlier years are different. We've learned so much, but for example, what I'm trying to do with The Row is a lot of work and a lot of time—and a lot of new learning. It's a whole other learning curve.

DvF: I hear your stuff is very nice. People tell me it's very good.

AO: Thank you. It's the most rewarding thing I'm doing right now.

DvF: You both should apply to the CFDA.

AO: We've thought about it seriously, and are keen to do it when the time is right. I want people to know that we're serious.

DvF: I should go and visit you and have you show it to me. Since I'm the president I have a lot to say and then I can speak, I can explain what I saw.

AO: I would love that. That would be amazing.

DvF: We'll find time. Maybe next time you come visit me here I'll come with you to your office afterwards.

AO: That'd be great. That'd be really helpful.

MKO: Well, thank you for having us over today. We're excited about the Met.

AO: Yes! Thank you for inviting us!

MKO: I'm excited about our table, too [at the Met].

AO: Is Christian [Louboutin] coming? I'm so excited. I went with him last time.

DvF: I know. It's always a magic night.

ABOVE:
Diane von Furstenberg's genius lay in the simplicity of her designs and in the fabrics she chose.

OPPOSITE PAGE, CLOCKWISE FROM TOP LEFT: At a premiere in 1973; a colorful DvF at the airport; at "La Belle Epoque" party in 1982; with her first husband, Egon von Furstenberg; pretty in purple on the red carpet; with her friend Christian Louboutin; with Egon; at an awards ceremony in 1987; backstage at her Spring 2008 runway show; receiving her Lifetime Achievement Award from the CFDA in 2005; a picture that Bob Colacello took of DvF with her mother; at a charity fashion show in 1976; with a model in her designs; in country-western gear at a Studio 54 theme party.

John Galliano photographed
by Jean-Baptiste Mondino.

Many designers live for fashion. Arguably that applies to no one more than John Galliano, the designer of his own label and the brilliant mind behind the couture and ready-to-wear labels of Christian Dior. John embraces the future and is passionate about moving it forward. He brings extravagant fashion fantasies to life; his shows make you feel as if you were experiencing fashion history. Mary-Kate went to a show in Paris recently in a Buddha-themed garden of golden ponds, gilded statues, and impossibly beautiful men and women sprawled out on throw pillows and lounges—it could easily have been the set of a new techno *Lawrence of Arabia* film. As the sound track pounded, models vogued onto the runway, posing for the audience and dancing in the fountains. And the clothes, when one remembered to look at them, were breathtaking. A Galliano show is an experience. Born in Gibraltar, raised in London, trained at the iconic Saint Martins fashion school, and now based in Paris, the designer has made his name synonymous with fashion. We're not his only fans—Kate Moss, Charlize Theron, and Linda Evangelista call him when they are in need of something decadent. When we met up with John in Paris, he told us about his fervent search for inspiration all over the world.

3/5/18   PARIS
DATE   LOCATION   INTERVIEWED BY

MKO: **Because you're considered one of the most influential fashion designers working today, we want to know how you're constantly inspired.**

JG: I am influenced and inspired by life, by the people I meet, people I work with, and people I aspire to and hope to meet—people like you! I read, I go to the movies, listen to music—I am just the same as everyone else, only I am always looking for inspiration, looking to create. I am always searching, always on a quest for beauty, for ideas and a muse to seduce me.

AO: **How do you find references for your collections? I read somewhere that you go on adventurous inspiration trips around the world. Do you like to travel?**

JG: I love travel. I've always been obsessed and very curious: Travel indulges this. Each collection is different; we go to different countries, cultures, but as much as that; we are open to find different characters. You can't say where or when inspiration will strike, but you can encourage it.

MKO: **Have any of your travels been more extravagant or more memorable than others? How do you integrate these trips into your collections?**

JG: All of my trips have been memorable in different ways, for different reasons—for where you went, who you met, who you went with, and what you saw, as well as for the end result. The collections are the memories, mood boards, postcards of the adventure brought to life! I remember watching the torero Miguel Abellán dressing before he went into the ring in Seville. He let us witness this intense ceremony, this sacred ritual before he entered the rink for what could have been life or death. Dancing with the monks in China, and flying the acrobats over to perform at the show and traveling around rural China with my team in the back of a van—the women were out working the ground, listening to pre-communist music, and we were bouncing along in a van through the fields. That was one of the most romantic things I have ever done.

MKO: **Speaking of moments, your bow at the end of each show captures such a memorable moment for the audience. Is that moment just as important for you?**

AO: **Yeah, your bow at the end of a runway show is as much a part of the presentation as the models and the collection itself. How much time do you put into your own last look?**

JG: Oh my God! People always ask me this question!! It's absolutely mad! It's so weird to me as I want you all to focus on the designs—I can't believe people really notice me.

MKO: **Of course we notice you! It's such a moment!**

JG: Yes, I do, of course, think about what I wear—I have a lot of people out there to impress—but honestly, I am thinking more about the fittings, the hair, the makeup, the total look, and of course how the clothes look on the girls! I want them to look and feel major!

MKO: **But each one of your looks is so completely different—how do you decide what character to play each season?**

JG: I make an effort. I can't lie—this is my seasonal curtain call, the fashion designers' red carpet, if you like, and it's all for me! You girls know you only get one chance to make a first impression, so I want to, have to, look my best! But as well as it being a photo op, this is in a way a chance to finish a chapter of my life, to celebrate what I have just been immersed in, to say hello and goodbye. I think the most crucial thing about what I wear is that it enhances and complements the spirit of the muse, the inspiration and the icon that I am accompanying up the runway. It's a bit like method acting—I have to immerse myself in the world of the character we are creating so that I can believe and understand and empathize with them, and so the collection has integrity. I blame it on working in the theater as a stagehand while I was at [the legendary London fashion school] Saint Martins—it's all about the right entrances and exits, and I was the best ironer at the National Theatre.

AO: **Is it rewarding for you to be as well known as your designs? How much are you aware of your own personal iconography?**

JG: I feel very fortunate to be at Dior, to be in Paris, to have met the people I have and to be continuing the legacy of such a fashion revolutionary. I love designing, I love creating fashion. I don't really think of myself as famous. You girls are famous, you girls are in the public eye. I am happy to be there as the guy that dressed these girls. The clothes are the stars, not me.

MKO: **What is the relationship between spectacle and fashion? And theater and fashion? Do you have any favorite plays or theatrical events?**

JG: I love going to the theater—whenever we get to London I make sure we go to a gallery, a movie, and most of all the theater! I love going to the theater. It is there to tell a story, to dress a character, to be your armor, your uniform. Fashion should empower you as much as it dresses you—it should make you a femme fatale one moment and a romantic the next. Fashion is there to transport you—it's escapist and seductive. You have to be a showman at heart in this business.

AO: **More than those of any other designer, your shows feel as if you're at the theater. Do you have one favorite show of your own?**

JG: Of my own? Wow! I couldn't possibly say that. It would be like asking a parent to choose their favorite child—you just couldn't! I love working with my team, with Bill Gaytten, the kids, with Stephen Jones, Jeremy Healy, Michael Howells, and bringing an adventure and an idea to life. We have done a cabaret, gone to the opera, the races, the future, to Versailles, to the "Diorrent Express" to Xanadu—I just want to keep going, to keep riding this roller coaster and see where I end up!

MKO: **I love the romance in your show. Would you consider yourself a romantic?**

JG: Absolutely. I am a real, true romantic at heart. Always. That's what it's all for, isn't it?

Ashley bought this robe, which John wore at the end of a fashion show, from her favorite vintage store in Paris.

MKO: **You also play a lot with historical periods and eras gone by. Our twenty-first birthday was a black velvet 1920s-esque garden party. Which eras do you identify with most? And which historical figures?**

JG: I love plundering the past and the decadence of days gone by. I also love the '20s as much as I love the '30s and '40s. I love so many eras; there is so much to be excited by. I love Great Gatsby style, Brassaï, Cartier-Bresson, as well as looking at the jazz era, or further back to other Belle Époque eras. If I could host a fantasy party, it would mirror Truman Capote's infamous black-and-white fancy dress soirée. I would invite him, Marie Antoinette, Napoleon, Lord Nelson, Oscar Wilde and all his dandies, Botticelli, Leonardo da Vinci as well as Andy Warhol, Leigh Bowery and Picasso, Diana Vreeland, Jackie and JFK—as well as all my mates today, Kate [Moss], Gisele, people with style, people who made a mark, people with panache. I'll have to think who I would set you two up with!

MKO: **Yes, please!**

AO: **How would you define personal style? Who do you think are the women and men that look good right now?**

JG: My own style is ever changing and ever evolving. But I am lucky—I now have Galliano Homme, so I am really spoiled for choice! The phrase "I have nothing to wear" doesn't exist now—I design it!

AO: **Is that why you started your label?**

JG: It's me. I am a chameleon; so it is impossible to describe my look; it changes too much. And who do I think looks good? Kate, Gisele, Stella Tennant, Drew [Barrymore], Cameron Diaz, Sharon Stone, Charlize Theron, Penélope and Mónica Cruz, you kids . . . I could go on and on! Basically people that are themselves and are great at it! Style is conviction, that is the secret.

MKO: **Do you think that people get dressed up enough nowadays? I get the impression—because your look is always meticulously put together, or meticulously disheveled—you would like to see people embrace the playfulness, or the originality, or the glamour that fashion has to offer?**

JG: I think people should have fun with fashion, should enjoy wearing beautiful clothes—but also not save everything for best. Fashion is there to be enjoyed, to be indulged—to wow in. Don't save it for Sunday best only. Get it out of the tissue paper and be sensational every day.

AO: **I love the fact that Kate Moss and other top models walked your runways for free when you were a younger designer. Can you tell me about your relationships with some of the other familiar faces of fashion? Are you and your girls an intimate circle?**

JG: I am so so lucky. Kate, Linda [Evangelista], and Naomi [Campbell] were there right at the start. I was incredibly fortunate that we were all starting out at around the same time, all trying to get a break, make our mark, and we've been on this journey together. The first show Kate did in Paris was for me, for Galliano. They are really such

Ashley wearing the robe in Paris.

beautiful and loyal girls, I wouldn't be anywhere today without their support and that of people like Anna Wintour, André [Leon Talley], Mrs. B. It's the people that you meet at the start, that open the doors and get the fairy tale off to an exciting start—they are the ones you never forget, and are always there. The people I am with and work with—we fit, we work. I am a very loyal person—it's the Latino in me, and I am an all-or-nothing personality—and the people that are with me are too. My team is my family, and that is why the shows are so special, because you get to see them, and all your extended family—and you get to put this show on. It's one big family celebration of beauty and imagination!

AO: **Kate [Moss] is iconic for her personal style. When did you meet her, and Linda, and Naomi? How important are these women to your design and the realization of your vision?**

JG: I met these girls when I was still very early in my career—Kate and I are both from South London. Like I said, I was the first show she walked for first in London, then her Paris debut. Naomi is another South London swan and Linda . . . well, Linda is just the source of so much inspiration. These women really do deserve the title "super". I was very fortunate that I had iconic Supers blossoming and starting their careers at the same time as I was. We grew together, they looked amazing in anything they touched, and thankfully they loved what I was doing!

MKO: **What do you find to be the most beautiful part of a woman's body?**

JG: That all depends on the woman: her smile, her eyes, her neck, her curves, her joie de vivre.

AO: **Who are other women you admire? You've vocalized your appreciation for the female form in the past—do you have a muse?**

JG: A muse is ever evolving, ever changing, ever elusive. The perfect woman is out there, and she is many things,

Galliano F/W 2008.   Dior F/W 2008.   Dior Couture S/S 2008.   Galliano S/S 2008.   Dior S/S 2008.

Dior S/S 2007.

Dior Couture F/W 2008.   Galliano Men S/S 2006.   Dior Couture F/W 2006.   Gall

Dior Couture F/W 2007.   Dior Cruise 2008.   Galliano F/W 2008.   Dior Couture S/S 2007.

F/W 2005.   Dior S/S 2005.   Galliano S/S 2004   Dior Couture F/W 2003.   Dior F/W 2001.

JG: Next! No, seriously, I would say to them, Come and have a look at it, come and try it once—look at the work, look at the idea. You cannot please everyone but you also cannot be narrow-minded. Live a little, feel the cashmere, look at the embroidery, understand the technique, time, travel, and luxury.

MO: When you design, do you have the spirit of the Dior brand in the back of your head? Or are you just concerned with pushing fashion forward? How do you meld your own aesthetic with that of the established Dior brand?

JG: Well, I design for my own name—Galliano women's, men's, and kid's—and I design for the house of Christian Dior. I actually work on fifteen collections a year—but when it's fun who's really counting? At Dior his spirit is very much still present, and it is my role to keep his dream alive, but as well as this to keep it modern.

MKO: Do you think he would be pleased with what you have created and accomplished with Dior so far if he were alive today?

JG: If Mr. Dior were designing today, I think we would share a similar approach—I think he would be pleased with where we have taken the house. He was a revolutionary in his day and this is what I want to bring to Dior: beauty, seduction, romance, and rebellion. You have to push fashion forward—we are all constantly moving forward. Time waits for no man, so you have to embrace the future and dress for it.

MO: What is fashion's place in modern culture? Is it expression, is it practical?

JG: Fashion is an expression of the now, yes. Sure, it is one part practical, as we are all wearing clothes, but it is also a business of creating dreams, art that you can wear. It is escapist and indulgent; it is a snapshot of society today.

MKO: So, what's next for John Galliano?

JG: The next adventure is only just around the corner—who's to say what it is, or when it will happen? But whatever it is I can't wait! You have to be ready for anything—who knows! What about you girls? That is what I want to know—what's next for you? Who is your influence?

MKO: Well, you are! But you'll have to get the book to see who else is. Thank you so much for everything.

JG: Good luck with the book, and thanks for asking me to be a part of it.

xo: You grew up in Gibraltar, went to fashion school in London, and now head up a fashion label that is an icon of French style. How has your own life influenced your aesthetic?

JG: I think you have to be influenced by everything and be reckless enough to gamble all or nothing to follow your dreams. You have to believe in what you do as much as love it. You only get a short life, so take chances, follow your dreams, and go where the winds of fate blow you. I have been a gypsy of life and blessed with luck—I am always ready for the next chapter.

xo: Can you remember the moment that you knew you wanted to work in fashion?

JG: Even before I consciously knew it, I knew I was going to work in fashion, always; it's been my destiny since I was born, since watching my sisters, my mother, my grandmother. I was always going to be a designer—I am just lucky I get to do a job that is not a job but more a way of life, that gets me out of bed, keeps me awake, alive, excited, and young! Fashion is what I eat, sleep, dream, breathe!

xo: Let's talk about couture. Your Christian Dior haute couture shows are the hottest ticket on the calendar and have galvanized the couture industry. What are your thoughts on couture? And the future of it?

JG: Thank you for saying that! Thank you! That is what I want Dior to be! Couture is the heart and the soul of Dior. I think couture is such an important part of the fashion industry—it is the center of it all. We work in a pyramidical effect at Dior, and everything stems from the top; the starting point is couture. Couture is, if you like, the eau de parfum—the pure elixir where nothing is distilled. It is raw, exciting, innovative, and beyond luxury. It is the difference between real diamonds and costume jewelery. Detail. Quality. Excellence. Couture is where the idea starts. It is the melting pot, it is where we let our imagination and inspiration run wild.

xo: How do you respond when people say your collections are too over the top?

The designers Lazaro
Hernandez (far left)
and Jack McCollough of
Proenza Schouler.
PHOTOGRAPH BY
NORMAN JEAN ROY.

Lazaro Hernandez (the gregarious Miami native with kohl-lined eyes and charming smile) and Jack McCollough (the one with big baby blues and a boyish charm belied by his tattooed arms) are hardworking, down-to-earth, modest fashion designers. Since meeting at the Parsons School of Design while studying fashion design and showing their first collection as their graduation collection (which Barneys bought), they have consistently presented collection after collection of fantastically imaginative and popular womenswear. Their shows are consistently innovative, their designs have retained integrity, and they've evolved from a small company into an international fashion powerhouse. As a testament to Lazaro and Jack's already established careers and aesthetic, they won the 2007 Council of Fashion Designers of America award *with* Oscar de la Renta, a designer who is most respected in the industry and has been for generations. The Proenza Schouler aesthetic can be described by a series of seemingly opposite adjectives—sexy, strange, aggressive, beautiful, embellished, simple—all at once. I visited Jack and Lazaro at their studio, an old building in Chinatown they used to live in, until the company became profitable and expanded onto other floors. Although we're friends, it was nice to hear about their unique collaborative design process.

2/13/08   CHINATOWN NEW YORK CITY

DATE   LOCATION   INTERVIEWED BY

MKO: So, Jack—where did you grow up, and where did you go to school?

JM: I was born in Tokyo. My parents and I lived there for five or six years, and then we moved to New Jersey.

MKO: Do you speak Japanese?

JM: I spoke a tiny little bit when I lived there, but now I don't speak it at all.

LH: You should see the pictures.

JM: I lived in Tokyo and went to preschool there. Then I moved here when my dad started working in New York. We lived in the suburbs, and I was mostly raised in New Jersey. Went to high school there, was kicked out of high school there, and then I went to boarding school.

MKO: When did fashion become a part of your life?

JM: Not until college, actually. I was more interested in sculpture and fine art. I thought I'd end up in that arena. I went to the San Francisco Art Institute for a minute; I was doing painting and glassblowing.

MKO: Had you visited Venice?

LH: What?

MKO: Where they have the glassblowing stuff, that place called Murano.

JM: No, I hadn't gone to Venice before. I don't really know why I started doing it—it was a weird little thing. I think it was more of my hippie days. I had dreadlocks down to my nipples when I was sixteen. I was a big Grateful Dead head; I went on tour with the Dead. I went to maybe 250 Dead shows.

MKO: I'm jealous.

LH: You should see pictures of Jack from that time: He's twenty pounds lighter, with dreadlocks down to his waist, and a *green* face.

MKO: Okay, where did you grow up, Lazaro?

LH: I was born and raised in Miami, and that's basically it. Went to high school there, went to a Catholic school . . .

MKO: Were you into the arts?

LH: Not really. Actually, when I graduated from high school, I thought I was going to become a doctor and was premed at the University of Miami for two years. I'd always gotten good grades; I always thought that school was kind of easy for me. But then I started blowing school off and living an unhealthy lifestyle, if you know what I mean. So I finally asked myself why I was fucking up, and I realized that something needed to change. I came

to New York for a summer. I'd always been interested in fashion, but for me it was always in magazines or on TV. It was a world that I associated with media; I didn't know that it was real. Then I came to New York and I saw it; I realized there is a world in fashion, there is a fashion industry, there are people doing it here. When I went back to Miami, I decided that I was going to apply to Parsons, and if I got in I would move to New York and do fashion. And if I didn't get in, I'd just keep doing what I was doing. I got accepted.

MKO: [To Jack] Did you go to Parsons?

JM: I went to Parsons too. I transferred from San Francisco, and that was where I met Lazaro. Our freshman year.

LH: Well, before that we met at Light. Remember Light? You might be a little too young, MK. Anyway ,we went to this place called Light on Bleecker Street before we started school. We met there randomly and started talking. We both realized we were starting Parsons in the fall and we were like, "Oh cool, I'll see you in school." The first day of school we walked into class—the way Parsons works is you have sections, where you have every class together with the person—

JM: It's very first grade. You have every class with the same group of kids.

MKO: I love that.

JM: Yes, so you become really close with the people in your section. And I walked into school, and we were in the same section. The only two people that we knew were each other, so we sat next to each other the first day of class. And it started from there.

MKO: Did you admire each other's work at that point?

JM: Lazaro really admired me!

LH: Very funny. You know, we became good friends, and we just started hanging out all the time together. Those were just kind of the development years. We were just starting to find out what we liked ourselves, and what we didn't like, figuring out what our aesthetic was. And we spent so much time together that we realized we mostly had the same self-references, the same eye in a lot of ways. We liked the same things.

MKO: What was your first collaboration?

LH: It was our senior year of Parsons. We had grown and developed as designers to a point where we had very similar aesthetics, so our senior year we asked Tim Gunn—

MKO: *The* Tim Gunn?

JM: Yes, him. Tim is amazing, but it was before that show [*Project Runway*]. He's pretty major now.

MKO: Did he always speak like that?

LH: Yes, it became a joke. He really talks like that. It's amazing.

JM: [*Imitates*] "Could I be any gayer? Make it work!"

LH: So Tim let us do our senior year project together. Before that we would do our homework together all the time, so it wasn't too much of a stretch, and the collection was double the size of any one student's collection. We were proud of it—we had really good fabrics and great quality. That show, our senior year show, Julie Gilhart from Barneys heard about the collection.

MKO: Did she come to the show?

LH: No, Peter Arnold came.

JM: Peter Arnold, who was the head of the Council of Fashion Designers of America at the time, came and really liked it. He told Julie, who bought the whole collection when she saw it. We were still in school at the time.

MKO: For Barneys? That is great.

LH: Yes, for Barneys—it was just our senior school project.

JM: So that's kind of how everything got started.

LH: And then we never went back to school!

JM: That was the fall collection, and then everyone was asking, "Hey, you're going to make a spring collection, right?" *Vogue* started shooting our stuff. And when *Vogue*'s shooting your stuff and Barneys is buying your stuff, other people became interested and started knocking on our door.

LH: Colette [the store in Paris], which hears about everything before anybody else does, came and bought it too. Suddenly, we were servicing Barneys and Colette.

MKO: How did you manage to keep up with the business side?

JM: Shirley Cook [the CEO of the company, who was Jack and Lazaro's roommate in college].

MKO: When did Shirley come on board?

JM: Shirley was working at Helmut Lang, but when we got these order forms we didn't know what to do. We were like, "Shirley, here's a receipt, and another one. Can you file it?"

MKO: How did you keep up with production and deliveries on time?

JM: She did it. She was the logistical mastermind.

LH: In the beginning it was really kind of grassroots, I guess. We did everything, and all our friends would come after their own jobs to help. They'd come here—we used to live here—and they'd help us cut our entire collections. We literally cut our first four fashion shows. It was a really, really fun time. You felt like you were thrown into this world and anything was possible. And it was a time in New York when—

MKO: American fashion was starting to come up.

LH: Yes. We were just lucky. A lot of it was luck; we had just happened to come about at a time when—

JM: I think there are so many young designers in New York now, but none of that existed then.

MKO: It was after September 11, when the fashion industry kind of came together.

JM: Which I feel was a good thing. It was an awful time, businesswise, if you already had a business. Many people lost a lot in the aftermath. But in terms of starting a business right after September 11, it was such a great time because everybody was rebuilding themselves. We were grateful to ride that wave of growth.

LH: It was a time when Calvin [Klein] and Donna [Karan] were super-super-mega-brands. The young designers underneath them were Marc Jacobs, Narciso Rodriguez, Michael Kors—who are amazing, but they're not in their twenties anymore. They're in their forties. All of a sudden they became the establishment, and there was this drive for something new that would support what was young. It was like us, Behnaz Sarafpour, Zac Posen—this whole young fashion world sprang up out of nowhere, and we were just lucky enough to be there at that time.

MKO: What's the design process between the two of you? Who takes care of what, where do you get your inspiration, how do you start a collection?

JM: We're starting resort now, this week. We basically just start with a dialogue about what the mood is, and what kind of silhouette fits that mood. Then we start researching images. We used to go to the library, but now we just kind of use the Internet: We Google Image pretty much everything from color to weird underwear from the 1930s. Anything.

MKO: Yes, I can spend hours in a bookstore.

LH: It's an addiction.

MKO: The hours I've toiled at the Strand [on Broadway].

JM: I love the Strand. You can get lost in there.

LH: The Strand has a good fashion section, actually.

MKO: Well, I like to explore the old films and fashion sections.

LH: This is kind of how we designed the fall collection you just saw. Every season is different, but for fall we went to Texas to see the Donald Judd exhibit and the rest of Marfa, Texas. We formed this idea of, well, the contrast between these really beautiful stark shapes in the middle of this rugged desert terrain. That contrast really appealed to us because our whole aesthetic is based on a general idea of contrast and the idea that what we're arguing with this couture sensibility, this midcentury thing, this notion of elegance that doesn't really exist anymore, and a world filtered through the minds of two men who grew up in the nineties. So it's that. It's high-level, for lack of a better word.

MKO: You have the conversation—then do you sketch separately?

JM: We used to do more so. Now we sketch together because we find we'll get ideas from each other in the middle of the process. Before, we used to split up, and then we'd get back together and edit the collection. It'd be like some of mine and some of his. A lot of times we'd sketch the same thing, which is kind of weird. I'll sketch something and he'll see my drawing and do a version of that, but slightly different, and then I'll go back to my drawing.

LH: We build on each other.

JM: Right. It's more of a dialogue.

LH: And every season we put together these huge inspiration volumes of color and what we like on the street and other images. Then we make two copies and sit down in the country somewhere—right now we're spending a lot of time in the Berkshires. We're obsessed with going out to the country, getting away from

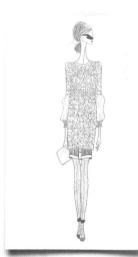

ABOVE: A look into the Proenza Schouler sketchbook.

LEFT: Proenza Schouler, Pre-Fall 2008.

Proenza Schouler,
Spring 2005.

Proenza Schouler,
Spring 2007.

everyone, because you need to be alone. And then we just sit down there for a week, and we just draw from these inspiration things.

мко: Do you sketch?

lн: Yes. But for this collection, the way it evolved was we were making paper airplanes. Here, look at this from fall—all the opening coats are based on the ideas of these things that look layered, but they're all actually cut from the same piece of fabric.

мко: Boys are so good at doing these sorts of things—this technical, ingenious type of folding and draping.

lн: All these layer dresses in the show were actually just one piece of fabric.

мко: The last time we talked, you were trying to put something together without a seam.

lн: Yes, exactly. All those dresses just have shoulder seams, but not layered seams.

мко: It's very mathematical and very cool. It only looks layered from the back.

lн: Like these coats: They look like vests thrown over longer coats, but they're actually just one piece of fabric with no seams at all on the inside.

мко: It's fashion origami.

јм: But they were based on paper planes.

lн: Every collection is really different, and Jack and I just take these really simple ideas and then—well, for us it's not so much about just clothes or fulfilling a woman's needs—

јм: It's a process of creativity.

мко: You do what you want. You have your audience and you have your supporters who trust you enough to be that inspiration for other people. You can be the inspiration for other people, which is kind of great. The fact that your stuff is copied so frequently is a testament to your designs.

lн: The more often that stuff like that happens, the more we want to do things that are harder to copy, the more we want to change. They'll never figure out this construction from a picture. And I think that's what the designer customers look for these days: really special stuff that you're not going to see on a mass level, whether it be gorgeous fabric or hand embroidery or the construction.

мко: Are you inspired by objects or photography or mood?

јм: Yes. Pretty much anything that you see.

мко: I saw a hamburger bun the other

day, and I said, "This is the color that we need to do for spring." It was a hamburger bun, like burnt honey. It's what started the ball rolling for spring/summer.

lн: One piece we did was based on bark. *Bark.*

мко: Do you ever have muses?

јм: No. Not really. It's weird—people always ask us that. It's always bits and pieces of friends, sure, but it's never so specific. It's not that girl, it's more of a hodgepodge.

мко: It's creating a fantasy world. It's going to places and thinking, What would you want this person—if she were standing in the middle of that field—what would you want her to wear? What's her personality? And what the fuck would she be wearing?

lн: There's a group of people whose style we like—Camilla Nickerson, Carine Roitfeld, Chloë Sevigny, you and your sister. These are the girls who don't really follow things. To be honest, we like freaks. They make their own rules, and as a result they become some sort of icon because they become leaders—as opposed to outsiders. I think that's so interesting. People who make their own rules usually feel kind of alone, left out, but in reality they become leaders. They become what everyone else follows.

јм: That's essentially our process. But it's different depending on the season.

lн: Very early on we learned that, for something to be successful, everyone should just focus on what they know how to do best. Whenever you try to do too much at once, you stretch yourself too thin and you can't compete with those who are focusing 100 percent on any one of those areas. We don't know shit about business, but we're not really interested in business. We could give a shit about money—we care about having freedom. What we care most about is having the freedom to sit around all day at our desks and make paper airplanes and do whatever we want to do. If we want to make our collections based on paper airplanes and bark, we can.

мко: And you have worked hard enough to be able to get to there.

јм: Not that we didn't pay our dues, necessarily. But we're starting to get to that point.

lн: That's what we value: independence. That's why, as a young designer, you're

offered all these design positions at established houses that need a designer. They can be really enticing, but you sacrifice—

мко: Integrity.

lн: Yes. Your freedom. Your freedom to do what you want to do. And I've always said that that designer ends up designing pink sweater sets. Because they sell.

мко: Pink is the highest-selling color, or so I'm told.

јм: It's so weird. I don't ever see anyone in pink, but I always hear that's the highest-selling color.

мко: The worlds outside of New York.

јм: Yes, like the Midwest. We did a great collaboration with a retail giant, but we wanted some dome buttons on our jackets—

lн: —and they were like, "Dome buttons are so LY."

мко: What's "LY"?

lн: Last year. Duh. Ha.

јм: We didn't know how a dome button could be LY. It's just a button. They really didn't want to do a dome button because dome buttons were really big the year before.

lн: And we asked, "Who cares about that?" There are so many extra things you have to think of if you're going to be working on that market level.

мко: To be a young designer and then earn your respect in the fashion world—was it a struggle?

јм: Well, being young experience wise was strange. I think it really comes down to experience, whether you're young or old. And it's been hard not having any experience, being thrust into this fashion world, and being critiqued. We're compared to some major people, like Karl Lagerfeld. We're still trying to get there; we look up to the people we grew up with. And we're still trying to figure out exactly who we are and what we stand for and what our vibe is and our aesthetic. But everything you do is up for public scrutiny, at least within the fashion world.

lн: They group all of these designers into one world. We were nominated for designer of the year with Oscar de la Renta and Marc Jacobs. C'mon! It's weird when you find yourself in those situations. We know that we're still learning; we're still deciding what we have to say. You cannot compare us. We were like, "Give it to Oscar. Oscar deserves it! We're kids and we're still learning."

94

ABOVE: The designers at Art Basel Miami Beach.

LEFT: Celebrating their CFDA Award for womenswear in 2007.

MKO: But that can be good too. I think in other industries there's not much attention paid to the younger generations, to the next group. It feels different in fashion.

LH: That's what's cool about fashion specifically. Very few industries want to support the competition. This industry, the older designers and the older editors really want to support young writers and young designers. I can't think of another industry that wants to support its young in such a way that could potentially cause competition. But the fashion world welcomes that somehow.

MKO: Is it hard being so close and working together?

JM: Yes.

LH: Of course.

JM: We work together every single day, plus we have a social life together outside of work, so it can get really annoying.

LH: Not working together is not an option. Not hanging out together is not an option, so trying not to crowd each other is the only option.

MKO: That's what my sister and I had to do.

LH: Yes. And it really works. You get your own space—

MKO: —and then it's more like a choice of when to spend time together.

LH: It's definitely hard, but at the same time, when we're traveling in Europe or we find ourselves with a random person in a random room, that's when we are so happy to have someone to love and trust to be there with you. Sometimes I'm not in the mood to talk, and he'll talk. And vice versa.

JM: At least you have each other.

MKO: What's the biggest learning experience you've come across through this?

LH: Learning responsibility, taking control of your own life, and learning your limits and boundaries. I think this business tests you: You're offered everything, and unless you know where your boundaries are and your lines are, you get lost really easily.

MKO: In life, or in business, what's been the biggest accomplishment?

LH: Whoa. I don't know. I would say just sustaining what we've built. It's one thing starting something, making something, doing it—it's much harder to sustain it. The novelty dies quick.

JM: It does for the stores and the press too.

People don't even really care that we're young anymore. We're not even that young anymore. People aren't going to be as kind to us, so we just have to perform, make stuff that they like. They're not going to be flattered by our smiles.

LH: Even though it started that way.

MKO: That's how you pull them in!

JM: You have to be talented at the start, sure, but it's a series of a lot of things.

LH: It would be one thing to do shit when you're young, but now we can't have less than perfect quality.

MKO: If you weren't doing this, what would you want to do?

JM: Blowing glass.

LH: Having a crisis about what am I doing— that's why I had to redefine my life. I think I will have a crisis again, too. I know that I don't want to do this for the rest of my life, and there are so many other things I want to do. I'd love to just be a nomad for three years. My dream is to just travel as much as possible and have full weeks when you can really explore a place. That's very interesting to me.

JM: I'm the same way. So yes, I could see us doing something completely different in ten years.

Lauren shot by
Fred Seidman.

OPPOSITE:
a childhood
portrait.

They just don't make 'em like Lauren Hutton anymore. Lauren has opened our eyes to the world in an entirely new way. We had been obsessed with her style for years, but we never had the chance to formally meet her in person. After Ashley rattled on about how amazing she thought Lauren was to a mutual business acquaintance, we were finally given the opportunity for an introduction, which we quickly took advantage of. Needless to say, Lauren was everything we thought she would be. In every aspect of her life, Lauren is a pioneer. She refused to correct the gap between her teeth when she entered the modeling scene in 1964, and this "imperfection" became one of her most recognizable and beloved traits. She was one of the first models to negotiate a major cosmetics contract. She founded her own brand of cosmetics, "Good Stuff." She posed nude for *Big* magazine at the age of 61. Whether she's crisscrossing the globe to hike, camp, or simply explore, there's just no stopping her. Lauren is one of the wisest, most compassionate, and most free-spirited people we know. She juices the joy out of everything she touches. She even calls herself our "God-Granny." So when we were selecting the model for The Row's Spring 2008 look book, we knew there was no one else to ask but Lauren.

11/2/07

NEW YORK CITY

DATE   LOCATION   INTERVIEWED BY

AO: Let's start at the very beginning. Can you tell us where you were born and who first discovered you?

LH: I think you discover yourself.

MKO: Yes, absolutely, and you have a strong sense of self.

LH: I was a poor Southern white girl—we weren't born in a barn, but we got there soon enough. My mother went to school with Gloria Vanderbilt, and I went to school with a bunch of deep country kids. Seriously rural. Or kids that were just first-generation Floridians, coming straight from New Jersey. Old-time crackers and first-generation everybody. It was a little dangerous amongst teenagers.

MKO: So you had street smarts at a young age.

LH: Swamp smarts is what I'd call it. I hadn't really seen any streets before I moved to New York. More like dirt roads.

AO: You had experience, though. Moving and traveling was a form of education in itself.

LH: Well, I was born and lived in Charleston, South Carolina, then Miami, then the swamp outside of Tampa, helping to raise my three half sisters.

MKO: Who was the first photographer you worked with?

LH: Dick Avedon. Diana Vreeland asked Dick, who had seen me three times and not booked me, to shoot me. She saw something in me—basically what she saw was that I was one of those kids who didn't wear bras, or too much makeup. I was a newfangled youthquake. I wasn't one of these big, giant European models. She had seen us in the street and wanted to cash that moment. So when I got to Dick, I wasn't up to the quality of his models—I didn't know as much as the other girls. He asked me where I had come from and I told him, and we developed a technique of me running and jumping. Like a kid in the swamp. So all my early pictures are of me jumping. Finally, when I landed, I learned how to model.

AO: And you're still modeling.

LH: Yes, I am. I just did a Lord & Taylor campaign.

MKO: Do you think you changed the ideal aesthetic of a supermodel at that time?

LH: I think I made it more natural as I used less makeup. The makeup was very heavy in those days, and I looked bad in a lot of makeup. I looked bad in heavy eyeliner. We did our own makeup in those days. More importantly, I changed fashion when I signed my first Revlon contract.

MKO: How so?

LH: Contracts didn't exist at that time; campaigns didn't exist. I saw the sports guys getting contracts and figured we should too. It made it about money rather than prestige, and that changes everything.

MKO: Yes, but those were beautiful magazines back then.

LH: In New York I was waitressing at night to keep myself alive, and then I did Christian Dior.

AO: Dior was your first ad campaign?

LH: No, at the time, they didn't have campaigns. I was a Dior NY showroom model. I'd finally learned to look in the want ads to get a job, and I was determined to never be a cocktail waitress again, because it was too debilitating. People would look at you funny and think you were a B-girl and I wasn't one of those—

MKO: And they felt free to talk to you in a certain way—

Mary-Kate and Lauren shot by Peter Lindbergh.

LH: Yes. And treat you disrespectfully. And you had to grin and take it, because you were working for tips. And six hundred dollars back in 1962 was a tremendous amount of money. But I was willing to do any modeling job just to save money so I could get to Africa.

MKO: Were you looking for a man at this point? Or did you feel like you always needed to take care of yourself?

LH: When I came back to New York, I had teas. I had already had one bad man, twice my age—it was a classic situation where I had never met my father and was looking for that figure—and I didn't want to waste my time. So when it came to men, I was looking for something else, for art and museums and travel. The outside world. Tribes and bugs and nature and stars. A guy had fifteen minutes to make his case at tea; I was looking for someone who was interested in all these things, someone I could learn from. More brains than beauty. One of my goddaughters says I invented online dating—it was like that, except it wasn't on a computer. You talk to someone for a few minutes and then blow 'em off. Until I met this one guy—he was the thirty-ninth tea. Maybe he was the fortieth. His name was Bob, and he knew about everything I wanted to know about. And thank God I followed my instinct. And him.

AO: He taught you a lot?

LH: Boy, he was my Aristotle. He taught me that men's and women's brains evolved from their genitals. We were simple creatures that evolved into more complex beings, into two sexes. And that wasn't for fun—we saved each other. Men are short-term hierarchical thinkers. Women are about feeding and warmth and safety, and it's beautiful. You need both of those in the world. We're long-term linear thinkers. And I learned that living with nine hunter-gatherer tribes. But men are fun, they have ideas, and they're wild. They're an exotic animal. I just love men.

MKO: I love men.

AO: Me too.

LH: They're a whole other species. And a whole other animal. They have different brains from us. But be careful. Because—

MKO: Because you have to know what to pull from them. And you have to know what you're giving them.

LH: That's true, but what we're talking about gets relearned all over again by each succeeding generation of women, if it gets learned at all, so it feels almost entirely new with your generation. It's hard to know without going through it. Experience. A lot of women stay with guys they shouldn't out of pity. I think most of my goddaughters have learned that. Intimacy is so intimate for us. And that is the natural double standard.

AO: Define "natural double standard."

LH: Well, we are meant to know the seed that we're taking, because nature wants to make a masterpiece every time. We're genetically bioengineered to make a masterpiece. But I think men are built to spread their seed all over. A girlfriend of mine wrote a song line that says, "I fall in love every time I see the ceiling above me." She's saying she falls in love every time she's intimate with someone—and I think a lot of girls do that. But I don't think it's the same case with men. We really have different agendas biologically.

MKO: Especially in relation to intimacy.

LH: We've got to be very careful about who we have sex with. So you

Lauren as a young
"wise woman."

better know whom you're spreading the seed with. Even if there's no seed being spread.

MKO: I love that you love men so much, and you can still keep your beliefs about your self in the forefront of your life.

LH: Well, I'm always looking for guys my own size—mentally.

AO: I think that's great. And totally true.

LH: There's so much pressure on us women, because of all that we've talked about. And so much pressure on us as people. I'm looking at you both now, who have been celebrities since childhood. And you have weathered so many storms—we're talking tsunamis. I'm very proud of you. Where are your people from?

AO: We are part Norwegian, French, English, Italian, and Sioux Indian.

LH: Oh, so you all have a great tribal mix. That's one of the reasons that I was popular—it was because everybody could identify with their people in my face. That's the greatness of America, is that we're all tribes. But more important than knowing ourselves as tribes is knowing ourselves as women. All women need to know is what's happened to us women in the last three thousand years. I always say there're only two races—men and women. I came to that idea when I lived alone on the Bowery, when it was a cracked-out avenue in the 1980s. When I would wake up, that would be the first thing I noticed: There're only men and women. We should share everything we learn.

AO: Knowledge.

LH: It's the most important thing we can do. More important than personal love, more important than children, more important than money. It's the most important thing we can share.

MKO: It just occurred to me that this interview is not going to be about fashion.

LH: No, there's no such thing as fashion. Fashion is an idea to make you think that you're not in it at all times. Fashion is what you're offered four times a year by designers—and style is what you choose.

MKO: But I like that you transcend fashion. Your story, and your talk with us today, isn't about just fashion. It's about your life story, how you've influenced us, your beliefs, and about influencing women in general.

LH: Good, good. Thank you.

AO: "Thoughts from a Wise Woman" we should call your interview.

LH: That's funny! The very first interview I ever did was with Eugenia Shepard from the *New York Times*. She was a wonderful, kind fashion editor, and she asked me what I wanted to be—I think I was twenty-two or twenty-three when I gave this interview—and she said, "What do you want to be when you grow up?" And I thought for a second; and then said, "I want to be a wise woman." I didn't want to be a rich woman or a married woman or this woman or that woman. I wanted to be a wise woman. And everybody laughed at me when they saw it in the paper.

AO: Why?

LH: They thought I was being pretentious. But I was real. I still want to be one. I guess they thought our wise women were little crones who lived in the woods....

AO: They were wrong. Wise women are beautiful women who've experienced a lot and have a lot to give back just with words.

ABOVE: A vintage picture of Lauren shot by Fred Seidman.

FILMSTRIPS: Lauren modeling in our Spring 2008 look book for The Row.
PHOTOGRAPHS BY KT AULETA.

A self-portrait of
Karl Lagerfeld.
© CHANEL.

OPPOSITE:
The elaborate carousel
set for Chanel's Fall
2008 fashion show.
© CHANEL.

Karl Lagerfeld—the man behind Chanel, Fendi, and his own Lagerfeld Gallery line—is famous like no other fashion designer. In Japan, his personal appearances have been known to incite riots. That's because, more than any other person in the history of fashion, Karl has single-handedly raised the profile and respect of what it means to fill a woman's wardrobe. His look is iconic, his designs constantly contemporary, his ideas always modern, and his intelligence beyond measure. He speaks four languages fluently, he shows a minimum of ten collections per year, he is an accomplished photographer, and he moonlights as a book publisher with his own imprint with Steidl. Born in Hamburg, Germany, Karl moved to Paris in 1952 and quickly became a designer for a variety of houses—including the couture houses of Pierre Balmain and Patou, and later the labels Krizia and Chloé. He joined Chanel in 1983, and his image quickly became synonymous with high fashion. Long before it was appropriate for us to wear Chanel, we were obsessed with the label's quilted bags and hip yet bourgeois look—Chanel is our first high-fashion memory. Lagerfeld asked us to meet him in the Chanel studio on the Rue Cambon, high above the apartment that Coco Chanel herself kept in the building. It was like climbing up to couture heaven.

2/28/08
DATE

CHANEL OFFICES ON
LOCATION RUE CAMBON IN PARIS

INTERVIEWED BY

AO: What we want to know is, who are some of the people that inspire you? In fashion and in photography?

KL: It's interesting. I like some photographers from the past, yes. The early days. But I'm not really inspired in that sense—because I don't want to do what other people did. The real inspirations to me are the people in the pictures. I have one beautiful portrait of Isadora Duncan, the American dancer who danced in Greek dresses. She was the one, in fact, who suppressed the corset before fashion did. But she ended very badly—she ended in a car accident when her scarf got caught in the wheel of a speeding car. In those days the wheels had a wire, which caught her scarf and strangled her. Very sad.

MKO: Yes. So you like portraits.

KL: Yes. I like to do portraits. I love it. But today you have to be careful—the photographer has to be very careful—because all the pictures start to look the same because of Photoshop. There is this man in New York who works for everybody, and all the pictures he does now look the same. They don't look human anymore. That's okay if you're an older face that is distinct, but the younger people lose all expression. They look the same.

AO: That's what Lauren Hutton was telling us. Now she's an older woman and gets the work that she wants, but she said it was very different when she was younger. She had her own look when she was young—and had that very distinctive face and gap teeth—it was sometimes hard for her to find work, because everyone started to look the same—perfect teeth, perfect skin.

KL: But then you have to face the reality one day. Some people I know—I will not mention them by name—make advertisements and campaigns with photos of themselves from 20 years ago. And then they go and stand next to the ad and you don't even see that's it the same person. Ha! You have to update, or make an effort to stay in shape.

AO: What do you do now to stay in shape?

KL: Nothing. Diet is something that has to be made to order for you, for each person. You may be twins but your systems may be different. Men are very different from women. I have a doctor who I made a book with that sold five million copies all over the world [*The Karl Lagerfeld Diet*, by Karl Lagerfeld and Dr. Jean-Claude Houdret]. Every country bought one, I think, in Russia and Italy and everywhere. But I don't get it—I don't know what Japan is going to do with a European diet book!

MKO: Ha!

KL: And I must say that now I only like to eat what I'm allowed by my doctor. Since I started my diet, which was like eight years ago, I haven't touched what I'm not supposed to: sugar, cheese, nothing! I don't even look at it. It looks to me like *plastic*. And the funny thing is, I know when it's eight in the morning, or one o'clock—I don't even have to look at my watch. I'm hungry. At eight in the evening I know it's time to eat. And if I'm hungry in between—it never happens—I have a very special protein my doctor has made. Twice a week I have to eat meat, which I'm not too crazy about, but it's good for you. You know, the most dangerous diet in the work is macrobiotic. Don't touch that.

AO: I couldn't even think about it!

KL: I knew a Finnish girl once, who was stunning. She started [the macrobiotic diet] and one morning she woke up with a pimple. The next day her hair, then her face and her skin—it was all changing. In three weeks it was over—forever. She could not get the face back. Never.

AO: It messes with your system.

KL: I think she started as a housecleaner, and now she is probably that again. She started modeling when she was young—nowadays you start to model because you're young. Now the girls are sixteen, seventeen, fifteen, and Russian. They are like from another planet.

AO: They can look very bizarre!

KL: I hate all these tall women. They are all giants!

MKO: If only I were a little taller—that would make me happy!

KL: You are one meter fifty-one. You are taller than that?

AO: We're five feet and one inch.

KL: Oh, I thought my office told me that you were four-foot eight or something. Not that it matters. What you need is a face. If you have a face you don't need height or a voice. Models know this; that's why the good ones don't need to talk much.

MKO: So how did you get started in the fashion business?

KL: I won a contest. I was in school—not fashion school, I was never in fashion school. I moved here for school, and was in school for one year. Then there was a huge culture affair, and a contest for the International Wool Secretariat, which asked for sketches of things like coats and dresses and boots. There were 200,000 people doing it, and I won the first prize for my coat. It was pure accident, everything. And then the house of Balmain produced my coat, which gave me quite a lot of money for a schoolboy in those days. They asked me what I wanted to do later on; I said I liked the idea of working in fashion—but I didn't say that I was still a schoolboy. So Balmain asked, "You want to join [our couture house]?" And you know in those days you dressed like a grown-up person even if you were not. So they asked me to come. My parents said, "Okay, you are in school, so go there, and if you don't like it you can go back to school. We don't want you to say one day you missed the chance of your life." I went there, didn't like it too much, but I said to myself, Who wants to go back to school? So for two years it was the idea of going back to school that kept me in fashion—I was not crazy about school.

AO: How do you pick your team, like the people who support you?

KL: Well, that is very difficult to say. By feeling, through people I know, through the recommendations. For every person here it is different. But some of them I have been with for twenty years. Like there is one who has never worked for anyone except Chanel, and another one I met while I lived in Monaco—I met an English woman who had a neighbor in the countryside who had a daughter who would love to work in fashion. And oh, Pascal over there [*motions to a man in the studio*], his aunt was my assistant for twenty years and he has never had another job since he was seventeen or eighteen. It's just wonderful. I got her [*motions to another girl in the studio*] when we found her at school in Belgium. I have found good people in Belgium. Very gifted. Very funny. But in a good way. I hate normal people.

MKO: Normal? No! That's very important.

AO: And it's great that you're giving other people—younger people—opportunities.

KL: I like to work with models for a long time.

Posing with Karl after his show. PHOTOGRAPH BY OLIVIER BORDE, COURTESY OF CHANEL.

Sitting front row at the
Fall 2008 Chanel show in
Paris with Mario Testino
and Claudia Scchiffer.
PHOTOGRAPH BY OLIVIER
BORDE, COURTESY OF CHANEL.

The merry-go-round set from
the Fall 2008 show was full
of Chanel's iconic symbols,
including the label's cuff,
pearls, interlocking *C*
logo, jacket, gardenias
and quilted bag.
© CHANEL.

FOLLOWING SPREAD:
ALL PHOTOS © CHANEL.

Karl always has big ideas, like this oversize Chanel tweed jacket that was the centerpiece of the runway from the Spring 2008 couture collection. © CHANEL.

Sometimes the girls change, but some girls I work with for years and years. With male models it is different. I hate working with male models.

AO: Ah, well, boys come and go!

KL: And I hate doing castings and things like this. "Oh no, you're not right"—that's horrible to say to someone. I never do castings. Other people do them, and then I see the result of the casting. It's humiliating for the models.

AO: How do you separate your work from your different collections? You design so many collections—for Chanel, for Fendi, for yourself—that it must be hard to focus.

KL: It's not. It all just comes. It's very strange. This is something I cannot and I do not try to analyze. It honestly doesn't cost me any effort. I don't even think about it.

AO: Do you take time off, though?

KL: Time off? You have seen the number of collections that I do. How could I?

AO: I know! That's why I ask. Don't you ever just want a vacation?

KL: But why should I? You have to take time off if you have a boring job. But my job is perfect. I do it in the best conditions. I never have to think about business. And there is no ego—I couldn't care less about that. You know, in Europe I can't even cross the street. I need ten bodyguards to cross the street. And it's even worse in Japan. So I don't even think about those things—the company runs the business. And the money? I could not care less. What I like about the *job* is the *job*.

MKO: Do you get inspired by people?

KL: Oh sure, yes. You cannot say no. That would be a lie. But you cannot say which people because you always must mix the expected with the unexpected. The trick is to keep your eyes open. The people around me are only people I like. I don't work with people I don't like. I don't have people I don't like around me ever.

MKO: You don't have to.

KL: Even the assistants, and the assistants of the assistants—I've got twenty-five girls here. I don't work with many men. I don't want to ask the men about the fashion. Their opinion doesn't interest me.

MKO: And women are your target audience—they're the ones buying the clothing.

AO: And they know their bodies and how a fit can be flattering or not.

KL: I like more classic [shapes] now. Best thing to do for skinny people to wear tight dresses. Although jeans are becoming too tight.

AO: Ah! Yes, it's becoming a problem. It's the worst.

KL: You can kill yourself in these jeans.

MKO: Ha, I'd rather stay inside with my friends than limp out in tight trousers.

KL: Maybe you'll stay inside with a baby. Do you want to get married? Children? Two perfect mums, yes?

[*Mary-Kate and Ashley look at each other*]

KL: Ah! Don't worry, you have time. You're young. Don't you want to get married?

MKO: I don't feel the need to get married. But Ashley wants children. I'll be a great aunt or godmother.

AO: To my child.

KL: [*To Ashley*] Are you planning?

AO: No. I don't even have a boyfriend. You have to plan that first, right? Figure that out first?

KL: If you get a boyfriend it doesn't mean that! Today you can have a baby first. If you want. I never liked the idea of a family at all. If it's a woman—it's more fun for a woman.

MKO: Were your parents in the fashion business at all? Are they artists in any way?

KL: I can tell you, when I was a beginner it was really horrible. My parents' generation? You didn't work in fashion. Very unpleasant.

MKO: When you were little did you ever sketch?

KL: I was born with a pencil in my hand. I always sketched but I never went to art

school. I don't understand how other people cannot sketch —but they can write. For me sketching and writing is the same thing. It's something I like to do. I love paper—that's why I have paper all over the place.

[*Mary-Kate slips on one of Ashley's rings and feigns she will steal it*]

KL: You are afraid she's going to run off with your ring? Ha! But you have a nice one left on this finger.

AO: Mary-Kate gave me this diamond for my birthday and then I designed the setting and had it set.

KL: Where?

AO: In New York.

KL: And this pink one? Ah, it's Chanel. I like the mix of fake and real. You know, there's a beautiful place in Paris for rings, you must go there. Do you know the shop Goyard? They make luggage. The next store, on the same side, three or four down. That is my favorite place. Divine. And the woman is nice. This came from there too [*pointing to one of the enormous rings on his fingers*].

AO: It's beautiful.

KL: Yes, they're sapphires.

MKO: I love sapphires.

KL: Me too. You know what I like also? Antique-cut stones. They don't have the same value, but I love them.

MKO: I love rose cut; it's my favorite.

AO: They're not valued, but at the same time, they're so beautiful.

KL: You don't buy the stones to impress other people, though—you buy them to please yourself.

MKO: Exactly.

KL: I love rings. Sometimes with no gloves I wear even more rings. But I put my rings most of the time here [*up on his knuckle and under his gloves*], because when you say hello to someone it hurts. Sometimes people are rude and sometimes they really scream!

MKO: You know the store Scarlet? She had a collection of your original full-finger costume jewelry. I bought every one in the store. They're unbelievable.

KL: They're the best. I love antique jewelry.

MKO: I love my jewelry.

AO: Do you get involved in the jewelry here at Chanel?

KL: Yes, but the team works from my idea. But for me I really like the very old pieces.

AO: What era?

KL: I like eighteenth century. I even collect things I

cannot wear because the stones are too big. I like stones. You know, if you have a big stone here [*pointing to his necktie*] or here [*pointing to his lapel*] people don't even look in your face anymore. Ha! I had one giant stone for a party at the Met from the Belle Époque and everyone just stared at it.

ʌo: But that's not necessarily a bad thing, right?

ʙʟ: They don't look at your face—they only look here.

ʌo: I should start doing that more often!

ʙʟ: But the trick with those big stones is to treat it like nothing

ᴍᴋᴏ: I hear you. Look, one of my emeralds already fell out.

ʙʟ: But that can be redone, no problem.

ʌo: You think that the real luxury item is one you use all the time? Good to know, cause I have a Birkin [bag] that's beat to shit.

ᴍᴋᴏ: Do you collect anything specific?

ʙʟ: I collect too many things. I collect a lot of things. Coming across things is very exiting, so I keep these things. I have several houses even in Paris. I have my Heartbreaker Hotel, the town house next to it for guests, and then I have my studio, which is a huge place, my studio, but it's also a library—a bookshop in front and behind my private library, only there are over a hundred thousand books. You have to see—it's nothing to believe. These are books that I don't sell.

ʌo: What kind of architecture do you like? Do you like modern?

ʙʟ: No, no I like eighteenth-century French—and something completely modern, like Zaha Hadid and Rem Koolhaas. We did this thing for Chanel [with Hadid] that will be a modern art container, which I love—it starts in Hong Kong, then it goes to Tokyo, and all the art is put in a container and shipped from one place to the other. It comes to New York for fall. It's great, it's really great.

ʌo: I studied architecture.

ʙʟ: I love architecture. I will take ten years to build a house if I want. I just built a modern house in Paris. It's an eight-room apartment with a big balcony. I tore everything down; I had to rebuild the building including the floor. One level is completely glass, with a glass floor.

ʌo: So it's very modern.

ʙʟ: Beyond modern. There's not one piece of furniture designed before 2000.

ᴍᴋᴏ: What is it filled with? Do you collect art art?

ʙʟ: Art? I have no space. I have only books. I have so many books that there is no space left for art! Ha! I bought an apartment in New York in Gramercy Park and I made a collection of this early German art. I don't know if I really need the apartment—I bought it something like three years ago and redid it. And someone said to me they'll give me five million more than I paid for it, but my business manager said I don't have to sell it. I don't need it but I love Gramercy Park. It's great. Gramercy Park is beautiful. And the building is attached to the [Gramercy Park Hotel], so there will be room service. But I never spent one night there. It's done, everything is there, but not the furniture, but I never spent one day there.

ᴍᴋᴏ: I feel like I always see you at the Mercer when you're in New York.

ʙʟ: Being at The Mercer is like being at home. I like the idea of doing up [new apartments, like the one in Gramercy Park]. "Doing" is fun; "Having done" is a bore, no?

ʌo: Do you spend time in LA?

ʙʟ: I love LA but for me there is no reason to have a house there. What is the security like in LA?

ʌo: It's tough. I won't lie.

ʙʟ: Security is important. Here, because next door is the former president of France Jacques Chirac, and if you're president of France, for the rest of your days you have bodyguards, we have policemen in front of the door night and day.

ʌo: That's perfect.

ʙʟ: When people recognize you in the streets, they don't talk or anything like that? Or do they?

ᴍᴋᴏ: No, they talk to you. They say things to you to get a reaction, and often it's not the most polite things to say to a woman.

ʙʟ: That's awful. That's what I don't like. I mean, I love LA, I love the life, but I hate the idea that you cannot walk around the streets in the city. That's why Miami is more fun. It may be trashy, but it's fun. How bad does it get for you?

ᴍᴋᴏ: It can dangerous when you're driving particularly, because they follow you in cars and scooters. That's bad. That's not easy.

ʙʟ: I had two accidents where I fell asleep—after that I thought it was better that I don't drive. I'll get a driver. I'm a bad driver because I want to look there, there, there, and up there. I get bored easily—so twice I fall asleep, and twice the car is destroyed. One was a Porsche and the other a Mercedes. One hit a pole next to the highway, and the other against a tree. I had nothing [wrong] with me—but both cars were destroyed. After that I thought, Now, we've had it. I haven't touched a wheel in years. I'm not even sure I still know. But it's like swimming—you don't forget.

ʌo: Or like riding a bike. Even though I forget every single time I'm on a bike! I'm not great at that.

ʙʟ: But you know the bicycles in Paris [a new service aimed at getting Parisians to bike around the city on bicycles] —several people got killed because some people don't know the rules, they don't know the circulation, they don't look left and right. I think it's okay in the summer.

ʌo: No, I'm not a bike person.

ʙʟ: You know I went to school as a boy for—how many years? Eight years. Eight years I went to school—six miles there, six miles back. Very good for the legs. It's true. I've never had a problem after that—I'm still built like this [*raps on table*]. Everything you get very early [in life] is good. I could make a shorter way, but then I'd have to walk—walking across the fields was only three miles, not six—but I don't care to do this. The fields with the bulls and the cows and all that—nobody thinks that I'm a country boy, but my childhood was in the country, which I think was a very good thing for sure.

ʌo: Do you ever visit the place you grew up?

ʙʟ: No, no, no. Never. Because when I was a child I only had one ambition: Let's get out of here. I wanted to be grown-up and everything. So, when I left my parents didn't like the place anymore. They had only bought it to put the children there; they hardly went there—my sister married very early when I was still a child. So I grew up there alone. It was perfect that way: I could read, sketch, and the children in the village were idiots, so I hardly went to school. But when I was moved, I thought it was good move, and I did not look back. And I still haven't.

Karl is constantly decorating his hands
with unique jewelry and gloves. This
accessory showed up in a 2008 collection.
PHOTOGRAPH BY STÉPHANE FEUGÈRE,
COURTESY OF CHANEL.

VOGUE

JAN
£2·20

THE 1990s
WHAT NEXT?
COLLECTIONS
THE NEW DECADE'S NEW SHAPING
PRINCE IN PICTURES
ENTER THE VOGUE AWARD

I've always believed that you have to put in your time in order to succeed in whatever you want to do. No one has made this idea more clear to me than the photographer Peter Lindbergh. At twenty-seven, Peter first picked up his camera; more than thirty years later, he is known for helping invent the supermodel phenomenon of the 1990s and is regarded as one of the most iconic fashion photographers of our time. Peter shot me for my first solo cover for *Harper's Bazaar*, and since then, our relationship has continued to grow and grow. (I loved the pictures from that shoot so much that I asked to keep the prints.) We even collaborated on a personal video project together, just for fun. He has the ability to make a woman feel both totally natural and totally beautiful in front of the camera. His pictures are known for their studied honesty, no matter what he chooses to focus his lens on. And in my case, he has captured a side of myself that I don't always see when I look in the mirror every morning. (Thank God!) Peter never wants to take anything from you other than the truth; because of that, I trust him completely. In talking with Peter, I found that this search for realness marks not only his professional life but his personal life. Whether he's taking a photograph of a model like Helena Christensen or a circus elephant, you feel his wisdom in everything he does.

3.11.08   SOHO GRAND HOTEL, NY

DATE   LOCATION   INTERVIEWED BY

AO: **The way that you photograph a woman is really something else. You always manage to capture a natural beauty. You just get it.**

PL: I very much like that kind of trueness in a person. That's what's amazing to me. It's the act of being in love each time, in a way. And it's really something—it's not something stupid and funky. I'm a little old now, too. So you have to feel you really understand someone well, no? I'm at a really good moment in my life—for the past few years, I've started to really *like* people. I'm really able to like people for who they are.

AO: **How did you get there? [*Laughs*] How did you get to that place? Tell me!**

PL: I have no idea. Someone just said to me, "There is something different between you and everybody else I know." He wanted to know what was between all these people and me. I said, "I don't know. It's probably because you feel that I like you." He told me that nobody liked him because he's a little pain in the ass. So I told him it's probably because I understood *why* he's a pain the ass, and I don't take it personally. People feel that. Then they feel comfortable and they open up—it's a really amazing process. There's no technique for something like that.

AO: **Do you think this ability to connect with people is what has made you such a successful photographer?**

PL: I got started in photography *after* art school. I had worked for a few years as an artist, but then didn't feel like it was the right thing for me. When I stopped it was the first time in my life I didn't really know exactly what I wanted to do. I was twenty-five. I stopped for six months. Then someone I knew, a photographer, was looking for an assistant. I became his assistant, and then about a year and a half after I said, "My God, this is so easy. I can do it myself." And I did it. [Laughs]

AO: **I remember you told me you did a campaign for a perfume once, and how you were very particular about the final product. The story was that you were photographing a woman with scars on her face, and the perfume people wanted you to sign off the rights to airbrush it. They wanted to airbrush it and you didn't. Do you remember that?**

PL: Yes, and I'm really so pissed with the retouching. It's so horrible. I've done jobs in France where they retouched her so much. I got so mad I went over to the CEO from the company, and I said they killed the emotions of the picture. I called them about how it was very embarrassing and how they had to be careful about what they did, because women were going to *hate* them for the image they were projecting, this kind of creature from Mars who didn't exist.

AO: **You seem to bring out a truth in every single person. Especially for women. Has the digitalization of photography affected the way that you shoot?**

PL: It's the opposite of before. Every idiot in the studio—the assistant hairdresser even—is giving comments about the pictures. And I get more and more pissed about it. I just decide not to use that, so nobody can look at it.

AO: **Block it out.**

PL: Because when you work on something with someone, you cannot have someone saying, "Wow! It's great!" I'm like, "What do you mean it's great? I'm just starting. You want me to stop?" It's funny. It's a process. Of course, it's a miracle that you push a button and see a picture on the screen, but that doesn't mean it's as far as you can go. That changed so much from before. In the past you were alone; nobody knew what you were doing. You were insecure.

AO: **It's almost like that feeling of insecurity was more intimate in a way.**

PL: I always say photography is not democratic. "Sorry. You like it? I don't care if you like it. Let's just continue."

AO: **[*Laughs*] But what about working for a major magazine that uses a lot of airbrushing?**

PL: It's an ongoing fight—and I'm going to win the fight.

AO: **They're your photos at the end of the day.**

PL: No computer work. Just photographed like that—nothing retouched, no Photoshop stuff.

AO: **Everything you photograph has an Old World feeling to it. It has a certain, what I guess I would call, *Vintage warmth.***

PL: I'm older.

AO: **[laughs] It's something else. It's not perverse; it's timeless.**

PL: It also comes from never following anything else. You have to find your own angle. Every generation, in the beginning, there will be, like, twenty photographers. Take today—you can easily mention twenty photographers who are shooting today. But in fifteen years there might be two left that we really remember. At the end of the day the most beautiful thing is discovering something.

AO: **Right, it's almost a personal thing that you learn from yourself. I think a lot of people tend to think looking inward is a big, spiritual journey, but it really comes down to the small things that you do for yourself.**

PL: I never look at magazines. I never think, "Wow, I'll do that too." That's boring, no? I always make a plan for what to do next season. I just say, "Give me the camera and I'll try something."

AO: **You work with a lot of models and actors. I have to ask: Which do you prefer?**

PL: At the moment I prefer actors.

AO: **Who's your favorite?**

PL: One of the most impressive persons I have worked with is Jeanne Moreau, the French actress. She's eighty years old.

AO: **Yes! Lauren Hutton once sent me a postcard with her on the cover of it. It said, "From one wise woman to another." I have to show it to you.**

PL: Eighty years old. Totally young in the head. She does a lot for young directors and other people doing things now, and she's a legend at the same time. Just a lovely lady, very sharp. You don't bullshit her. I did a film with her with still lifes and lots of photographs. It wasn't fashion, but more diverse with a beautiful story.

AO: **I did a video for The Row last year. It was about getting dressed and undressed, moving through a house. It was about nothing really but movement. It was good, something different for me.**

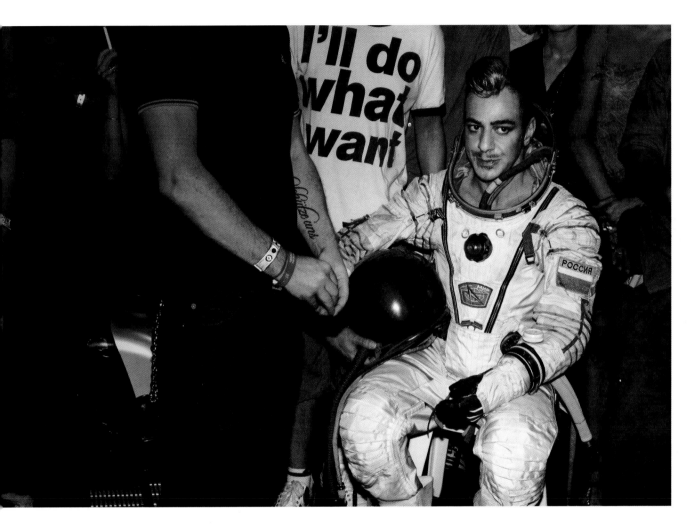

ABOVE: A snapshot of
John Galliano after the
designer's show.

PREVIOUS: Peter told
us this shoot inspired
his "narrative"
photographic work.

I always feel comfortable in front of Peter's camera—even in the rain.

PL: The film I did with Jeanne started like an experiment. Like, great, we have $100,000 and let's do a fifty-minute experiment. New ways to photograph pictures and film pictures and all that. And then it was five years later, and it cost us $400,000, then $600,000—

AO: **It sounds like fashion, in the way an idea can grow so quickly. I wanted to make the perfect T-shirt and it's escalating into a business with ten employees and a company!** [*Laughs*]

PL: My agent, who is very respectful and doesn't ask many questions, asked me, "Why do you want to do a film?" I said I didn't know, that I just wanted to do it. I'd like to see what it is at the end. I told him I knew it was expensive, but it didn't matter. Then he asked what I was going to do with it. I didn't know, but I had to do it for me. Then it showed at Cannes.

AO: **I need to see it. . . .**

PL: It's seventy-three minutes, so you have to be very patient. It's very slow, very deep. Jeanne is saying the text. She had to change it to say it, which was an amazing process. And then I bought ten minutes of *Mademoiselle*, this film from the '60s that Anthony Richardson did with Jeanne Moreau, so suddenly the images start to move. We have these ten minutes that we spread over the whole film, some of the films moving and others still. It was a really amazing experiment.

AO: **What else stands out to you in your career as something that you are really proud of?**

PL: There is one photograph that started lots of other things; it's of a little Martian with Helena Christensen walking in the desert.

AO: **Why that picture?**

PL: That was the start of my storytelling. There was an exhibition that was about storytelling in fashion photography and they were all young photographers—nobody asked me to the exhibition. And then I read about the exhibition in the *New York Times,* and the article was like, "God, what are they talking about? Storytelling's a new thing? Storytelling started with that picture from Peter Lindbergh in the 1990s—that Martian. That's when storytelling started." I found it very funny.

AO: **What story were you trying to convey?**

PL: I was in the dentist's waiting room in Paris when I got the idea for the story. On the table was a Xerox copy of a story on UFOs from a magazine. Someone had left it, but I looked at it and thought it was great. There was nothing visual in the story except for those signs in the sky. I asked myself, "Why not do something with a Martian?" The idea was that Helena was driving her Volvo in the desert, and she found this Martian and took him home. She lived in a trailer in the desert, so it made sense. They didn't fall in love, but they liked each other. Then she went to LA, and she showed him the beach and the sea.

AO: **Who knew getting your teeth cleaned could be so inspirational?**

PL: I was so fed up with what was happening, so I decided that was the year to change things—for one year I would do something really different. I did all these stories like crashes in the desert, with explosions and Martians running all over.

AO: **I remember some of those. A lot of them are with Amber Valletta—you use her often, don't you?**

PL: Yes, since the beginning. She and Kate [Moss], they are the last ones of the old big girls. When Kate and Amber came up, things started to change. The first book I did was called *Ten Women.*

AO: **I have it.**

PL: It was Kate and Amber and Claudia [Schiffer]. Karl Lagerfeld helped.

AO: **I love Karl.**

PL: Yes, you can only love him. I've known him thirty years. He told me that the only ones out of those ten who have the key for the future are Amber and Kate. It was true.

AO: **He called it.**

PL: He just said it. The key for the future, that's what he said. It's really something funny.

AO: **Do you tend to take inspiration more from your peers or from more abstract ideas, like art movements or books?**

PL: I'm influenced a lot by all the Germans, like the Bauhaus. And then the Fritz Lang movies; his film *Metropolis.* Old black-and-white films. I'm very inspired by all this cinema.

AO: **Do you collect art?**

PL: No. I don't collect anything. I hate the idea of collecting, because in the everyday life, so much stuff comes together and piles up everywhere. I just can't collect anything.

AO: **I've never collected any specific person. I'm pretty broad in that respect. I try and only buy the things that I love. So what's on the walls of your house?**

PL: The walls of my house don't have much. There are old pictures that I bought when I moved in.

AO: **Okay, so which artists do you like even if you don't collect them?**

PL: I was never into Andy Warhol or artists like that. I much more like Joseph Kosuth and Donald Judd. I like Schnabel a lot.

AO: **I have two paintings from him. They're maps that he's painted over. They're the most beautiful things.**

PL: Sometimes people say that Schnabel is too decorative, but I don't think so. I really like it.

AO: **I try not to really listen to people when they critique art.**

PL: They are mostly people who don't do anything themselves. So they don't know what it means to do anything like that.

AO: **I've been getting really into Clemente and Picasso, particularly his sketches.**

PL: Where I live in Paris there are two houses right together. My house has a courtyard, but the other one has a courtyard all the way up on the roof. On that roof is where Picasso painted *Guernica,* his most famous painting. It's amazing when you see the little place where he did it. The room was so small he had to paint it diagonally.

AO: **He had to think inside his apartment walls. . . .**

PL: You know, the most important thing I can tell you about creativity is to try to think originally. And try to look into yourself to find things. They're not outside. That is the most important thing.

"The most important thing
I can tell you about
creativity is try and think
originally," Peter told me.
Two examples of Peter's
originality are shown here.

Every time Christian Louboutin is in New York and every time I am in Paris, we make time to see each other. While I love him as a friend, I am in awe of him as a designer. His shoes are no ordinary heels; they are pieces of art. Who else can get away with making ankle boots with oversize spiked studs look just as chic on an uptown lady-who-lunches as on a young fashionista? I remember when I first caught wind of some designer named Christian Louboutin—his red-soled heels were a well-kept secret among shoe-fetishists like me. Now he has become one of the most recognized shoe designers in the world. Christian has taught me that when it comes to your work, you have to be fearless in order to succeed. While his company has exploded into the mainstream, he's never given up his singular vision. It's very French in a way. Christian is a man who embraces a woman for who she is—bold, complicated, and a bit risqué. His shoes are charged with a sexual energy; despite how feminine and gorgeous they are, there's always something kinky and humorous about them, too. I look to both his integrity and his my-way-or-the-highway attitude for inspiration. He sticks to his guns and never sells out his name. But most importantly, he understands the secret to the feminine mystique: Being a woman might be tough, but being tough is sexy as hell. As Christian would say, voilà!

3.11.08   SOHO GRAND HOTEL, NY   AO

DATE   LOCATION   INTERVIEWED BY

AO: Christian, your shoes are like mini pieces of art. But you're also in charge of an international mega brand. How do you negotiate these two aspects of your career?

CL: I wanted to do shoes. That was my thing. But, the funny part is that I didn't want what else came with the fashion industry. For me it was only about shoes. I never, ever thought of money. I never thought about company policies or shareholders. I had no consciousness that I was building a name.

AO: You just did it for yourself.

CL: I wanted to do shoes. It was as simple as that.

AO: How did this all start for you?

CL: I started first by working for showgirls—showgirls of cabaret, not escort girls—going up and down the stairs at the Folies Bergère and the Moulin Rouge. I was seventeen, and I really wanted to do their shoes because I thought a showgirl was like a bird of paradise.

AO: I can only imagine their amazing outfits!

CL: Lots of feathers and the most amazing shoes. The birds took care of the feathers, and I would take care of the shoes. When I was a teenager in Paris, I discovered that when you go to the theater there is an intermission, an *entre acte*, and that during the intermission everyone goes outside to smoke cigarettes. When everyone comes back, they try and get a better seat. I figured out how to sneak in during the second part of the show. I had no money, so we would see the second part but never the first part. And it became very interesting to try and understand what happened during the first hour when you weren't there. But with the showgirls it was much easier because it's just tableaux, it's not difficult. So that's what I started to do. It was the best school you could imagine.

AO: I bet they could teach a thing or two about women! [*Laughs*] Who else was an influence on you?

CL: The person who influenced me when he was alive was [the late French fashion designer] Roger Vivier. I worked with him, with the real man. He knew how to behave with women. Always, even when he was very old, he would open the door for a woman, run to open a car for a woman. He was well brought up and well educated. It's a thing that's lost now, and it's a thing that I really love. So apart from the amazing designs that we know, I love his vision of the '50s. I did everything with him: I was his secretary, I was his interpreter, I prepared his food. But I never designed for him, ever.

AO: Were you ever tempted to help him directly with his creative process?

CL: Yes. But I never designed for him, I never did a sketch. It's like if you're a young painter and suddenly you are going to work for Picasso and he asks you to help mix the color. You want to look at Picasso's work, you don't want to—

AO: You don't want mess with the best.

CL: And you also don't want to paint on a Picasso! [*Laughs*] You just want to learn from him, look at the paintings. Also, I knew that I didn't need to prove that I could be a little part of somebody else. I just wanted to be around him. I knew pretty early that I wanted to be myself.

AO: I like that. You have to surround yourself with creativity to be creative. I mean, no one said a perfect silhouette was easy.

CL: Voilà. The perception of the showgirls is all about the silhouette. It's all about the leg, it's all about the body, and it's very technical: When a normal woman goes down stairs, she looks at where she puts her feet. When you're a showgirl you don't—you look straight ahead. It's a real technique, how to walk, how to express your body language. I remember the girls always asked me for veal carpaccio. Veal carpaccio! I was like, "My God, they eat so much carpaccio." And they always asked for kosher food so it had no blood. I didn't understand why they were all kosher, so one day I asked one of the girls why they needed so much veal carpaccio. She laughed and told me that they weren't eating it—they were putting it inside the soles of their shoes as a pad. That's why it needed to be white and kosher. They kept the meat inside the shoe so when they went down the stairs it was cushioned.

AO: That's incredible! I'll have to try that one day. [*Laughs*] So tell me, when did you know that you were a success?

CL: In 1988 or 1990, I decided to stop working with Roger Vivier. I wanted to do my shoes, but I just could never do the business side. That was alien to me, so I stopped thinking about it. Then two things happened by accident. I was buying a piece of furniture in a gallery, and the owner asked, "What about your shoes?" I told him I had stopped designing and didn't want to work for anyone, so he said I should just get my own store, that one was available near him. So I said, "Why not?"

AO: What was the other thing that happened?

CL: Looking back, I can see now that it was the passing of my mother. I really adored my mother, but when she died I had to become an adult. It's not like you turn eighteen and automatically become an adult, as I'm sure you know better than me. Suddenly I realized, if I'm an adult, I have to work, I have to be responsible. I felt that in her death she would really want to see me succeed.

AO: Was she the main influence in pushing you to take your career to the next step?

CL: Yes. I built a company because of the death of my mother. This I realized recently. When she died I really believed there was this energy, her energy back in me. It's funny because I barely speak about this, but yes, she's ultimately my influence. Not from a fashion point of view or a style point of view but—

AO: Emotionally.

CL: Voilà.

AO: And now your success has redefined what anyone could imagine a shoe company to be.

CL: It's funny because when I'm designing it's always the next shoe that excites me. When somebody asks me what my favorite shoe is, I always say, "The one I haven't yet designed." I don't look at the past. I guess I don't have a goal—not a precise one, anyway.

AO: I like that: You don't know what you want, you just know that it'll end up in the form of a great pair of shoes.

CL: I'll give you an anecdote: Not a long time ago, I flew from Paris to New York. This girl that I know turned to me and said, "Ah, I love fashion," and said how she had loved fashion her whole life. Then she asked me what magazines I read, and which ones influenced me. I thought about it, and I realized that I've never looked at a fashion magazine. Never. I realized that my thing was really not fashion at the beginning. I was interested in the fashion of showgirls, cabaret, cinema—but not what the fashion industry has become today.

AO: So if you try not to look for outside influences, do you have a personal mantra that keeps you going?

CL: I think that to be happy is to be free. Liberty! The people who have been really inspiring to me

Some of the many Louboutin shoes I've collected over the years.

RIGHT:
The "Monica" boot.

BELOW:
The Christian Lou-
boutin store
in Paris.

OPPOSITE PAGE:
A page from
Christian's
sketchbook.

are people who are free. I know what I'm about. I don't necessarily want to be the biggest company. I'm not working for revenge on my childhood, or to prove something to someone. My parents were great, and I never had to prove to them that I could do something. Really, I never worked against people; I've always worked for people.

AO: And for the love of the game.

CL: It never works if you do things just by reaction. Work should be done for pleasure. Everybody is different, but for me this is most true. My father was a carpenter, and he would always say the wood has one grain, one direction. If you want to sculpt the wood, go with the grain, and you can create something beautiful. If you go against the grain, you break the wood. My philosophy in life is like that: Go in the sense of things, in the sense of life, in the sense of people.

AO: And not feel pressure from other people to do something that might challenge your artistic integrity.

CL: Absolutely. But then again, I'm always curious. You want to know why people want to buy you. You want to know, you want to listen—

AO: Why are they buying me? Why are they buying my brand?

CL: And at what sacrifice does this brand come? That is tricky. But I would not sacrifice independence for a little bit more money.

AO: You're not going to sell your company just to get a private jet.

CL: Exactly.

AO: 'Cause I would! [*Pauses*] Just kidding. [*Laughs*]

CL: I've learned some lessons from great business-people. Another anecdote: At one point I was going to do a line that was not really interesting—but I was going to do it anyway because I had seen a vacation house that cost a certain price. When they approached me for the line I asked for this price. Basically, if they bought me the house I would do the line. So they said yes. And then I thought, When am I going to go to the house? I have no fucking time, I have to change planes to get there, it's a pain in the ass. Oftentimes we end up charging ourselves with a lot of responsibility. I thought, What's the point? I don't need that. I don't need the responsibility.

AO: Exactly—for what?

CL: I decided to rent a house for a month. And the investors thought I was crazy: I had asked for a ridiculous amount of money, and when they said yes, I said no.

AO: You're about quality over quantity. You want to respect the brand that you've built, and you don't want to sell out.

CL: Right, I did not build a brand for money.

AO: And to think it all started with a couple of hardworking showgirls. . . .

CL: Absolutely. Like the French saying, "You have to suffer to be beautiful."

Glass Heart Platform

Bijouterie

↓

Laura & I are making
the glass pieces in France

Two of my favorite
designs by Christian.

OPPOSITE:
An early photograph of
the entire Missoni clan;
Margherita is in the
left foreground.

Whether she's at the prestigious AmFar dinner at the Cannes Film Festival, at lunch at a random café in Paris, or at a rock concert in grungy bar in New York City—Margherita Missoni is always impeccably dressed. That should not be too hard for the fashion heiress: As the ambassador of the family business, Missoni, which her grandparents Rosita and Ottavio founded in 1953, she has her pick of the hottest clothes right off the runway, and one of the best fashion archives in the world at her fingertips. Pairing the family wares with her own quirky polished Euro-class style always produces an admirable look. She is known for mixing Missoni pieces with other designers, from Gap shorts to Givenchy accessories—and her outgoing, boisterous personality helps too. She's a free spirit, and creative beyond the limits of the fashion industry. That's why she can also dabble in acting and modeling, all the while fulfilling her duties as the unofficial muse of the family empire. She's the first person I look for at a fashion party—'cause if she's around, I know I'll have a good time. I caught up with Margherita in her apartment in New York, just months before she moved to Paris.

1/25/08   NEW YORK CITY

мко: When did you know that fashion was a part of your life?

мм: I don't think I can pick one moment when I figured that out. I spent all my afternoons as a child playing in the factory where the Missoni clothes were made, playing with pieces of fabrics and the models and taking Polaroids. There was never a separation between fashion and the rest of life.

мко: But was there ever an exact moment when you knew that Missoni was Missoni?

мм: I can recall a moment when I realized that my grandparents were famous: I was leaving my grandmother's garden in a car, and I suddenly had this intuition—like I finally became aware—that people knew them. I guess I just always knew that we were part of fashion, but that was the moment I was sure of it.

мко: And that was fun for you?

мм: Well, it was at the time! They let us experiment with the fashions, which wasn't always a very good idea.

мко: What does that mean, "experiment"?

мм: They never told us what to wear or how to wear it. So I would wear three bows in my hair and go to school. We of course got made fun of, especially my sister, who was more eccentric. She would wear these knit tights and gold bodysuits that my mom had put in the show but made for us in smaller sizes. And oh, a boa, too.

мко: What would your mom say?

мм: Oh, if she or the nanny ever told us to take something off, we would turn to them and say, "What do *you* know about fashion?"

мко: I guess you realized how much she knew about fashion when you were older. Are you going to take over Missoni design one day?

мм: I don't know. I get asked that a lot, and I just don't know. It would be unique if I did, though—I would be the fifth consecutive female head of the company, which is interesting 'cause there weren't that many women working when it started in the 1920s. My great-great-grandmother, all on the mother's side, had this company that did embroidered shawls and fringed kimono robes. Her husband was doing the financial while she did the fashion part. Then, when the Second World War started, they hired a seamstress who always had fashion magazines—*Vogue*—around the factory. So my grandmother grew up looking at these types of things.

мко: It was her, your grandmother, who then came up with Missoni, right?

мм: Yes, and it's a cute story how she became Missoni: when she was fifteen or sixteen, she went to London with her school to learn English. At the time it was the 1948 Olympic Games. My grandfather was an athlete when he was young—and was once the fastest man at the four-hundred-meter dash in the world, before the war.

мко: Are you fast?

мм: Not in these shoes! But my grandfather, he was fast. And when my grandmother saw him win one of the qualifying races she said to herself, "That's the man I'm going to marry." By chance, the next week they met under the statue of Cupid in Piccadilly Circus.

мко: How romantic.

мм: I know! And then they started writing letters to each other and doing the courtship. She was very young. At the same time, though, he started producing the suits for the Italian track-and-field team. When they got married she was into fashion, and he had the machines to make a few things. She got from her family's factory all the extra yards of fabric, which had only been poorly dyed, with all the lines and colors bleeding. That's how we have those traditional Missoni patterns now, 'cause that's the only thing they had. It started at their house, and slowly they got bigger. And then one day—this is funny—they finally got a window in a store. The mannequins that were wearing the Missoni clothes in the window were blindfolded. When my grandparents went to see them for the first time, they were standing there, with pride, and an old Milanese man came up and said, "Thank God they can't see what they're wearing."

мко: Ha! Were they upset?

мм: No, not really. They were fine with it. That's something that I think Missoni should go back to now—that it shouldn't be pretty at the first moment. I want people to have to think about it to get it.

мко: Do you design now?

мм: No, but I'm moving back to Europe, so I can be closer and more involved. It's really easy for me to show up in Milan just before the shows and tell my mother, "Ah, that's ugly."

мко: But you went to school for acting, right?

мм: Well, yes. Everyone thought I was going to be in fashion and was really pushing me. All that pressure made me want to throw up.

мко: I know about pressure, honey.

мм: Exactly, and it can ruin something. I always loved fashion, but I never wanted to have to work in it. I hate the idea of predestination, when you can't make choices. It was not just my family either; it was everyone around. When I was studying philosophy in Milan, a paper wrote, "What a great loss for fashion." I really didn't want to do it—but now my mother has so much more responsibility, which she fought hard for. But she doesn't have the time to be scouring art schools and design schools for fresh talent anymore, or see what everyone is wearing, or have all these meetings about trends. We were kicked out of fashion week at one time, the original one in Florence.

мко: What does that mean? Why were you kicked out?

TOP:
The cover of
Arianna magazine
with an early
Missoni look.

BOTTOM:
A look from a
Missoni runway
show.

OPPOSITE:
Margherita,
Rosita,
and Angela
Missoni.
PHOTOGRAPH BY
KIM ANDREOLLI,
© MISSONI.

Margherita, who recently moved to Paris to be closer to the family operations—although she's keeping mum as to whether she'll follow in her mother's footsteps—spent her first twenty-five years collecting daisies. (Her name translates into the flower in Italian.) Now sick of them, she's moved on to collecting daffodils. Her other passion is travel, but not just for work. Every year she goes to a far-away locale she hasn't been to yet—and heads straight for the markets. She says local markets are the best place to learn about a local culture.

Rosita, the matriarch of the Missoni dynasty, resides in Italy. Since handing the reins of the family business over to her daughter she's busied herself scouring flea markets around Milan and collecting mushroom knickknacks and vintage pieces to add to the already impressive Missoni archives. But her biggest tip for staying fit and looking healthy is swimming; she diligently does fifty laps every morning.

Angela, the current creative head of both the women's and men's departments of Missoni, splits her time between the family estate in the northern part of the country and Missoni's Milan headquarters. A self-described shoe addict, she has pairs that she's never worn but keeps in places of prominence in her closet for their beauty. (Much to Margherita's dismay, mother and daughter are not the same size.) She also counts interior design as a hobby, and rearranges her house every summer.

MM: Originally, fashion week was in Florence, but we started Milan fashion week with some other designers because we were kicked out when my grandmother accidentally showed nipples on the runway.

MKO: You're kidding me.

MM: No, she did this look and didn't know that with the lights on you could see straight through to the breasts—but this was before the '60s, so at the time it was a very big deal. There was this headline that read, "Missoni Brings Crazy Horse to Florence," in reference to the famous strip cabaret in Paris called the Crazy Horse.

MKO: That's the look you want to go back to?

MM: Well, not to the Crazy Horse, but to something new, something that's not very nice.

MKO: I think only you can do that. This is our generation, and I'm sure you would bring a lot to the table.

MM: Yes, my hands are itching right now, 'cause I know what could be done.

MKO: That's what my sister and I used to struggle with when it came to fashion, and why we started our own lines—

MM: Which are really good, by the way.

MKO: Ah, thank you. But we have to evolve it ourselves, with our own hands. Not until you have that control over the product do you feel that satisfaction, when you produce something and then see it out there in the world.

MM: I know what you mean. I had signed a deal to do my own jewelry line but pulled out of it. I did all of these designs, and after every meeting they kept taking things away, making it a bit cheaper. It got to a point where I just quit.

MKO: Good for you. You don't want your name on something you don't believe in.

MM: I don't want my name or my passions stifled. I'm an actress, I'm creative—that kind of stuff is important to me. I love jewelry. When I'm old, that's what I want to be known for: my jewelry. At least that's what my psychic told me!

MKO: Tell me about it.

MM: I can see that you like jewelry too!

MKO: Yes! Ha! What school did you go to?

MM: I studied philosophy in Milan first, and then at Columbia University here in New York, but only for two and a half years. I really wanted to move here because I wanted to study acting, but I couldn't do both. It was the hardest time of my life; I was literally not leaving my place. And then my mother told me she would stop paying for my shrink if I didn't go back to acting, which was very clever of her.

MKO: How did your mother know you were upset?

MM: Ha! She knew it was bad 'cause I stopped asking her to buy me clothes. That's when she said she knew it was rough. Not even Balenciaga boots—that's when she asked if I was okay. I would only wear polar fleece tights under jeans and huge sweaters, and always sunglasses.

MKO: Going to college can be a tough process; it was for me, for other reasons, too. I'm always learning, though, and I will go back to school—but hopefully when I'm made to feel more comfortable in that environment.

MM: I heard Anna Strasberg was giving classes at some fashion event in Milan, so I went to check it out. I met Anna, and she asked me to do an exercise with her. That's another great story: During this class there was someone in the audience who stopped me afterwards and said really nice things to me—that I was an honest talent and stuff—and asked for my parents' number. So he called my mother about me, and then I got a call from my mother asking why Dennis Hopper was calling about me! I didn't know it was him.

MKO: That's wild.

MM: He helped me get an agent and was like a mentor. And now I think I'm moving to Paris—

MKO: To become a French actress?

MM: In Paris they're very supportive of Italian actresses. Many Italian actors have moved to Paris and made it—the new Bond girl used to be one of those girls that walked around with numbers on TV shows in Italy, and then she moved to Paris.

MKO: And then you're more respected when you come back, and you can use that accent.

MM: Ah, I can't do an American accent—if you only knew how much time I spent in speech classes trying to do an American accent. I can speak French and Spanish without an accent, but not American!

MKO: And you'll work for Missoni when you're there too?

MM: I'll figure that out when I get there.

MKO: Take it day by day; you should be doing everything. Do whatever you want.

MM: Exactly—I don't want to do one thing that takes up all my time. And I hate waiting for other people's decisions.

MKO: Just utilize your creativity, work with your strengths, have good advisors—those are the only things you can do.

MM: My mother is very supportive; she really lets us follow our passions.

MKO: When you go to your events, do you design your own clothing?

MM: Well, often it's Missoni, but what I do mostly for the brand is buy pieces and send them over as reference pieces, buying old stuff from vintage fairs. Looking at the past, both in our brands and in fashion history, is an important tool. I found this old woman who has all this old Missoni that we don't have—so I have to buy it all back!

MKO: But I bet your archive is impressive.

MM: Oh, you have no idea. I have all the old Missoni, obviously, but then I have all this other stuff. My

Angela Missoni, Margherita's
mother, with her parents
after a runway show.

grandmother was buying vintage in the '50s, so I have stuff from the early parts of the century, and then original Balenciaga and Dior couture pieces. It's like going into the best vintage store ever, every time. I can remember three years ago Alaïa was back, so I called and asked them to send me all the Alaïa and this huge box just full of Alaïa showed up.

мко: That makes me so jealous.

мм: It's amazing.

мко: But do you have to wear Missoni?

мм: No, and I think that's important. I wear what I like, and people know that. If people say I have good style, I want it to be because I can wear what I want—not because I have to wear this brand or that brand. Lucky for me Missoni makes good stuff, and I can wear vintage Missoni and new Missoni. But I wear what I like. And my grandmother has always said that fashion is for the young—people like you, who have a real passion for what's going on in the arts and the rest of the world. And then how to digest that into clothing. I love what you and your sister are doing. My grandmother was always curious—she would go to Studio 54 just to see what was going

on. But then she got to a point in her life when she wasn't curious anymore; that's when she knew she shouldn't be in fashion anymore. Fashion is like this—[*snap*]—it's not like art; it's split-second. It's of the moment, of the time. Missoni was selling really well in the beginning of the '90s, but it wasn't fashionable. Yet no one wanted to change because it was selling well. My mom had to fight to change, 'cause of course when you change you have to lose some of the old customers to get some new ones.

мко: That's going to happen at first, obviously. When did you know that what your mother was doing was the right thing?

мм: I can remember it exactly: When I was eighteen, all my girlfriends kept asking me for discounts.

мко: There're so many people politically, even in the fashion industry, that you have to please, be it clients or partners. People have to be ready to take the risk. It's a big game, with a lot of players. And numbers.

мм: But it's a world and an art that I love, and that I feel fortunate to be surrounded by.

An image from 1968 of an early Missoni collection, shot by Patrick Rouchon.

Robert Lee Morris at
work in New York studio.

OPPOSITE:
Ashley snapped this
picture of Robert's
work in progress.

I first really began to understand the genius of the jewelry designer Robert Lee Morris at the Council for Fashion Design Awards last year. During rehearsals for the event (I had been asked to present one of the awards of the evening), a video was screened honoring Robert's groundbreaking career. While I had been aware of his longtime collaboration with Donna Karan, I was shocked that I didn't know more about the man himself and his influential designs. The next day, I called Robert directly to shamelessly express my adoration of his craft. And I've been a customer since. While some jewelry can feel clunky when you wear it, Robert's innovative designs fit over your body like a second skin. The materials he uses and his approach to design are organic, so it's impossible not to feel plugged in to the power of the natural elements when rocking his pieces. Like a master magician, Robert can make a huge chunk of silver feel both buttery soft and sturdy at the same time. His jewelry ages with your body and evolves with your style. I know I'll have his pieces in my jewelry box for the rest of my life. I've even asked him to collaborate on a jewelry line with Elizabeth and James in the hopes that more people can experience his out-of-this-world originality. He understands that beautiful things should be for everyone. And, there's no arguing with Robert.

3·28·08   RLM'S DESIGN STUDIO, NY   AO

DATE   LOCATION   INTERVIEWED BY

AO: So tell me, what's new with Mr. Robert Lee Morris?

RLM: We're in the middle of a complete reinvention of our brand. I have never worked so hard in my life. We have this new president, this new manager, who is finally the right person. He gets what I do and he gets my history, he gets my influence, he gets all of that. He is the guy who turned [the jewelry retailer] Bailey, Banks & Biddle completely around. And now he's working with us because he thinks that we could be this amazing turnaround picture.

AO: Wow. That is so exciting!

RLM: Well, I mean, it just takes so much work.

AO: And it takes time. I'm dealing with that now with The Row and Elizabeth and James. Fashion is what I want to do now. This has become my life.

RLM: That's your groove.

AO: But yes, it takes time to build the respect, to build the brand, to build the following.

RLM: It's like [the designer] Doo.Ri when she competed for the CFDA/Vogue Fashion Fund [an award created by *Vogue*'s Anna Wintour and the Council of Fashion Designers of America to sponsor and mentor new talents in the fashion world]. She went through it twice and should have won it the first time, but the talent was so great that when she won it the second time it was like, *finally*. I mean, she's like [the legendary designer] Geoffrey Beene's ghost come back.

AO: Absolutely.

RLM: And so she and I have a very special fondness because I did Beene when she was just a baby. We touched in the cosmic world at that point. Because [Beene] would never have come to me if he didn't like my sensibility. He was literally the emperor of fashion. That kind of heritage has proven itself over the years.

AO: Was he someone you really look up to? Your number one?

RLM: Yes, he's like Picasso, Brancusi, or any of those modernists. He was all about the line and invention and creating brand-new concepts all the time. He had a lot of champions in the press, so for me he was a big influence. But on a similar level, to really get to the point, I had very particular mentors, and I have very particular names in my head that I always turn to. They're like spirit helpers. They're like ancestors. I've been guided to them—they always put me back on track. And one of them is [the American sculptor] Alexander Calder. I just focus on Alexander Calder's work—the complete unification and the joy that it brings when you look at it. And I thought, Okay, here's a good example of an A-to-Z artist who not only designed sculptures and mobiles and did paintings and did drawings and did toys for children, but he also did fly swatters and gadgets for the bathroom towel holder. He would make things for his grandchildren, and he would make circuses. And everything he did looked like Calder.

AO: Consistency.

RLM: He had a way with the metal that he put his personality into every twist, every curl. And that becomes the personality you leave behind. And I have found that to me that's the most important part of my career. Make sure that everything I do comes from that place of pure Robert Lee Morris–ness. That's the beacon of light that I have in me that inspires other people.

AO: That's true. You are consistent in everything you do.

RLM: As long as I stay firm, then I maintain a standard for other people to observe and say, "Yes, it really works."

AO: How do you do that while staying true to yourself and your image? Surely it's difficult to mix artistry with the commercial demands of the market. I guess it always comes back to that age-old question of how to balance your paycheck with your passions.

RLM: I'm sort of going at it the opposite way. I already have a broad-based business that has cannibalized my existing business in some ways. The buyers get so voracious when they come here; they want everything they see. In order to meet the goals they set, and knowing the business is so fast, we end up giving them things that we've discontinued but that are really signature Robert. So we've blurred the lines between the two collections. It's really more about price point. Not material—the materials are the same; it's mostly silver.

AO: How do you differentiate between your lines that aim to appeal to a higher-end market and your lines that are for a broader audience?

RLM: The difference between the two is sometimes very hard to tell. Like with a ring. A ring on QVC has the same weight as a ring that you'd buy at a department store. It would be exactly the same feeling; there'd be no difference. The ring on QVC would cost $60; the ring at a department store might cost $160. Or $260. Or $460! Or $860. I mean, they can put any price they want on it, and people don't know, or they don't want to know, that you could also get this ring, this same exact ring, on QVC, for $60. They don't ever want to hear that. So they have to be convinced that there's no way I'll ever do similar things. That's why this collection has been sleeping in my drawer for thirty years.

AO: The one you do all by hand, you mean?

RLM: I finally brought it out because I had management who would know what to do with it. We're sort of gunning for the relaunch with my earliest archival pieces, which are some of the best designs I've ever done. So if people are worried about my jewelry now, they are really going to be in trouble once this collection comes out. If they find it kind of weird,

Robert's work is both organic
and out of this world,
evinced in the elaborate
pieces shown above.

this'll weird them out even more. But if they think that it's kind of cool, this will take them to the next level of cool.

AO: The next level. How could someone possibly think your pieces are too weird? I think they're beyond beautiful.

RLM: Today I was thinking about how people's views of beauty are so different. I'm reading the reviews on the boards at QVC—thousands and thousands of reviews—and there is this massive fan club for extremely saccharine-looking super bling in which every square inch, every square centimeter, is covered with some activity going on that would make a sparkle. And then these giant big stones—prongs that have diamonds on the prongs and then there are diamonds on the diamonds. It's all Diamonique, mind you, fake diamonds. They make these amazing pieces, and there are still a lot of women who just live and die for this bling jewelry. When they see my simple things they go, "That's too simple for me. I can't wear it."

AO: I'm discovering that, in terms of creativity, it always comes back to these two ideas that you're hinting at. There's this really natural sensation that doesn't require you to look to other sources for influence; it's more from your own creative process. You come to mind in this respect. And Peter Lindbergh, Francisco Costa—

RLM: These are all originators.

AO: Yes, and all these people don't really read magazines; they don't follow what's in or what's current.

RLM: They're visionaries.

AO: And then there's this complete other group of people who are constantly looking for inspiration and flash. They read magazines and know what's happening in all parts of the world. Karl Lagerfeld did an anklet based on all the alcohol-monitoring bracelets that young actresses were ordered to wear by the police. Look at Terry Richardson's work, or John Galliano's fashion-shows-as-spectacles. Peter Beard falls into that category as well, and then there's George Condo, who's really pop-oriented. It's really distinct, in a way. Everyone's kind of falling into one or the other—

RLM: Category, yes. But the one thing they all have in common is they're all visionaries. They all see what they have to do, and they're just doing it. And there's no right or wrong. We're just doing our thing; this is what we're here to do. And they can see it. That's why they're so inspiring. I think that's why people like Picasso blew everyone's mind—work after work, painting after painting after painting, he just kept going higher and higher and taking everyone with him. He left us with this entire world of beauty that we get to look at forever and ever and ever. So that's the other part—to not die in obscurity when you

know you shouldn't be. But people like you are helping to prevent that from happening. Like this book.

AO: Exactly, it's really about finding out how much work actually goes into a person's work. It's about knowing where it originates.

RLM: If you do what you say you want to do, then you're proving what you're saying to be true. And that's your modus operandi.

AO: I have to think about this a lot because of The Row and how simple it is. It's T-shirts, beautiful cashmeres; it's just really about—not about the clothing. It's about making that person look as beautiful as they really are. And that's the whole point of the collection in general. In that sense, yes, some people pick it up and they say, "This is too simple. I don't understand it, and I don't understand this price point—for a T-shirt? Or for a skirt?" You put it on, though, and it feels like something completely different and personal.

RLM: It's great to see that kind of conviction, because you're going to need a lot of it. It's like you're creating a very clean uniform base. Like a wardrobe of pieces that are all hip enough to not be uniforms, but that are all so easy to wear that you can just pick and choose any of this to be your daily wear and then become yourself on top of it.

AO: That's exactly what it is, and that's the mentality. Is it something you can wear every day? Some people can, some people do, some people pull it off—but some people don't. In a way, I want the clothes to serve as complements to other designers. I wouldn't do a fashion show because this is about the personal experience. It wouldn't translate. You have to try it on, you have to put it on, and you have to feel it.

RLM: I brought a piece out to show you the inspiration I had from my mentor in high school. See that chariot right in front of you made of metal? Can you grab it? That was made by my mentor George Garner, and he was my teacher of art in college. And George was like Alexander Calder. Every single thing he made looked like George Garner. And he did a wide variety of products, including these little constructions that looked like chariots and war vehicles with moving shields and spinning helicopter things. I love that the wheels move. He started making jewelry, and the jewelry was so cool looking, like something out of *Aliens*. It really got me into the concept of doing jewelry as art.

AO: He helped plant the creativity seeds in your brain.

RLM: George Garner and Alexander Calder were the two living artists that flipped the switch in me. I began immediately to focus on this one side of myself, which were memories of a Celtic lifetime. I started going into my more spiritual center. I was twenty, I guess, and beginning to see myself as the

154

became a synthesis of ancient tribal culture, modern urban life, and future designs. It's—that's what I do. That's my purpose.

AO: You have to be able to keep this sense of purpose open to others, to people who want to be provoked by your jewelry just as much as they want to just wear it.

RLM: Yes, and that's why for this collection I'm working with these razor-sharp flying shapes. It's like an "I dare you to wear these" kind of thing. They're almost kind of like elegant barbed wire. Talk about a punk, young feeling. This ain't for any old woman.

AO: Well, maybe a chic one.

RLM: Yes, like Lauren Hutton.

AO: Exactly.

RLM: Pieces like this are museum pieces.

AO: You really do inspire my clothing design. You totally did. It's a mentality—it's like filtering. I really like your stuff because your stuff is just so *you*, so personal and organic.

RLM: That's the big lesson for anyone who reads the book—everyone in the book is pursuing their dreams without compromise and standing up for what they have to stand up for. It's when people compromise that they get weak and they no longer inspire. They just tire.

AO: You're not tired, are you Robert?

RLM: No, and neither are you.

Snapshots of
Robert in his
own designs.

descendant of the metalsmiths of ancient tribes, making shields and fires and pelts and bison and God knows what. I was thinking of those people with big collars around their necks and grunting, rutting people and mud and furrowed grasslands. I was just like, "I know this period. I was there." And I was beating out the swords. I was making the metal, and I was creating all these things for people that lived a long time ago, eight thousand years ago. But when I first made this journey, I decided I was going to start making jewelry that looks like it's from this period. I was directed. I was focused. I knew what I was doing. I had made this existential decision that I was not going to be an artist unless it was my being my true self.

AO: What year was that?

RLM: This was '65, '66. It was just a wild time of faith and no faith; life is what you make it. I went, "Oh my God, I might as well kill myself now. I didn't ask to be here, God." It was like original sin or something. Throughout college I worked a way out of that, that possible living in horror all the time. I came up with a reason to live that was my true calling, and it was to be this liaison between the spirit realm and ordinary people, and to go up there and get my ideas and bring them back from the future and from the past. Then I

Robert told me:
"I came up with a reason to
live that was my true calling, and it was to be this
liason between the spirit
realm and ordinary people,
and to go up there and get
my ideas and bring them
back from the future and
from the past." His one-of-
a-kind jewelry, above and
opposite, reflects his
visionary approach to life.

Whether she knows it or not, my sister has been my greatest teacher. At a young age, we had very distinct personalities; like a teddy bear, she was quiet, affectionate, and loving—which are adjectives I wouldn't necessarily use to describe myself at that age (*feisty* and *stubborn* would be more appropriate). But by merely observing her demeanor, she taught me another way of being: I learned how to be affectionate. I learned how to compromise. I learned that tough love is not the only option. As one matures, personalities become more complex. In Ashley's case, she evolved into a woman with a strong work ethic (she works twelve-hour days or more) and determination (she was the one to convince our parents to buy us our first pair of heels—red one-inch platforms with cherries on them). Her most dominant characteristic would be her natural business mentality (without a prior relationship, she got Lauren Hutton to do our Spring 2008 look book for The Row)—and those are only minor examples. Passionate and true to her convictions, Ashley is an admirable woman who lives her life with a great magnitude of integrity, loyalty, and love. It's been an honor to watch her grow and evolve on this twenty-two-year journey all the while fulfilling her roles of CEO, fashion designer, business partner, and sister. Possessed of a pure heart, unrelenting dedication, consistent drive, and endless innovation, Ashley Olsen is a person who has—and continues to influence me and the people in her life to do better, work harder, laugh more, live longer, be stronger, and know that anything is possible.

—MARY-KATE OLSEN

"I wanted it to be

"... one woman ..."
LAUREN HUTTON

"I always knew the woman I wanted to be."

DVF

Your most marked characteristic?

POSESSING A ~~CREATIVE~~ CREATIVE BUSINESS MIND

The quality you most like in a man?

SENSE O HUMOR

The quality you most like in a woman?

~~PROCEED BY~~ NOT STRONG SENSE SELF (SENSE OF HUMOR)

What do you most value in your friends?

HONESTY + LOYALTY

What is your principle defect?

SOCIALLY AWKWARD

What is your favorite occupation?

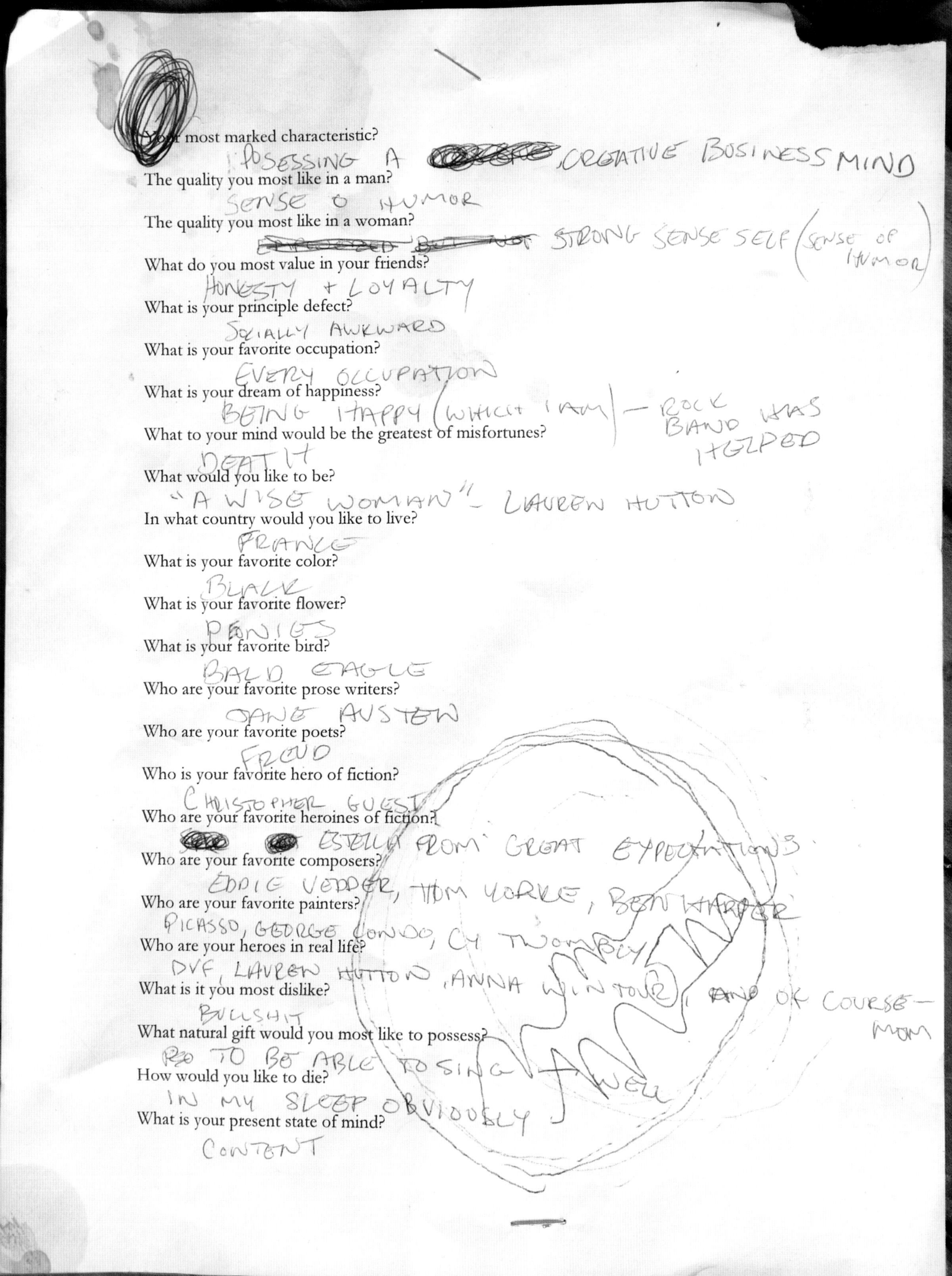

EVERY OCCUPATION

What is your dream of happiness?

BEING HAPPY (WHICH I AM) — ROCK BAND HAS HELPED

What to your mind would be the greatest of misfortunes?

DEATH

What would you like to be?

"A WISE WOMAN" — LAUREN HUTTON

In what country would you like to live?

FRANCE

What is your favorite color?

BLACK

What is your favorite flower?

PONIES

What is your favorite bird?

BALD EAGLE

Who are your favorite prose writers?

JANE AUSTEN

Who are your favorite poets?

FREUD

Who is your favorite hero of fiction?

CHRISTOPHER GUEST

Who are your favorite heroines of fiction?

ESTELLA FROM GREAT EXPECTATIONS

Who are your favorite composers?

EDDIE VEDDER, THOM YORKE, BEN HARPER

Who are your favorite painters?

PICASSO, GEORGE CONDO, CY TWOMBLY

Who are your heroes in real life?

DVF, LAUREN HUTTON, ANNA WINTOUR, AND OF COURSE — MOM

What is it you most dislike?

BULLSHIT

What natural gift would you most like to possess?

TO BE ABLE TO SING WELL

How would you like to die?

IN MY SLEEP OBVIOUSLY

What is your present state of mind?

CONTENT

To what faults do you feel most indulgent?

WORK TOO MUCH

What is your motto?

~~WORK YOUR WAY DOWN, NOT UP~~

DREAM BIG. WORK IT OUT FROM THERE.

Your Name or Pseudo

~~SMASH~~, SMASHLY, ASH, MOM, MOM, COA MOM

"Part of being a genius is taking everything from everyone around you."

BOB COLACELLO

Alexandra Hamil

Your most marked characteristic?

giving advice, usually beginning with: "let me tell you something" OR "LISTEN".

The quality you most like in a man?

maturity, trustworthy & being geniune

The quality you most like in a woman?

self determination, independent success

What do you most value in your friends?

their sense of humor, their uniqueness their loyalty.

What is your principle defect?

~~scribbled out~~ works too much!!

What is your favorite occupation?

friend, business lady woman

What is your dream of happiness?

to have a family and good friends

What to your mind would be the greatest of misfortunes?

not being able to spend time w/ the people I love.

What would you like to be?

an intelligent, rational, happy woman (lady?)

In what country would you like to live?

In the United States.

What is your favorite color?

i dont have one but maybe greys or blues, black or white, maybe ALL!

What is your favorite flower?

peony

What is your favorite bird?

peacock

Who are your favorite prose writers?

F. Scott Fitzgerald, Joan Didion

Who are your favorite poets?

Alexandra Hamile

Who is your favorite hero of fiction?

Bobbi of "Bobbi's world", Cartman, Corky from "Waiting for Guffman".

Who are your favorite heroines of fiction?

Parker Posey in "Waiting 4 guffman"

Who are your favorite composers?

Dave Matthews, Pearl Jam,

Who are your favorite painters?

Basquiat, Julian Schnabel.

Who are your heroes in real life?

Lauren Hutton, Alex Hamile & my father.

What is it you most dislike?

disloyal people

What natural gift would you most like to possess?

mind reading, ~~the sense~~ the power to sense a liar from a mile away.

How would you like to die?

naturally, of old age, or any way so long as i was able to say goodbye to ones I love.

What is your present state of mind?

focused, determined, stressed out(?)

To what faults do you feel most indulgent?

shopping but ~~not~~ not for clothes, for things for my house or art.

What is your motto?

~~Need to read the team~~ Dream big, work it out from there!!

Your name or Pseudo

Smash + TRASHLey

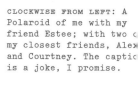

CLOCKWISE FROM LEFT: A
Polaroid of me with my
friend Estee; with two o
my closest friends, Ale
and Courtney. The captio
is a joke, I promise.

RIGHT: A favorite pastime
of mine? These Deepak Chopra cards.
They really get you going.

BELOW: An album my great-grandmother put
together documenting my career until I was
six. It's the most valuable thing I have.

WHERE'S CARRIE
BRADSHAW?

GREEN STOCKS STILL WORTH THE HYPE | **THE NEXT PERK** A $5,000 PHYSICAL | **HONDA** DESIGNING THE SAFEST FACTORY | **BASKETBALL'S HOTTEST FRANCHISE**

DECEMBER 24, 2007 | WWW.FORBES.COM

Forbes

Smart Collecting

Chinese Painting,
Fashion Photography,
Diamonds, Cigars
and more

The Beauty of
Custom-Built Bikes

Trading Art:
How One Family
Made Billions of Dollars—
and Plenty of Enemies

The handmade
Franken Knuckle, $50,000
(Lauren Hutton not included)

$4.99 CANADA $6.99

FAR RIGHT: Me in
The Row at the 2007
CFDA Awards,
at which I wore a
silver cuff
designed by Robert
Lee Morris.

RIGHT:
A collaboration
with Robert for our
Elizabeth and James
jewelry line.

NATIONAL GEOGRAPHIC
Memory
Why We Remember,
Why We Forget

The Economist

Castro's legacy

GQ *UPGRADE YOUR STYLE
ERIC BANA
F KILLER GOOD LOOKS

A couple of m
favorite magazines

TOP: Lauren wearing The Row's stretch leather pants
and T-shirt for the cover of *Forbes*

LEFT: Me, MK, and Alex in high school. Weird.

I wear this Cartier watch just about every day; it keeps me on time. I slip on this gold Rolex when I go out.

LEFT: My must-have travel essentials.

ABOVE: I traded a Fendi bag for this Fendi bag from my friend Estee; I think it is stunning.

ABOVE LEFT: with Johnny Depp, Snoop Dogg, and Orlando Bloom at the 2006 Teen Choice Awards.

LEFT: This Picasso, a gift from MK, hangs in my bedroom. © 2008 ESTATE OF PABLO PICASSO/ ARTISTS RIGHTS SOCIETY (ARS), NEW YORK.

FROM TOP: A great pair of vintage Levi's; some of my coffee-table books.

RIGHT: My living room. My leather club chairs are clearly falling apart, but I refuse to have them fixed.

BELOW: The funniest birthday note I received for my twenty-first b-day was this one from Will Ferrell.

RIGHT: A Polaroid Eddie Vedder sent me for my birthday.

BELOW: A sketch from an architecture class I took while studying at NYU.

Happy Birthday Ashley, Eddie! Co.

Ashley—
You're a class act. I've always said that.
Happy Birthday

THE KAUFMANN HOUSE

BY RICHARD NEUTRA

ARCHITECTURE
DONNA GOODMAN
ASHLEY OLSEN

GARDEN STATE 78

RIGHT: At the wedding of one of the closest people in my life, Jill Collage. It was my first time as a bridesmaid.

FAR RIGHT: I collect records; I love the cover of this Stones' album.

Ash—!
It was fun—No?
Made this postcard
wrote
in New Mex + never
sent it. No address
tomorrow for...
Leaving ZAMBULLA!
ZAMBOWANGA! ZAMBIA!
Will call when
back mid Sept. Have
just more fun
Lauren

Lauren Hutton sent me this note and postcard; I'll keep them forever.

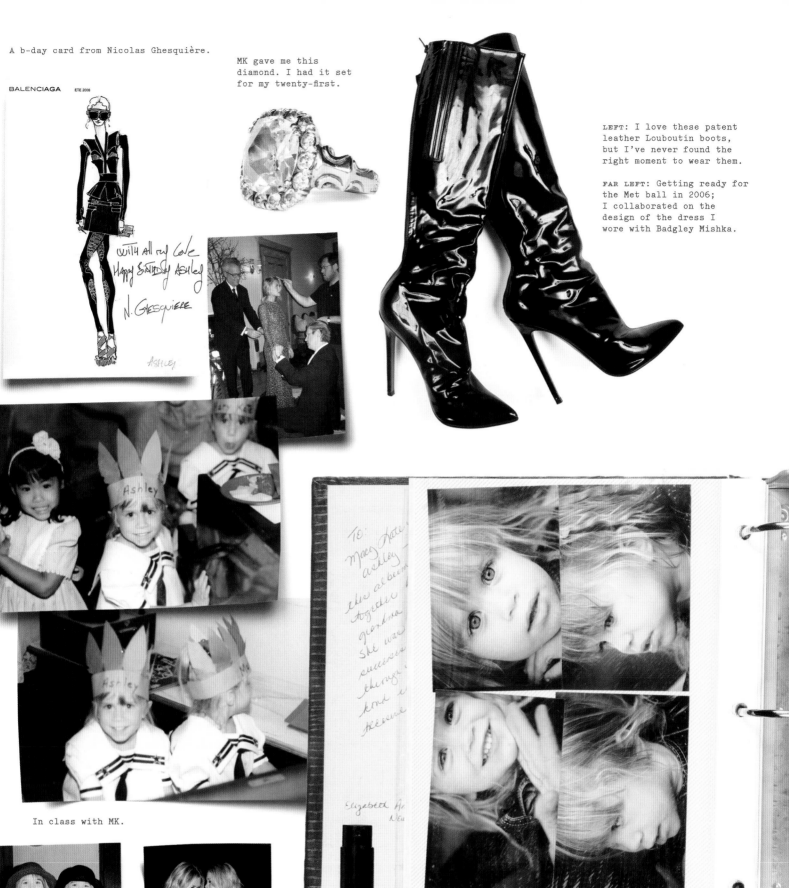

A b-day card from Nicolas Ghesquière.

BALENCIAGA   ETE 2008

With All my Love
Happy Birthday Ashley
N. Ghesquière

ASHLEY

MK gave me this
diamond. I had it set
for my twenty-first.

LEFT: I love these patent
leather Louboutin boots,
but I've never found the
right moment to wear them.

FAR LEFT: Getting ready for
the Met ball in 2006;
I collaborated on the
design of the dress I
wore with Badgley Mishka.

In class with MK.

Awkward!

Conquering my
fear of public
speaking during
my twenty-first-
birthday speech.

BOIS D'ARGENT
COLOGNE
CHRISTIAN DIOR
PARIS

MURE ET MUSC
EAU DE TOILETTE

Two of my favorite
scents, Christian
Dior's Bois D'Argent and
Mure et Musc from
L'Artisan Parfumeur.

One of my favorite pieces
from my closet is this
hand-painted velvet
robe I got from Scarlet, a
vintage boutique in Paris.

My first T-shirt sample from The Row.

The first piece of clothing my sister fell in love with was a pair of black spandex shorts with black fringe down the side. We were just six years old, but I remember she refused to take them off no matter where she went. She loved them and that was that. But that's the thing about Mary-Kate: She alone makes and breaks the rules for her life. I remember in high school—I think it was for prom or a winter formal—my sister wasn't happy with a kimono-style dress she was going to wear. So she did the only thing she knew how to do. She grabbed a stapler, totally reconfigured the whole thing, and made it her own—visible staples and all. She possesses that rare gift of individuality; she doesn't need approval from anyone or anything. I trust her to always call it as it is. Part of what makes my sister such an honest soul is her unwavering loyalty to her friends and family. Whenever there is a dinner party or special occasion, my sister has to spearhead the whole operation. One time for a friend's birthday, she got down on her hands and knees to blanket the house in moss. It was just one of the many magical things she does for people she cares about. This book is all about influence; it's been a journey for me to figure out who I admire and for what reasons. And every step of the way, Mary-Kate has been along for the ride. Out of all the amazing, talented, and awe-inspiring people I have been blessed to meet in this world, the connection I share with my sister influences me the most of all. Just by being herself, Mary-Kate teaches me something new every day. Looking back, I see that my sister has always worn herself on her sleeve—just now, it's no longer fringe.

—Ashley Olsen

"BE RECKLESS ENOUGH TO GAMBLE ALL OR NOTHING TO FOLLOW YOUR DREAMS."
— JOHN GALLIANO

" CHIC IS WHEN A WOMAN IS IN HARMONY WITH HERSELF. "
— GIAMBATTISTA VALLI

4/24/08
4/29/08

FINAL DRAFT
5/4/08

Your most marked characteristic?
MEDIA: BIG SUNGLASSES AND STARBUCKS ~~FRIENDS & FAMILY:~~ SARCASM CHARTEUSE JEWELRY

The quality you most like in a man?
~~ALWAYS CHANGING~~. TOO MANY (AND THEY'RE ALWAYS CHANGING)

The quality you most like in a woman?
~~TRUST, TOO LITTLE~~ TOO FEW (BUT TRUST IS ALWAYS UP THERE)

What do you most value in your friends?
~~NON JUDGEMENTAL~~ NO JUDGEMENT, NON JUDGEMENTAL

What is your principle defect?
GIVING PEOPLE THE BENEFIT OF THE DOUBT

What is your favorite occupation?
NOT HAVING ONE, ~~HER~~ BEING A FULL-TIME GEMINI

What is your dream of happiness?
I DON'T UNDERSTAND THE QUESTION

What to your mind would be the greatest of misfortunes?
TO BE TAKEN ADVANTAGE OF, TO LOSE TRUST IN ONE BUT (OR) "EVERY MOMENT OF LIGHT AND DARK IS A MIRACLE" — WHITMAN

What would you like to be?
TALLER

In what country would you like to live?
I NEVER STAY IN ONE PLACE FOR TOO LONG

What is your favorite color?
DEPENDS ON MY MOOD, DOES BLACK COUNT?

What is your favorite flower?
MOSS AND BLACK MAGIC ROSES.

What is your favorite bird?
BLACK CROWS, ~~RAVEN~~ A BLACK CROW

Who are your favorite prose writers?
PLATO, FRANZ KAFKA

Who are your favorite poets?
WILLIAM BLAKE, WALT WHITMAN JIM MORRISON

Who is your favorite hero of fiction?
ODYSSEUS, MARC ANTONY, ROMEO

Who are your favorite heroines of fiction?
APHRODITE, CLEOPATRA, JULIET

Who are your favorite composers?
NEIL YOUNG

Who are your favorite painters?
HENRY DARGER, BASQUIAT, EDWARD RUSCHA, MARTIN KIPPENBERGER, LARRY RIVERS, DE KOONING, WARHOL JOHN BALDESSARI

Who are your heroes in real life?
PEOPLE WHO LIVE WITH INTEGRITY

What is it you most dislike?
THE MEDIA

What natural gift would you most like to possess? THE ABILITY
CONCENTRATION, ~~BEING ABLE TO~~ CONCENTRATE

How would you like to die?
IN YOUR ARMS

What is your present state of mind?
SARCASTIC

To what faults do you feel most indulgent?

N/A WOULDN'T YOU LIKE TO KNOW

What is your motto? EVERYTHING HAPPENS FOR A REASON

~~BE CURIOUS, NOT JUDGMENTAL~~
~~WHITMAN~~

Your Name or Pseudo

MK

"IT'S HARD TO TELL WHERE REALITY ENDS AND ILLUSIONS BEGINS. THEY BLEND — THEN THEY SEPERATE"

LIND GOODMANS, GEMINI

— AS FOR ME, ALL I KNOW IS THAT I KNOW NOTHING
— SOCRATES

DO NOT DWELL IN THE PAST, DO NOT DREAM OF THE FUTURE, CONCENTRATE THE MIND ON THE PRESENT MOMENT
— BUDDHA

IT IS NOT LENGTH OF LIFE, BUT DEPTH OF LIFE
— RALPH WALDO EMERSON

ALL LIFE IS AN EXPERIMENT
— WHITMAN

BE CURIOUS, NOT JUDGMENTAL
— WHITMAN

— EVERY MOMENT OF LIGHT & DARK IS A MIRACLE
WHITMAN

— I ACCEPT REALITY AND DARE NOT QUESTION IT
— WHITMAN

— EVERY ARTIST WAS FIRST AMATEUR
— EMERSON

— FEAR DEFEATS MORE PEOPLE THAN ANY OTHER ONE THING IN THE WORLD
— EMERSON.

" EVERY DAY WE FEEL DIFFERENT;
SOMETIMES WE'RE HAPPY; SOMETIMES
WE'RE SAD. BUT TO PHOTOGRAPH
SOMEONE AS THEY ARE IS MY
FAVORITE. "
                    - TERRY RICHARDSON

SIGMUND FREUD
The Interpretation of Dreams

Freud's seminal work in understanding the human mind
• His method of interpreting dreams
• The purpose of dreams in our lives
• The meanings of common dreams
• The most typical sexual symbols in dreams

Being the adventures of a young man whose principal interests are rape, ultra-violence and Beethoven.

STANLEY KUBRICK'S
CLOCKWORK ORANGE

ABOVE: Ashley and me receiving our preschool diplomas.
BELOW: You'll never be in a room of my home without an ashtray; I collect ones like this from Hermès.
BOTTOM RIGHT: On Halloween in 2006, my friends and I dressed up as droogs, the gang from *Clockwork Orange*. I'm a fan of Kubrick's work.

ABOVE: When I'm at home this pile is my uniform.
TOP: My dad and his three girls dancing on my twenty-first birthday.
RIGHT: This picture was taken at the CFDA Awards—this dress was finished on my body moments before the event.
BELOW: This bubble chair from the 1960s is one of my favorite pieces of furniture.

ROLLING STONES
TOUR OF THE AMERICAS 75

ABOVE: A treasured vintage t-shirt
LEFT: My bedroom in LA

BELOW: New Year's 2008 in Napa, California—the best New Year's yet.

ABOVE RIGHT:
This book was a present that I treasure; it's has a perfect description of my Gemini sign.
RIGHT: I use these 1970s Gucci glasses on special occasions.
BELOW LEFT: Jim Morrison is one of my favorite poets and songwriters; I wish I could have the opportunity to experience the energy of a Doors concert.
BELOW RIGHT: An antique emerald ring I found in a vintage shop on the Rue Saint Honore in Paris.

I have a sweet tooth when it comes to Tootsie Rolls and Swedish Fish.

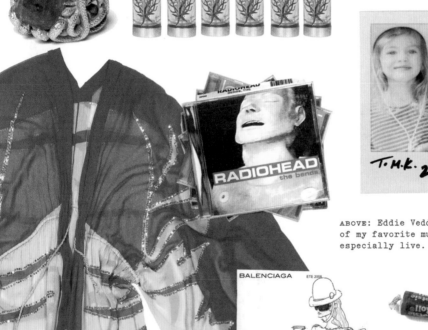

ABOVE: Eddie Vedder is one of my favorite musicians, especially live.

Wishing you The Best
Happy Birthday Mary-Kate

N. Ghesquière.

MARY-KATE

FAR LEFT: I collect Zandra Rhodes dresses and caftans—and wear them everywhere, from lounging around my house to special events.
LEFT: Nicolas Ghesquière did this sketch of me for my twenty-first birthday.

PREVIOUS: Two of my
favorite Warhol
Polaroids; on the left is
Andy in drag, and on the
right is Truman Capote.
FAR LEFT: A Zandra
Rhodes dress I wore in
a wedding.
LEFT: Channeling the '70s
at a pool party in LA;
Polaroids are perfect for
capturing a moment.
RIGHT: My favorite dress,
which I wore to the Met
ball in 2007, was picked
out days before the event
at Lily et Cie in LA. The
whole dress was feathers.

JESUS HATES IT WHEN YOU SMOKE

RIGHT: I love these battered Balenciaga heels so much I've worn
them for years—and even
under my Met dress in 2007.
LEFT: A trippy fairy tale
is always welcome.
BELOW LEFT: I've always been
a fan of sunglasses.

BELOW: Having
fun—in Lolita
sunglasses—at
a friend's
birthday party.

2-DISC SET
Walt Disney's
Alice
in Wonderland
THE MASTERPIECE EDITION

INCLUDES A VIRTUAL WONDERLAND PARTY

How did they ever
make a movie of
LOLITA ?

JAMES MASON SHELLEY WINTERS ... SELLERS ... SUE LYON
LOLITA

BOIS D'ARGENT

COLOGNE

CHRISTIAN DIOR
PARIS

NEUTRA
Complete Works

TASCHEN

The Chateau Marmont, with its Gothic features and long history associated with its famed rooms and bungalows, was the perfect place to talk with the artist Jack Pierson. Despite being quite familiar with the surroundings ourselves, we were still nervous about sitting down with the Massachusetts-born, New York–based sculptor, photographer, collager, and painter. While we have both long been admirers of his work, we had never actually met Jack Pierson before. In fact, he was the first person that we had ever interviewed—not only for this book, but in our entire lives. We didn't know how to hold a voice recorder, let alone turn the thing on. Thankfully, Jack seemed amused by the whole process and was the perfect first interview. He is probably best known for his giant "word sculptures," though both of us are fans of his other works, including his photographs and drawings. After he presented us each with a chunk of turquoise from his property in California (an interview subject bearing gifts is a good sign), Jack patiently took us through his story of growing up as a beach-town kid and moving to New York to chase the Factory and the Velvet Underground. Warm, honest, and full of an innocent sense of wonder, Jack is a lot like the art he makes.

10/19/07

DATE

Los Angeles

LOCATION

INTERVIEWED BY

MKO: **Where did you grow up?**

JP: In Plymouth, Massachusetts.

MKO: **Okay, how'd you get started?**

JP: In art, you mean?

MKO: **Yes.**

JP: I don't know; I was just always interested in it. Plymouth was a summer town. Everybody came to go to the beach in the summer. This one lady from New York came, and she knew all about artists, and somehow that made it reasonable to think about being an artist. That little thing, like you said, that influence did it for me.

AO: **Were you artistic as a child?**

JP: I colored in the lines. Stuff like that. I liked to make things, like spoon rings and crafts.

MKO: **Was your first piece the signs? With the letters?**

JP: That was a real "a-ha" moment for me with the signs, but I had started with photography. I thought I would be a photographer, and when I was in art school I did a lot of photography.

AO: **Which art school did you go to?**

JP: I went to Mass Art, which is like a little art school, in Boston, and studied graphic design. I wanted to do a little bit of everything. I never shut off anything and turned to a focus. I guess I just wanted to do a little of everything.

MKO: **I can tell! Who were you influenced by?**

JP: Well, for sure Andy Warhol. He's a big thing to me somehow, and when you talk about influence—I can almost tell you exactly how it happened. I lived out in the sticks, so only the biggest things got to me. At the time it was Alice Cooper. Do you know who Alice Cooper was, the rock star? He was sort of like the Marilyn Manson of my generation—crazy, heavy metal. And so I'd read about him and the articles would always talk about Andy Warhol's Factory, and that he was connected to the Velvet Underground. So through him I crossed into all that kind of stuff. I'd wonder, "What's the Velvet Underground?" And then I'd have to look it up. Sort of like Internet searches today. Andy Warhol was pretty big, though—people in the sticks had started to hear about him. He was in *Life* magazine and things like that.

AO: **He changed the media, in a way.**

JP: Exactly. And I got into those messages, whatever they were. The basic one was: "It's cooler in New York than it is here. Get there quickly."

AO: **Did you live in New York?**

JP: First I went to Boston because I was a little timid; I needed to ease my way into New York. And then I got to New York in 1983—I was twenty-three years old, so it took me a while to get things really going. I was thirty before I had my first show. I was there hanging out, and doing other things, going to nightclubs and meeting people and being a part of that little specific scene in the '80s. I had known Tabboo!, a drag queen creative type who needs no

explanation, and Pat Hearn, a big gallery dealer, who was a big part of the scene. She was one of the first people to bring art to Chelsea. And I was always at the Pyramid nightclub—I don't know if you've ever heard of it.

MKO: **Of course. It was a historic nightclub with irreplaceable art and the fact that it no longer exists is devastating!**

JP: Totally. I was there and I probably took it for granted, but it was a great moment. And there were a lot of little things around that time that you could be a part of.

AO: **There are a lot of allusions to fame in some of the pieces. Were you inspired by that? Was that a reaction to these groups? Your photographs have an element of fantasy to me.**

JP: Yes, definitely. This isn't necessarily my generation, remember. My parents are much older, and I had three brothers that were at least thirteen years older than me—this was more their generation. Again, it's that influence—their influence on me. When I was six they were all teenagers, and I wanted to really catch up and be into what they were into. I was like, "No, I don't want to play with toys; I want to learn about rock 'n' roll, music and cigarettes, and cars and stuff like that."

MKO: **That reminds me of Richard Prince's art issue with *W* magazine last year, especially the headshots. Do you think he got the idea from some of your pieces?**

JP: Absolutely! No, I'm just kidding. Seriously, though, his influence was already felt in New York when I got here. He's been doing that for a long time. His stuff is a little cooler 'cause it's modern day, but we're both definitely born from barroom culture, a little bit, anyway. When I first started going out you would go to old bars where they'd have a million eight-by-ten glossies [*see page 202*]. Or I don't know if you went—what's that place down here?

AO: **The Palm.**

JP: No, more old school. Like the Formosa. I love places like that. Part of the reason I make stuff is just to make it look like something I liked in my past. I said earlier that I moved to New York and didn't have my first show for the first ten years. But so many nights I would stand in the middle of a raging nightclub and be like, "Wow, this would be so cool. You should just put this in a gallery." And finally one day, I did. I was like, "Why can't it just be tinsel and the lights and cheap and sad?" Then I just did a piece like that. And that was a huge change for me: Instead of asking, "What if?" I just started to do it.

AO: **When did you realize you could turn your art into a business and an actual lifestyle?**

JP: I guess around 1990, because I had had my first show of photographs. Things take me a while to percolate, so I had ten years' worth of photographs. Since I had never really made them, printed them

PREVIOUS, LEFT:
In Every Dreamhome a Heartache, 1991, chromogenic color print, 40 x 30 inches. COURTESY CHEIM READ GALLERY, NEW YORK.

PREVIOUS, RIGHT:
On the Beach (Self-Portrait), c-print, 20 x 40 inches. COURTESY CHEIM READ GALLERY, NEW YORK.

RIGHT:
Silver Jackie with Pink Spotlight, 1991, Plywood, silver Mylar, electric lights, cigarette butts, paint, 96 x 48 1/4 x 48 inches. JPS#172, WALKER ART CENTER, MINNEAPOLIS. COURTESY JACK PIERSON STUDIO, NEW YORK PHOTO CREDIT: TOM WARREN

Heaven, 1991,
photographic collage
on canvas, 98 x 84
inches, JPP#17.
COLLECTION OF BILL
BLOCK, LOS ANGELES.
COURTESY JACK
PIERSON STUDIO,
NEW YORK.

RIGHT:
ELVIS 2008,
mixed media:
metal, plastic,
and wood found
letters,
E: 44 x 48 x 1/2
inches, metal;
L: 24 x 15 x 1 1/4
inches, metal;

V: 44 x 32 x 3
inches, plastic
and metal;
I: 14 x 8 x 1
inches, wood;
S: 23 1/2 x 20 x 4
1/2 inches, metal;
COURTESY CHEIM
READ GALLERY,
NEW YORK.

and made a show, taking that action and then seeing that people liked them—it made me confident. And with that confidence, I said to myself, "I'm going to draw." I had spent all my money on the photographs, so all I had left was paper and pencils. So I did drawings, and people liked those too.

AO: The drawings are my favorite.

JP: Thank you, that's so sweet.

MKO: The drawings, or the faces, they remind me of Francesco Clemente's works.

JP: Thank you. I love Clemente.

AO: Let's talk about your letter pieces, which we both love. When did you first start getting those letters?

JP: I was at a salvage store in New York—at the time my studio was on Forty-Second Street, which used to be very, you know, gritty—and they were tearing all this stuff down. Oddly, it was being moved to this area near where I lived, so on the way to my studio I stopped in and shopped there. I was with a friend once and these letters where there. On this trip I said, "I bet—if I could put these letters together . . ." I spelled *Stay*. That was the first word I did [*see pages 204–205*]. And so I said, "What if I could sell this for fifteen hundred dollars next week?" My friend said, "You probably could." So I responded, "I'm going to." And [the letters] cost around sixty dollars. At the time I had to ask myself, "Should I spend this sixty dollars?"

AO: Right. "Can I turn around and actually make it?"

JP: I said to myself, "Let's try it." So I did, and I put it on the wall of my studio. I called up somebody who had seen and liked my photographs. He made a phone call, told this really sweet lady that he had a piece for her. "You've got to see it, you're going to want it," he says. "How much?" the lady asks. "Fifteen hundred dollars." And she was like, "Yes, I'll take it."

MKO: You were just kind of playing it by ear.

JP: Yes. But again, it took me ten years to acquire that. Because I used to think, "Oh well, this work is just like somebody's journal; nobody's going to want this." I had to turn my attitude around.

MKO: The things that you write, are they things from your past?

JP: Sometimes it's past and sometimes it's present.

AO: It seems like there's a lot of present stuff.

JP: The drawings I sometimes have to let go of because I can get so into them—it's like acting to me. I have to summon up all this angst or remember some something that drove me nuts to get into it.

AO: It's an emotional thing. They're really personal.

JP: Yes, and then for a while, when I was really pumping the drawings, I felt a little exposed, as if everybody knew my stuff. So I pulled back. Now I want to start going back to them, so I'm glad you like them.

MKO: Are the pictures of the men personal?

JP: They go back and forth—some are really personal, but I know how to make it look personal. I wanted to make it look like you were in on a private moment, sort of. But I feel like you get pegged as doing one thing and people say, "Oh, they're personal, they're intimate, they're so real." And then I want to show them that I can do something that looks austere and professional, like fashion. For a while I got into this mood where I wanted to make it look like real Hollywood pictures, contemporary, like this could be an ad on a bus shelter. And so it oscillated between the two. And that's because I felt like I was being a little bit pegged as not knowing what I was doing.

MKO: And it was important for you to show diversity in your art.

JP: Yes. I like that I was at the beginning of this moment when people became enamored with a snapshot quality, because they believed it was more "real." Then it went out into the world and everybody started doing that. And, look, everybody's snapshots are interesting if you edit them well. That's why there're a million of these books nowadays where someone has said, "Oh look, I was a makeup artist in the '70s, and I took Polaroids at every shoot." They are totally interesting. But then everybody did it, and for awhile it became a snapshot aesthetic. I had to kind of pull back because what I was interested in was an anonymous quality, and at that point I could only achieve that by aping a sort of generic, professional quality. And that's how the self-portraits came about.

AO: That's funny because we're also interviewing Peter Lindbergh. And he's more of a professional—fashion photography, landscape photography. It will be interesting to see what he has to say about that.

JP: Is he fun?

MKO: Amazing.

AO: He makes you feel like you are the most beautiful woman he has ever photographed.

MKO: He loves women.

JP: That's nice.

MKO: A different kind of intensity, though. He gets the final say, especially in his magazine work. He did a photo shoot for the cover of a magazine once, and the magazine wanted to go back in and touch up the model's face—she had a huge scar and a couple of lines—and they ended up not being able to use the photos because they wanted to blow it out and he didn't let them. He said, "This is the only way you're allowed to use this picture, this is what makes it interesting, what makes it different." He wanted to capture a completely different moment.

AO: Where do you find your letters?

JP: Flea markets, antique stores. . .

MKO: Do you think of the work first, or do you find the letters first?

ST

JP: Both ways. I have many in my studio now, so sometimes I'll think, "I want to do this, how can I pull it together?" And then in the midst of that, one will end up next to the other. A cool *C* will wind up next to a cool *K* and I'll ask myself, "What word would make it so I could leave those two together?" And then I'll work around that.

AO: **I love your series that were called self-portraits.**

MKO: **You're clearly not the people in your self-portraits, so I'm curious about why you called them that. Is it a desire to be someone else, or are you trying to relate to traits you see in others?**

JP: Totally. I know you guys must go through this too, where you want to connect on a different level; it's like when you buy a pair of Calvin Klein underwear you think you're going to have that body. His advertising has been a huge influence since the '80s, since it started. With Bruce Weber, they totally changed advertising and the way shoppers associate themselves as consumer.

MKO: **Yes. When you buy their underwear you think you're going to end up like Natalia Vodianova, with a man lying on top of you in the woods.**

JP: Exactly. And there's this old cliché: Every photograph is a self-portrait. So it's this thing when you want to be that person in the picture; it's not even about love—you just want to be that person instead of who you are sometimes. Another big influence of mine was Mark Morrisroe, who died in 1989; we lived together and he was part of that early crowd that I mentioned earlier. He was an artist, he was a few years older than me, and when I came to the city he knew everything. People are now really into him; he was great. He had a piece once that said, "Sometimes I'd rather be a movie star than an artist." So I did an *Answer* piece that said, "Sometimes I'd rather be a photograph than a human being." I didn't set out like, "I'm going to take these pictures, these self-portraits." They were photographs from that period where I was doing professional photography and slowly I began to think, "How do I make this art?"

AO: **I love your series of naked men.**

JP: The collage? That's an early one.

AO: **And your neon signs? I always think of LA because so much of this city can get cheesy, with neon everywhere—**

JP: That was a big thing for me too because my first trip to LA did a number on my head. There's so much poetry out there, just driving around. The signage came really from the first couple of weeks I spent in LA.

MKO: **What are you working on right now? Anything inspiring you lately? What kind of direction are you going toward now?**

JP: It's off the wall and I can't account for it yet, but I'm suddenly into pottery. I've been making pots. I saw the work of this incredible potter in Belgium—his name is Alain Vernis—he makes raku, which is a Japanese form of pottery. It's very elegant and beautiful, and the part I like about it is that I'm making something with my hands, which I haven't done in awhile. That's the direction it seems to be going for me. It's all elemental as opposed to glamour. Maybe I'm going to turn into a mudman or abstract painter—I don't know.

AO: **But it's taking you to someplace new.**

JP: Yes, it just helps me relax.

AO: **Are you worried that you won't sell your pottery work? Do you work to live, or do you live to work?**

JP: Well, I don't think the pots are part of my artistic oeuvre, so to speak. It helps me relax. But I think it will affect my work, definitely. There is one artistic thought process that says, To be a true artist, one has to produce from within themselves. But sometimes I like to think of it like a fashion designer. "Okay, now what are the next three months going to be like, as opposed to my twenty-year career?"

MKO: **Like a season, or a trend?**

JP: "What is good for right now?" is a question I'll ask myself. That's why there's so much different stuff—which is not necessarily great when you're an artist. People like one thing about someone's work. That's why the sign pieces have really taken off, because people want a brand, they want a clear message, they want the Jack Pierson, and that's Jack Pierson. Because if they come upon one of my paintings that aren't so well known, they might ask, "Is this a Jack Pierson?"

MKO: **But that's why, I think, we really wanted to talk to you. That's something that you are doing, and people are responding and understanding.**

AO: **Well, it's like when an artist is in touch with the way society is culturally. It's interesting.**

JP: I'd like it to be more like that. I like to think I'm culturally relevant.

MKO: **That can be an inspiration in itself.**

JP: I'm touched that you like my work so much. The next time you're in New York, you're welcome to come to the studio. I'm working on my newest word pieces now, which are kind of abstracts and they don't really say anything; they're just broken letters that I hope look like symbols and you don't really know what they mean.

MKO: **I want to see them.**

JP: I'm in New York three fourths of the time. I come out here not even a quarter of the time. But I have this house in the desert, and I come out here and just chill out.

AO: **That's great. Get away from it. I think that's healthy.**

PREVIOUS:
STAY 1991, mixed media: metal, plastic, and wood found letters, 18 x 44 x 2 inches. COURTESY CHEIM READ GALLERY, NEW YORK.

LEFT:
Pink Badlands, 1992, chromogenic color print, 40 x 30 inches. COURTESY CHEIM READ GALLERY, NEW YORK.

OPPOSITE PAGE:
A car Richard designed, in
his Princeville studio.

Richard Prince is a studious, quiet artist—the type who broods over and debates his artistic actions before he executes them. Even the inspirational pieces that he's collected for decades (old romance novels, clippings from the *New York Times*, vintage Hollywood glamour head shots), which are catalogued in his studio in upstate New York, sometimes sit on a drafting table in his studio for years until he knows exactly what he plans to do with them. Richard grew up in a suburb of Boston, and after some travels in Europe and a stint at an art school in Maine, came to New York to begin his career as an artist. Along the way he worked in the tear-sheet department at Time/Life, a job that would influence his later works. Today his large body of work is celebrated around the world. What's more impressive are the several types of works he's known for: reproductions of vintage magazine campaigns, his Nurse paintings, his works with automobiles and car hoods, his Joke paintings, his Cowboy series and his Girlfriend series. Put bluntly, he's a modern art icon. (Marc Jacobs agrees, since he commissioned Prince to be his collaborator for his Spring 2008 accessories collection at Louis Vuitton). So it was with much excitement that on a sunny spring day I headed to upstate New York, to a town the artist affectionately calls Princeville, to tour his expansive property and discuss his life and body of work.

3/25/08   PRINCEVILLE, NEW YORK

DATE   LOCATION   INTERVIEWED BY

MKO: **Well, that was quite a road trip out here.**

RP: I wanted to live in the middle of nowhere.

MKO: **Mission accomplished. How many properties do you have out here?**

RP: This one, the studio, and then my house over there. We're about to get two more on this road, and then we have one in that little town down the road. I used to have a property on the other side, but I donated it to the Guggenheim.

MKO: **The one that burned down?**

RP: Yes, that's on the other side of town. There's nothing in it—it's just burned.

MKO: **How did it burn?**

RP: Lightning. Luckily there was nothing in it.

MKO: **Outrageous! So when did you start working as an artist?**

RP: I don't know really. I went to France when I was eighteen—on a boat full of students. It was pretty crazy. I left New York, and it was really a small boat just filled with kids. I had a ball. But then I landed in France, and I was supposed to go to a university, but I just didn't go.

MKO: **That makes sense. I'm not sure the second that anyone gets to Paris they want to go straight to a classroom.**

RP: I knew I wanted to study art history, so instead of going to school I decided to do that in my own curriculum. I bought a Euro pass, and I just went to every city and looked at all the art. When I came back to the US, I needed a deferment—in those days you had to get a deferment or else you'd get drafted in the Vietnam War. So I went to this hippie college up in Maine. I walked into the art studio when I was about nineteen, and I just thought, "This is for me. This is where I want to be." All the people who were there looked like people I wanted to be with, and the teacher was very influential. He became kind of a mentor. I never went to an art school; I didn't have that opportunity. Then I just went to New York immediately. I was probably twenty-two, and my teacher said, "If you're going to do this, don't go to art [school], don't go to graduate school, just go to New York and try to see if you can live there for awhile." I ended up staying in New York for twenty-five years.

MKO: **Growing up, were you surrounded by art?**

RP: No. My parents had one painting—they still have that same painting on the wall. They weren't art people, really. Never a book. My parents didn't read. It's kind of bizarre. I was the opposite, you know?

MKO: **What kind of pieces were in your first show?**

RP: I used to study the figure; I started by taking figure-drawing classes. There was this group show, and that was really fun for me because everyone else was a real artist. I think I had been asked to show some of my watercolors, and that was it. When I went to New York, I worked in a printmaking studio. When I wasn't working, they gave me use of their presses, and I would make collages and things like that. When I was a student, it was really hippie-dippy stuff that I was making; I was eighteen and reading *The Hobbit* and things like that. So it was weird things, like a—

MKO: **A hobbit collage?**

RP: Yes, yes. Ha! I don't know where any of that stuff is.

MKO: **You didn't keep it?**

RP: I gave it away or I would sell it for five dollars to another student or trade it. Some of that stuff has started to surface now, but for the most part—

MKO: **That was a good investment. Five bucks! Were you always attracted to ad campaigns, the media?**

RP: Yes, I love magazines. I'm a magazine junkie. I always used to tear magazines up and collage them. I remember being incredibly focused on the happenings that were just a little older than I was—for instance, the Swinging London in the '60s. I was a little too young for that, but I was very attracted to that whole mod look, the fashion, the haircuts, and the Rolling Stones. I was a little too young to participate in that, but I would tear up the album covers. Those were so important to me because I didn't have access to the clothes where I grew up.

MKO: **Where did you live?**

RP: I lived just outside of Boston, in a suburb. Everybody had crew cuts and wore chinos there. Then you would see a picture of what Mick Jagger would wear, and we would ask, "Where did he get those clothes?" It was always very appealing to me. When I was eighteen, I ended up in London, and I remember buying pink crushed velvet pants.

MKO: **That period is still attractive. That's one era I gravitate toward.**

RP: Well, it all comes and goes. Three or four years ago, I was thinking hippies, and now I'm sort of getting back into the punk thing. I'm not too sure where that's going to go, but a lot of my work revolves around that: beat culture, hippies, punks. I just bought a Jimi Hendrix archive—to me he was like the real representative of that era. Again, I was just a little too young for that; I was in high school when all that happened.

MKO: **What was the first ad you photographed and reappropriated in your work?**

RP: The first ad was "The Living Rooms," which were a series of ads that appeared in the *New York Times Magazine* a long time ago. They were one per page, and every week another one would come out. There were four in a row, and they were very strange looking, but big.

MKO: **One of those prints inspired my own living room in New York.**

RP: To me, they just really seemed to be what was going on at the time. In 1977, the sensibility was, like, the Talking Heads. And then they got a little bit more *Playboy*-ish, and then there was this one that was a little bit more modern. But I was photographing these photographs. When I first showed these works, the reaction was, "What are you doing?"

MKO: **When did you first show that?**

RP: That was about 1979. I had a little bit of support from other artists, but it wasn't exactly "oh my God."

MKO: **How would you describe your work now?**

RP: There's always a kind of hidden subtext to what I'm doing. I sort of share a sensibility with David Lynch. I collect things, and they'll inspire me much later. Like this [full-page advertisement from a 1990 *New York Times* newspaper of a television character]. I've had this out now for a couple of years and haven't done anything with it—there has to be something else to mix. And then this [framed collage of signed pinup photos of unknown ballerinas, kung fu artists and Old Hollywood starlets], a piece like this is a very simple piece. I collect images of ballerinas that are signed by them, and then I'll just hook it up with this gesture that's not ballet, that's more like a karate thing, but relates in movement. I didn't know

Bitches and Bastards,
1985-86, Ektacolor
photograph, Edition of 2,
86 x 48 inches.

214

Untitled (Kool-Aid),
1983, Ektacolor
photograph, edition
of 2 + 1 AP, 24 x 20
inches.

what publicity photos were when I started doing this, so some of the signatures are fake.

MKO: **They're pretty awful.**

RP: But that's what was fascinating about that type of photo to me. You'd go in and see them in the window of a deli or a nail salon, and I'd think to myself, That's an odd place for a head shot.

MKO: **I've run into some pictures like that of my sister and me, with signatures from when I didn't even know how to spell my name.**

RP: But that's interesting in terms of how a photograph can work. That's more interesting to me than, say, Ansel Adams. Also, it was something I could buy at the shopping mall.

MKO: **Do you ever look to buy these types of head shots online?**

RP: A little bit. I'm not very good on eBay because it takes too long. Now what I do is use memorabilia sites and get them in the mail. I look for the ones that I can use in my work. I try to get real ones now. I don't like to fake them anymore. Or I'll go to this thing called Glamourcon. There's one in Chicago. I went to Chicago once specifically for this Glamourcon that *Playboy* put on. All the models sat behind their desks, and you'd go up, wait in line, and buy their eight-by-tens in front of them and say, "I want this one and this one." And then you'd pay for it with about ten dollars. Then they'd sign it for you—you could tell them what your name was and they'd sign it there. I really enjoyed that. I loved the cheesiness of it. All these different cultures and subcultures have these things now, whether it's a comic book convention or *Star Trek—*

MKO: **When did you start with the Nurses series?**

RP: I started in 2001, but then I dropped them because when I began it started to get depressing. Then I discovered the idea of painting the mask on them. Once they became something I could paint, all the drips made sense.

MKO: **They were based on books.**

RP: I started collecting nurse books a long time ago. They were little paperback books that cost about ten cents. I noticed them one day at a flea market. There was a whole box of them. It got my attention because there were so many. I wasn't really aware that there were so many.

MKO: **A whole world.**

RP: There are literally thousands of them. They're like romances. People fall in love with a nurse or the nurse falls in love with a patient. I've never read one, but I have thousands. I just started painting them, but I had no idea that they would become as much of an iconic series.

MKO: **The Louis Vuitton show opened with your Nurses.**

RP: I didn't even know that was going to happen. I didn't know Marc [Jacobs] was going to come out with all those nurses.

MKO: **Were you at that show?**

RP: I was at that show. That was the first fashion show I've ever been to. I brought my daughter, my wife—none of us had ever been to a show. I designed the tent that the show was in; I designed everything. There was a part of me that didn't want to go, but I'm so happy I went, because I've never experienced anything like it in my life.

MKO: **It's pretty crazy.**

RP: I thought so.

MKO: **Fashion shows can either be a great, inspirational experience—or possibly the worst experience.**

RP: When they came out in their outfits and the Louis Vuitton

masks and the music, I was sitting next to Pharrell Williams—I think that's his name—and the music, I think it was Def Jam. It was amazing—the sound and all the photographers. It was like, "What am I doing here?" And then you saw the bags—that was another thing. I hadn't seen the bags; I'd only designed them, but I hadn't seen them made.

MKO: **What was that process like?**

RP: Well, I had no idea about Louis Vuitton, or what it was. I did know Stephen Sprouse had done the graffiti—I knew him—and I remembered him doing it a long time ago. But the only reason I did it was because of Marc [Jacobs].

MKO: **Did Marc call you personally?**

RP: Marc called me. But I didn't know much about the brand, the cult of LV. They sent you a history of Louis Vuitton, and it was kind of interesting. We spent all summer going back and forth.

MKO: **Collaboration can be difficult.**

RP: It was hard. But then they sent me silk screens of the monogram. After that I just sailed through it, gave it to Marc, had one meeting in a hotel room where we had everything laid out. He was amazing with what he did that afternoon. He did his thing and I did my thing, and then it was completed. Really quickly, actually. I didn't hear anything for a month. "Come to Paris"—that's all I heard. I knew he was busy; I didn't want to bother him. And then I got there, and it was like a performance piece.

MKO: **His fashion shows are like fifteen-minute performance pieces.**

RP: It's funny because Marc and I share a lot of friends, like Elizabeth Peyton and Kim Gordon. Marc seems to be this guy who's the daddy. I was very interested in it only because of him. I would never have attempted to do a fashion thing; I didn't know anything about handbags—but now I do. I'm going to make my own handbags, I think.

MKO: **So furniture, art, architecture, handbags. You're a busy man.**

RP: Well, the handbag now has become like architecture. Look at it, it's architecture. It's this thing that can look pretty, but you use it. You put things in it, so it's not unlike a little house.

MKO: **Do you have a hard time seeing your work go? It seems like you have such a vested interest every single piece.**

RP: Anything in this room is going to be difficult for me to see go. I want to try and hold on to as much as I can; everything I've recently made has really been a piece of me. I don't want to sell it because I want to spend a lot of time and think about it. I don't want to really sell any of these cars.

MKO: **Are you happy out here? Have you thought about moving back to New York?**

RP: We were thinking of Los Angeles, back to New York, or London. Those are the three left. I can't do anymore here, so it's time. My oldest child, when he goes to college, we can think about moving somewhere else. I wouldn't mind going back to New York at this point.

MKO: **What would you do to this place?**

RP: I don't know. We've just bought the field there and the house next door. So if we'd move I'd probably just stick someone at that road, a caretaker. And then I'll have the people who work here just continue to work, and I'll come up here and check on them. We're buying a house in Saint Barths. I've been going there forever and I love it.

MKO: **Do you go there over Christmas and New Year's? It can get very hectic, and very intense that time of year.**

RP: We do. We're so isolated up here all year that we don't mind, actually. I don't mind the craziness, actually. Up here we're literally by ourselves—the UPS guy and the FedEx guy are the only two guys I see.

MKO: **Do you keep up with the media and all the gossip? I feel like it has translated into several parts of your work. Like that spread you did in *W* magazine—the one with Angelina Jolie and Jennifer Aniston and Lindsay Lohan.**

RP: That was for *W*'s art issue. I just did what they gave me. I didn't totally understand it, to tell you the truth. I did some dicier signatures on those pictures, which they didn't use. I don't think anybody objected to what they ran though; I didn't hear anybody object at all.

MKO: **You mean from the people who were in it?**

RP: I don't believe the people who were in it objected.

MKO: **How do you stay updated?**

RP: We subscribe to a lot of magazines, and I do go online.

MKO: **Do your kids keep you up to date?**

RP: Yes. And I read Page Six [gossip column in the *New York Post*] every day.

MKO: **Well, hello. I'm Mary-Kate, nice to meet you. Don't believe everything you read!**

RP: Yes, I know a lot of that stuff isn't right. Like when they say that someone was somewhere with someone else. I've been in those places with some of those people, and then I'll read something that's so far off, saying that this person was there with someone else. Then I think, Well, wait a minute, they weren't there. I was there last night and they weren't.

MKO: **Exactly. That happens pretty often. Well, thank you so much for allowing me to come up here and see your space. It's truly something.**

RP: Well, I've loved having you.

MKO: **No, the pleasure was mine. It's been an honor. And an inspiration.**

ABOVE:
I was particularly drawn to *Las Vegas Nurse*, 2008, ink-jet and acrylic on canvas, 84 x 54 inches.
PHOTOGRAPH BY DEREK BLASBERG.

RIGHT:
Richard's workbench is still covered in paint and ink from his collaboration with Louis Vuitton.

RIGHT MIDDLE:
A gallery adjacent to Richard's studio is filled with his joke paintings and car pieces.

BOTTOM:
The personal space of Richard's studio.

Danger Nurse at Work, 2002
Inkjet print and
acrylic on canvas
93 x 56 inches
(236.2 x 142.2 cm)

Kate Moss, 1996.

The photographer Terry Richardson started taking pictures when he was still in high school and living with his mother in Southern California; at that time the punk aficionado would rather have been a rock star or, as he told us, a hairdresser, but after assisting a few photographers, he found himself addicted to creating his own images. He moved to New York with his father, Bob Richardson, an established photographer and a man Terry had a unique relationship with until his passing in 2005. In New York, Terry forged his own aesthetic niche and his career took off. Today, Terry counts major fashion magazines and fashion mega brands as clients, and supermodels and celebrities as regular subjects. And that's not including his more artistic personal works and pictures. We visited Terry's place on the Bowery, where he lives and takes the majority of his pictures against a blank wall near a window overlooking the notorious downtown boulevard. We had coffee and a good chat about his career and life. We discussed his photographic style (which has been called everything from ironic to cheeky to explicit), his relationship with his father, and the evolution of his body of work. His pictures often come off as sexually charged and graphic, but when we talked with Terry, we had the opportunity to experience his wit and his charm. And after the interview, we experienced what a great photographer he is to work with.

1/29/08   NEW YORK CITY

DATE   LOCATION   INTERVIEWED BY

AO: So, Terry, how did you get into photography? Were you interested in it as a child?

MKO: Yes, start from the very beginning.

TR: Okay, well, I was born in New York and then, when I was one, I moved to Paris with my mom and dad. My dad was a photographer, and he worked in Paris a lot so we moved there. I spoke French before I spoke English.

MKO: Really? Ddo you still speak French?

TR: Not a word. I don't remember it. I wish I did, and I've tried to get it back—I got the tapes, had the French girlfriend, everything—but I just can't remember it. And then when I was about four and a half we moved back to New York. Then my dad was introduced to this model, named Anjelica Huston, who was like seventeen at the time, and fell in love with her. He ended up leaving my mom and moving in with her; so my mom and I moved to Woodstock for three and a half years. She met an English musician, Jackie Lomax, married him, and then I moved to London for a year and a half with them. Then he got another record deal from Capitol Records, so we moved to LA, to Hollywood, and that's kind of where I spent my adolescence.

AO: How was Hollywood different in comparison to now?

TR: It was, you know, the late '70s, early '80s—lots of skateboarding and Black Flag and punk rock bands and punk rock shows and the metal stuff. It was cool.

MKO: So you were into music before you were into photography.

TR: Yes, I played bass in a bunch of bands, garage bands, and played parties and a bunch of other stuff.

AO: Tell the truth—you still have the bass, don't you?

TR: Yes, every once in a while I'll get the old bass out, put on the records in front of the mirror, do a bunch of poses. My dad's a photographer and my stepdad's a musician, so I kind of started doing music first and then started taking pictures. I was going to Hollywood High [School]. When I was nine my mom was in a car accident. She was on her way to pick me up from the therapist's office—I was really violent when I was little; I would always have tantrums and smash the house, so I was going to a shrink—and she was rear-ended by a telephone truck and put into a coma for a month. There was permanent brain damage, so her equilibrium was off. She could never walk again and had to retire at thirty-six. That happened when I was nine and getting into punk rock. By the time I was fifteen, my dad kind of lost everything and ruined his whole career. By the time I was sixteen, he was homeless—had nothing, broke, sleeping on benches. So the funny thing for me was that in the beginning, as a kid, there was lots of money, fabulous apartments, a Sony color TV that everyone was so jealous of; but by the time I was ten, eleven, twelve, my whole life had changed and it was like food stamps and welfare. And because my stepdad was broke, we settled out of court with the Pacific Bell Telephone Company, and my mother got nothing. She got, like, $300,000 for permanent brain damage. If they had appealed, it would have taken years. My adolescence was just spent drinking, getting high, punk rock, playing in bands. Then in the middle of my junior year at Hollywood, my mom decided to move to Ojai, which is this little town near Santa Barbara. And I was this total Hollywood High punk rock kid, threatening to move in with a friend. My stepdad was like, "You can't stay with me; just go with your mom." So I ended up moving to Ojai in the middle of my junior year, which is like a little town with cowboys and rednecks and stoner kids, and I started this whole punk rock scene there. I ended up doing a book recently of pictures I had found at my mom's house; she had given me a snapshot camera and I would just, with no ambition to be a photographer, take pictures at parties. And subsequently I ended up finding those pictures in my mom's house three or four years ago and did a book.

MKO: And that's when you got into photography?

TR: No, not really. I got rid of the camera and kept playing in bands. When I was eighteen, I went to City College for a bit, but I dropped out. Then I went to beauty school—Ventura Beauty School—and after about two weeks, I just thought, "I'll be a hairdresser, I'll move to Hollywood, girls, it'll be fun." Plus, my grandma was a beautician.

MKO: In a way, that's kind of genius thinking.

TR: It was not a happy ending, though. So I was in beauty school and I was going be a hairdresser, thinking, This is awesome, it's new wave, it's '80s, Hollywood, *Shampoo*, Warren Beatty. But then my grandmother, who was from Budapest and was a beautician, called me and was like, "You can't be a beautician because all of the guys who are beauticians are gay. So you're going to become gay." She wasn't exactly politically correct at that time. Anyway, she said that she'd give me $10,000 if I would drop out. So I took the money.

AO: And now you completely regret it.

TR: Yes, I totally do. It's one of my biggest regrets in life. I'm a beauty school dropout. I took the ten grand and went to Hollywood with it—well, I ended up having a fight with my mom and got thrown out of the house. The police came and I got arrested. I destroyed my mom's house; I had another episode/tantrum. That's how I left my mom's. Anyway, I went down to Hollywood with my ten grand, and I partied it away pretty quick. I was playing in a band and working as a busboy or whatever. Then, through my mom or someone, I met this guy who used to assist my dad in the '60s named Tony Kent. He said he would teach me about taking pictures, but that he would be putting me to work. I said okay and started assisting this guy

Batman and Robin,
1996.

Bob Richardson,
2003

with zero intention of being a photographer—I didn't even own a camera at this point. I was hanging out and was like, "Wow, this guy gets paid to do this?" Then all of a sudden I started taking pictures. My dad was kind of going in and out of my life at this time. We wouldn't speak for two years, or he would be homeless and I'd go rescue him. While I was taking pictures and hanging out in LA, I had been photographing Donovan Leitch and Ione Skye and Adrock and all that kind of LA scene in the '80s, taking portraits and hanging out. Then my dad told me I should move to San Francisco, where he had turned up, and he would mentor me.

AO: Did it come pretty easily?

TR: That's the interesting thing: When I look back at my old pictures, they were like snapshots. Once I started working with my dad, the thought was—that was like 1990 or something—the first thought was, How do you work for magazines? This was early '90s, though. There's now *iD,* but back then there was no grunge revolution; people were still really conservative. My father and I decided to do a portfolio together, and then come to New York, get into *Vogue,* and just make it. I remember I was doing this with him, and then I had this girlfriend—some seventeen-year-old model or whatever—and we got engaged. I followed her to New York. I got my portfolio, a credit card with a thousand-dollar limit on it, and the $1,500 or so I had gotten for selling my car. We got here, and then she split to Milan. I had my portfolio and I called a friend, who told me he was in a little studio that wasn't his and that I couldn't stay with him. Now I was sitting at some little Polish diner, and I was shaking, almost crying, totally terrified of big bad New York. So I called my mom, and she has a friend here, and she got me in a hotel where I paid—this Indian place on Park Avenue—where I just paid the tax. Then my girlfriend's booker told me there's a room on Christopher off Hudson for like $400 so I took that.

MKO: But you're here, and you're making it happen.

TR: Totally, I'm in New York, pounding the pavement, going to see *Vogue* and *Allure* and whoever else there is, and I'm getting these little pictures in the front of the magazine to illustrate these little stories like, "How Do You Do Your Hair if You're Going Out Tonight?" Sometimes it's a full page; sometimes it's a little picture. At this point it was like I'd abandoned what I was doing in the beginning, which was just shooting friends and partying and stuff like that. I was trying to do what I thought they wanted. I never thought about going to London or anything like that—I just thought I had to make it in New York. What's the saying—if you can make it in New York, you can make it anywhere, right? So I was like pounding the fucking pavement, going to see all

these people, and then my dad decided he wanted to move back to New York. I'm like, "Fuck." He's very manipulative and very seductive, but he showed up and he stayed with me. I got him a teaching job, and he was like, "You know, I have a great idea: We're going to work together, and we're going to be called the Richardsons." I was like, "Okay, that's great, I'm twenty-four. I'm trying to make a name for myself, and now I'm going to work with my dad. Whatever you want, Dad." So we would do a slide show. We would go on these appointments—carrying the screen, a 1972 slide projector with wooden paneling on the side, two carousels, a boom box with Nine Inch Nails blaring, "Bow down before the one you serve," just my dad and me. We'd smoke a big joint 'cause we'd always get high right before these appointments, get in the subway because we couldn't afford taxis. . . . I mean, they would just . . . I mean, jaws would drop. It was me and my dad—high—doing the slide show for Grace Mirabella at *Vogue,* making a big impression. Somehow we started getting these little things, little mini pages in Miami. We were kind of flying around and my dad—he was a real character and always super stoned and fighting—would always tell me how it was going to be.

MKO: You were kind of locked into working with your father as this photo team.

TR: Well, meanwhile, a good friend of mine came from LA, and he asked me what the hell I'm doing. He told me, "This is not being a photographer. If you want to be a photographer you have to go and take fucking pictures—it's not about trying to get work, it's not about waiting for the phone to ring. You've got to become passionate about it and do it all the time." And he showed me Larry Clark's *Teenage Lust* and Diane Arbus and all this other stuff I had never seen. I was like, "Holy shit, these are pictures of people just hanging out and partying. This is like what I used to do." I started trying to figure out how to get away from my dad. It was like that Oedipal complex, in a way. *Vibe* had just started, and then it was a cool, really edgy, good magazine, very different than now. They gave us this fashion story. The night before the shoot I called my dad, and I'm like, "I can't work with you anymore. I'm doing it tomorrow on my own. Don't show up." He said to me, "You can't do it without me, you'll never be anything, if you go to that shoot tomorrow without me I'll never speak to you again." I was like, "Okay, don't speak to me again." He said, "Fuck you," and hung up. The next day, it was a nice shoot, and I was just praying, "Please don't show up, Please don't show up." I did these pictures and I told the models not to change clothes—let's get all the kids dressed and we'll go out, hang out, and go roller-skating, boxing, drinking in the streets. I wanted to just photograph them in that kind of element, and that would be the story. That's what I did. When that

story came out, it won this award in the *Festival de la Mode* or something, and then [Phil Bicker] said he had seen the pictures in *Vibe* and asked if I wanted to do the [Catherine Hammond] campaign. I'd been hanging out in Tompkins Square Park every day just photographing kids. I broke away from my dad and just went out every night and day and took pictures, started documenting people and myself. So I sent this one story I had and these pictures and got the campaign. They came to New York and we shot the campaign in my neighbors' apartment and all over the East Village.

AO: That's when you started to form your own distinctive aesthetic.

TR: I did a picture—I think that was in '93 or early '94—of a girl and she had her legs open. It was dark in a bar, but she was very hairy and she had her legs open and you could see everything. When I took the picture I didn't see it because I hadn't gotten glasses yet, so I didn't know I was blind, which explained all these out-of-focus shots I had at the time. But I got the contact sheet and, holy shit, that was a trip. I sent them and they ran the image, which caused a big stir—that's how things started to open up. Then I would go to London and work for *i-D* and *The Face*.

MKO: Did you feel as though you had found your niche?

TR: My dad had taught me how to deal with all the magazines and all this fighting, but it was also my friend telling me, It's not just about that. It's like, if you're an artist or photographer, you do it all the time, and you do it because you love it, and you don't know what else to do. You just have to. It changed for me at that point, Because I just did it no matter what.

AO: Do you start with concepts?

TR: Commercially there're concepts and there're layouts, and there's all this stuff. But I'm more of an emotional photographer, and I like to make things up as I go along. Sometimes there's a little, like, "Let's shoot in this place," or maybe, "Let's get a funny prop," but I kind of just like to see what happens and photograph someone as they are on that day. Not so heavily directed—which is scary at times, especially with models, because if I don't have a connection, I'm screwed. I don't rely on retouching and beautiful light and all this stuff; if I can't get any sort of vibe going I'm screwed. That's why casting is everything. It's about just making a connection—that's what I rely on more. I could do my straight-up, standard simple picture, but especially with fashion, with models—well, some of them are just so young they don't have anything to say. If they're used to being posed it's really hard for me because I don't do that. It's all about this connection with people.

MKO: And your subjects inspire you.

TR: I'm inspired by everything. You have to be a sponge and just see things. I think anything—music, film, art, life, people. My dad gave me some good advice: If you're working and you don't know what to do, just stop and take a walk and look at people. For me, that's what I should be doing; I should be photographing people as people. Just see how people move and what they do. That's why it's funny when you're working with models, because you're like, "Just be like a human being! Like when you're walking down the street or when you go buy a coffee or hail a cab or get something to eat—just do that." People forget the minute when there's hair and makeup and a camera—they lose a sense of themselves.

AO: I do. Absolutely.

TR: You become a robot?

AO: A little.

TR: But the coolest thing is to capture someone's soul or spirit or something or an energy. For me that is the most interesting moment. Every day we feel different: Sometimes we're happy; sometimes we're sad. But to photograph someone as they are is my favorite.

MKO: What are some of the pictures you're most proud of?

TR: I guess a few have become classics, in my mind, anyway. Like the Batman and Robin, or the Kate Moss with the sunshine between her legs. Recently I shot Robert Downey Jr., whom I've always wanted to photograph. And that was incredible. There was just this beautiful energy there; I mean, we're the same age, been through similar stuff and this and that, so we just had this really cool connection. That's amazing. And when I'm photographing I get to the point where I don't think about it. Everything else disappears besides what you're doing and it's a high—like a really good opiate or something. It's the most amazing high where there's this groove going on; it's an incredible thing, such a beautiful thing. And I think you see that in pictures.

AO: What do you think specifically about your work has inspired other people?

MKO: That's a good question.

TR: I like it when people think I do American Apparel because it looks like I did it. It's cool that people think I did it, even though I didn't. So much of commercial advertising is boring and bland, so I think that when people are able to push things through, it changes what the norm is, which I think is cool. Maybe what's inspired people is a DIY aesthetic; like, you can just pick up a camera, a digital camera, and anyone can do it. Obviously when I first did snapshots it took a while to get good ones, to make it an extension of myself. But it's a point of view that develops. What do you guys think?

MKO: I see things like American Apparel, which is from more of an advertising standpoint. But you have a lot of street credibility, and you see other

Mary-Kate and Ashley Olsen, 2008

people trying to re-create your aesthetic. But you've done it in your own, professional manner, and others tend to do it in a more explicit way. Like, you've gone this far, but they're going to take it even farther.

AO: And it's so easy to be a photographer now, with digital cameras, the Internet, and MySpace.

MKO: You don't use digital, do you?

TR: I do a little bit, like the snapshots and things, but mostly film. I always like film; I like the way it feels and I like waiting. It becomes obsessive-compulsive—you shoot and you look, you shoot and you look. I like the idea of not knowing what you're getting, because accidents are very important. Like that first image, the pubic hair thing—it was an accident. I think that in photography or in any art form, accidents are great; they're beautiful and they're unexpected and so natural and organic—and that's so important. I've noticed that if I use a digital, I'm constantly looking and thinking and analyzing it. It's nice to just shoot and wait and not know what you have. You work more off the feeling when you have the picture because you feel it, more so than having that proof.

MKO: Do you ever feel like you're compromising when you're working for magazines or for ad campaigns? How do you feel about that?

TR: Totally. I think it's a double-edged sword.

AO: It's business, though, so how do you deal with that?

TR: It's hard sometimes, but the key is to just not beat yourself up. I have a choice: I can either do something or not, I can say yes or I can say no, and if I say yes I have to deliver something that the client or the magazine can use. You can push it and try things, but the key is that they have to be able to use the pictures or it's just self-indulgent and pointless.

AO: And when you work on commercial products, there's a lot more to deal with, right?

TR: Yes, and when you're working with models or hair and makeup or having to shoot a product, if one person's off, the whole thing can fall apart. You get a bad hair day or something. Girls walk in here all the time, and they look amazing. Then after hair and makeup they look horrible. You can work with really famous hair and makeup people and they have a bad day and they make someone look terrible and they ruin it. There are so many elements that it can get frustrating. You try not to compromise, but I think the key is if you do something and you feel good about it, no matter what it is, that's the greatest satisfaction—to do something and be proud of it. Then if it reaches a broad audience and it kind of works, that's great. But the key is to be able to look at yourself in the mirror and be happy with what you've done. That to me is the greatest reward, and then the respect of peers, and then all of those other things that are kind of nice. At the beginning I used to beat myself up and be miserable on those kinds of jobs, but then it's like, I agreed to the money so I have to do this. This is the gig. And it's okay sometimes. You'd like to think that everything will be how you want it to be, and you wouldn't compromise, but the minute you say yes to something, that's a compromise. The minute you start to work with other people, you're

compromising, because when there are other people involved in your vision, it becomes different.

AO: When you walk down the street, do people know you? Is that irritating?

TR: Well, what do you guys think? I imagine it's a little bit worse for you two.

MKO: It depends. I mean, it comes with the territory.

TR: Well, it's different for you. Normally those guys are pretty nice to me—it depends on what neighborhood I'm in.

MKO: Well, sometimes it opens opportunities and sometimes it's flattering—

AO: It's one thing if you walk into a room and you're meeting someone, if it's a business or work environment and a reputation is preceding you. That's an entirely different thing than walking down the street by yourself.

TR: If you're just going to get, like, a pack of cigarettes or coffee, and people start yelling or harassing. But, for me, the scariest thing is when people run at you, run up to you, and you're like, "What?" And they're drunk or something, and then they ask, "What are you doing, man? You want to party?" And I feel like I'm letting them down: I'm like, "I'm just walking my dog and then I'm going to go home." But it's funny how, because of the Internet and magazines, people become overnight celebrities now. They're recognizable all of a sudden. Well, you two know more than anyone. You're in those magazines all the time, and people are harassing you all the time.

MKO: Do you ever think you went too far in one direction? I know a lot of people thought your work was going into pornographic territory. Do you regret going in that direction, or are you trying to scale back from there?

TR: Trying to? I have scaled back! I mean, I always did work that was sexually charged. Plus, when you start, at least in this industry, you have to do something to get attention. I mean, there're fifty thousand photographers or seventy-five thousand photographers trying to get work on any given day in New York.

MKO: Was it a conscious decision?

TR: When that one image happened it was an accident, but I kind of figured, "Well, wow, everyone in London is not doing sexual work. It's not horny, no one's making out." But they were beautiful pictures I started coming up with. I had my point of view and I had my thing. A lot of people weren't doing it at the time, so I was able to get in with that. People were like, "Oh, that's the guy who takes the kind of sexy pictures, the naughty pictures." And then I built on it. And then I became known for just that. But, I mean, I do pictures of kids, pictures that are just silly and funny and have nothing to do with sex, but people remember the powerful images. There's an aspect to an artist's work that is more popular than another part of it, and people remember it. They're known for this, so maybe something else might even be better, but this is what made them really famous, or this is the iconic imagery. It's good to try different things, though, and I think personally when I stopped drinking and getting high and stuff like that, then the whole sex thing came. Because when I was drinking I didn't care so much about sex. I just wanted to get high, and when I stopped that, it was like adolescence all over again. It kind of became another addiction or another rush or this kind of thing to go into.

AO: How did you start getting in your own pictures?

TR: I remember years ago doing a Sisley ad and there was one frame left on the camera, and I just stuck out my tongue and did something—or actually I had a Heineken—whatever, I had to finish the roll. But the client saw the shots and was like, "That's awesome"—and ran it. Then I did the self-portrait story, which was kind of organic in that sense too. It wasn't like, "Wow, you know what? I'm going to start putting myself in pictures." But then people were starting to recognize me, and it became a celebrity thing or whatever. It was just an accident—and then you build on it. In the beginning I'd put a hand in or I'd touch a girl's face. And then more would get in, and all of a sudden I had pulled myself in. And then the clothes came off.

MKO: Indeed! I've seen you nude in several of your pics, Terry.

TR: But even the first time I was nude in a picture, it was organic. I was shooting this girl, and I asked if she would run naked on the beach? It was beautiful, it was Malibu. But she was like, "No, *you* get naked and run down the beach." And, even though I was a little nervous, I said to myself, "Fuck it, I'll do it." Then someone else had the camera, and we just ran down the beach naked. It was this awesome, funny image.

MKO: That sounds spontaneous—and completely normal.

TR: Yes, it wasn't like I was always getting naked and doing it for lots of attention or something. It was organic, but then you build upon that and you become consciously aware of it.

AO: And that's where your influence comes from, right?

TR: I think the organic things are cool. People ask why someone did this or did that? And I'm like, "I don't fucking know—it was just instinct."

MKO: A spontaneous moment of creativity, if you will.

TR: To trust any thought that comes and just go with it. Go with it, man. Loosen up, don't be so uptight. Let's do it.

RIGHT:
Clown, 1998

232

A portrait of Giambattista
Valli, shot by Kate Barry.

OPPOSITE:
A torquoise necklace from his
spring 2008 collection.

Gambattista Valli never allows for a dull moment. He makes a point to see something beautiful every day. He has a great sense of humor and really strives for a well-lived life. I visited him at the Hôtel Crillon in Paris and when the staff couldn't find us a table to his liking, he suggested they arrange for a private dining experience to be set up in the empty, wood-floored, Baroque Marie Antoinette suite upstairs, which has a patio overlooking the Place Vendôme. He knows decadence! Only Giambattista could think of a way to make dining at the Crillon even more thrilling and indulgent. This characteristic is also brought to life in his designs—and his generosity is overwhelming. He was my date at a gala last year and we spent the whole day together, playing dress-up and listening to the same song on repeat. He's a passionate Italian. Born in Rome, he studied fashion there before working at a variety of other companies, including Emanuel Ungaro where he held the top job. He started his own fashion label in 2005—and I've been a fan since. His clothes reflect the confidence and exuberance of the women who wear them. Just before that decadent lunch at the Crillon we talked about his career in fashion.

3/4/08
DATE

HOTEL CRILLON
LOCATION

INTERVIEWED BY

MKO: Where were you born?

GV: In Rome.

MKO: Did you go to school for fashion?

GV: Yes, I went to fashion school, but for me, Rome was school. It is one of the most eclectic towns that you can find in the world. You can see the craziest things there—a square that could almost be Moroccan, a Baroque elephant carrying an obelisk on its back. There is old Roman architecture, fascist architecture, so many things that are classic, but then also Renaissance, Baroque—everything! Just the whole city was a school in fashion and shapes.

MKO: Who did you design for before starting your own line?

GV: I began with Cecilia Fanfani doing couture shows, and then I was at the house of Capucci. Then I went to Fendi for six years, and then I moved to Paris for six years to work with Emanuel Ungaro. I was the creative director of the house until I started my own line.

MKO: When did you start your clothing company?

GV: I started my own company three and a half years ago.

MKO: When you were younger did you make your own clothes? Did you like to dress up and wear crazy outfits?

GV: At that time, there was this old lady, a tailor, who would come to the house and stitch things for the whole family. There was not really the ready-to-wear yet, it was still the couture. It was the late '60s, early '70s when they started ready-to-wear, so my grandmother used to have a couturier come to the home and stitch things. She would get patterns from Paris. I remember I was a kid and I would obsessively watch these old ladies stitch, and I would ask them to stitch things for Barbie dolls. Not for myself, but for my collection of Barbies.

MKO: Every time I received a Barbie I cut her hair.

GV: Always. Always I was styling the hair.

MKO: I would cut the hair, cut up their clothes and change everything. Which I'm sure explains a lot about my style now.

GV: It's true! Ha. Are you enjoying Paris? You have to come open-minded to Paris, open-minded to Europe.

MKO: I love coming here and would like

to move here someday. But tell me more about your Barbies.

GV: Oh, right. I was doing Barbie dresses—I still have them, actually; I have a box in Rome.

MKO: You should do a presentation of all the dresses.

GV: Yes, probably.

MKO: Create a crazy white room for all your Barbie dresses. In a way, your show last week was kind of like a children's fantasy come to life. It was based on the tale of Little Red Riding Hood, but the little girl eats the wolf and then the wolf jumps out of her body.

GV: Exactly! I was working around volumes, specifically around the volumes of this woman. So it comes to me right away—this idea, 'cause of the fur, 'cause of the volumes, because of the effect that I wanted to use a lot of red in the collection I say, "Oh my God, it looks really like the fairy tale." I start with a cape. And then I say to myself that she should eat the wolf, but then the wolf will come out of her—so as it's indigested, it starts to come out of the stomach, from her back and on the side. Yes, the silhouette is more a precise moment of fashion—late '50s, the kind of egg line of Balenciaga and the kind of tulip line that's mostly Christian Dior and Givenchy. I wanted to mix those things together. And then I thought of this artist called Meret Oppenheim, who became very famous because she did this cup of coffee covered by wolf fur. So it all became almost like the artistic movement Dada, where you take an object and turn it into something else that's exactly the same. I took this classical story—"Little Red Riding Hood"—but turned it in a different way. I love to work on something that can be at the same time really beautiful or really ugly. The idea is to have that kind of aggression that is not too beautiful, not too ugly—if not, things are very boring.

MKO: I understand what you mean.

GV: I think you do, very well. You work these really interesting proportions that on you are so unique and fabulous. You and your sister can be in something really difficult, but it's something you never thought of, so it's fabulous. It's amazing. You are fabulous. You always work on this proportion, like you choose very sure

things—huge accessories or very, very small accessories. Or very, very short or very, very long. There is no—

MKO: There's never a happy medium.

GV: There's never normal. Very, very long and very, very small. I think what you guys do is amazing because it's like playing around. Mini, mini, mini, mini furs and then a long, long, long, long piece of dress. I mean, it's amazing; it's like working on opposites.

MKO: I've heard you use art for your inspirations often. Do you collect any?

GV: I always have an art reference. In every single collection that I did there was an art reference. I did one collection all based on the collection of Peggy Guggenheim. Another one before was Rembrandt. I love the idea of art. I love timeless things and I think art is something really timeless. I don't like trendy things. I like to work on style and not on fashion.

MKO: And you only want to show in Paris?

GV: Yes, because I think Paris is very classic. There are people from all around the world coming here, and they are the most talented ones. I don't like the idea of competition, but in Paris in the fashion world the competition is very high. In other big fashion capitals there are big trends going on, but here it's like everyone has their own trend. I love last year when [*International Herald Tribune* fashion critic] Suzy Menkes called Paris the MySpace city because everybody has their MySpace kind of style. You can go to Comme Des Garçons and then you go to John Galliano and then you go to Chanel and then you go to the new designer coming out—each one opposite of the other, each one faithful to himself. And anything goes.

MKO: Who are some of the designers you looked up to when you were young?

GV: Yves Saint Laurent. Monsieur Yves Mathieu Saint Laurent.

MKO: Why?

GV: Because of his obsession with silhouette. He was obsessed with the silhouette. There was one face of the girl—always the same—hair back and lipstick or hair like in a kind of '40s style, same silhouette. The shoulders were, from the first moment that he started until he retired in

Two dresses from
Giambattista's Fall 2008
collection.

238

JESSIE WILLCOX SMITH

Giambattista's collection for
Fall 2008 asked the question,
"What would happen if Little
Red Riding Hood ate the wolf?"
The result was a collection
of red dresses exploding with
fur and embellishments.

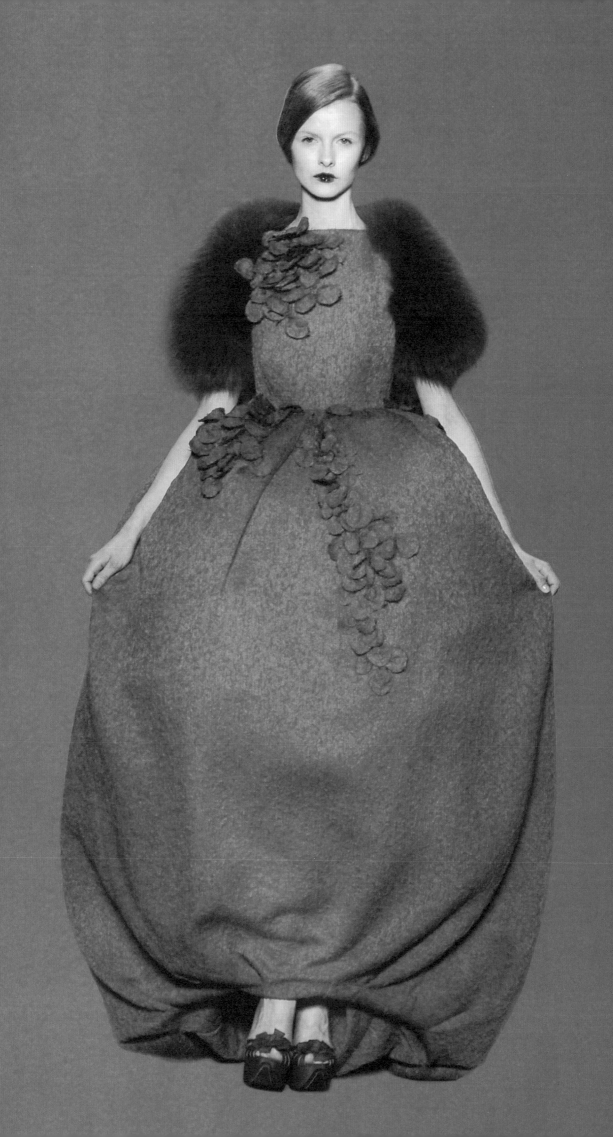

2000, his own shoulders. *That* silhouette. I love obsession.

MKO: And what designers do you like now, besides yourself?

GV: I adore Gareth Pugh in London, because it's something so personal and so unique and so dreaming. I love this kind of creativity on the scene. I love it. I adore. Then I think Miuccia Prada is fabulous.

MKO: She is fabulous.

GV: And many others too. Like, another one that I love is Marni. I adore. Because now I'm working with the family that owns Marni and I love the way they make things. They're really kind of freaky-chic-y hip.

MKO: Their furs are unbelievable. When I first moved to New York I mainly shopped at Marni. I bought a lot of print pieces and I have started to wear those prints again now, the ones from five or six years ago.

GV: For me, what I love about good fashion is that it gets old well. An Yves Saint Laurent gets old well. Right now I can say that even Cristóbal Balenciaga is very important to me. He was too dramatic when I was too young, so I didn't like him. But Yves Saint Laurent—it always works. Even, like, a really old feathered dress—

MKO: I wore one just like that yesterday.

GV: New or old?

MKO: Old. Vintage. To the floor, feathers. It was this long piece with slits for the arms. Gorgeous. It was for a photo shoot.

GV: You know what is really funny, and I have to tell you the truth right now, when I was at Ungaro—and this was like ten, no eleven, years ago and you were really, really young—I used to see your pictures and think, "These are the girls to dress." I remember a picture of you and your sister, and one of you was in a flowery long dress, like Laura Ashley, and you were on the red carpet. But you were really, really young, like ten years ago, honey. And I said, "I adore these girls. One day I would love to dress them." And when my public relations person Justo [Valli's friend and head of PR] showed up with you, it was my dream. But at that time you were eleven. That's why it's so amazing that you are here with me now. I can still remember looking at you—

MKO: I was probably miserable in that picture.

GV: I still remember being in my studio looking at pictures of you in *Vogue*. . . .

MKO: Do you ever feel uninspired? Is there any moment where you think, I'm done. I don't know what to do for this collection?

GV: No, no, no. Sometimes it's the opposite. I have too many things going on. But it's the same problem, when you have nothing or when you have too much, it's the same problem. I have too many things going on, and sometimes I have to stop and say, "Okay, which one am I gonna do?" You have to kill some. So no, at the moment I cannot say I've never been uninspired. But one day I might wake up and say, "Oh my—"

MKO: "I'm done."

GV: But hopefully by then I will have found something else to do. Like, do you know Hide Nakata, the Japanese football star?

MKO: Yes, I went to a dinner last night and he was there.

GV: I love him because he was kind of done doing football, so he started chasing other passions. One time he called me, and he told me he was learning how to drive an elephant in India. It's like what I want to do one day. If that day comes when I wake up and I have no more ideas, I will want to learn to drive an elephant.

MKO: I'll go with you. Let's do that someday. In couture.

GV: This is the thing that I really like. The unexpected.

MKO: What makes a woman chic?

GV: When she doesn't represent anybody else. When she is just herself. Chic is when a woman is in harmony with herself. I hate everything that is artificial bullshit, in a direction that is not you, that you're pushing to be someone else. Just accept who you are and work on it. When I was young I wanted to be blond, I wanted to be taller—but I am dark and I am short. Work with it. Do you know what I mean?

MKO: I've always wanted longer legs. I've always wanted to be taller.

GV: But then you say, "I'm like this and I'm fabulous." Do you know the artist Tracey Emin? One thing I really love about her is that she did this sketch of herself looking at her reflection in the mirror, so you see her from the back and then her in the mirror. And then it says, "Me, feeling beautiful." Sometimes I think about this and it's like, Okay, me feeling beautiful. I wanted to be tall, I wanted to be blond, I wanted to be short, or whatever. But I am as I am and that's it.

MKO: You are a chic man.

GV: Yes, I am a chic man.

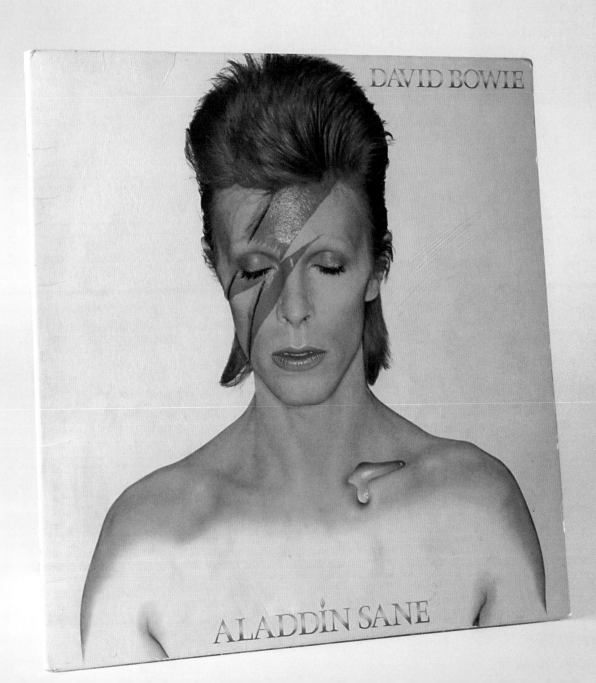

Giambattista
did this sketch
of Mary-Kate
in the dress
she wore to the
2007 7th on
Sale gala.

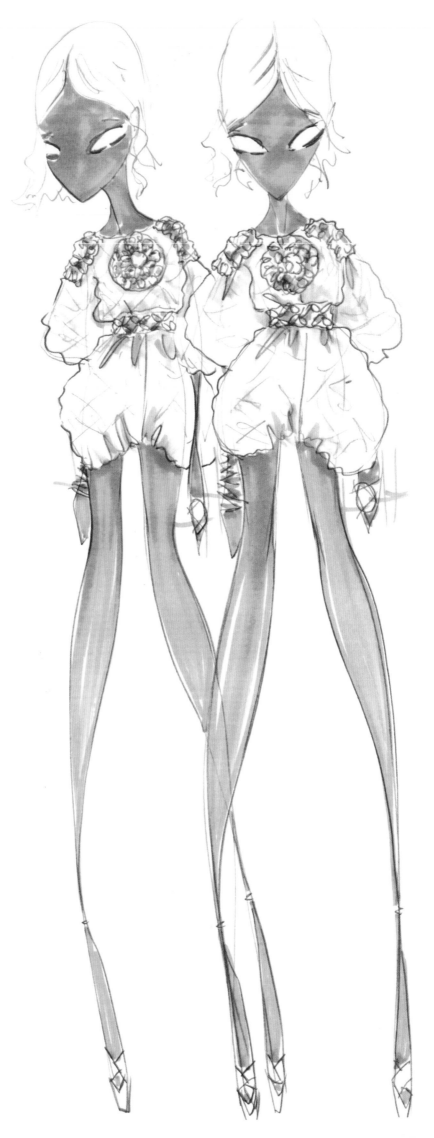

Giambattista
sketched Ashley
in the dress
she wore to a
party for the
2007 Golden
Globes.

When the Yurman company decided to switch from still-life campaigns to more fashion-oriented, sweeping publicity pushes they commissioned Peter Lindbergh to shoot the likes of Kate Moss (seen here) on the beaches of St. Barths in their jewelry. The images became some of the most well received advertisements in that field.

The first things that came to mind when I met Evan Yurman were the overwhelming gems, trinkets, stones and one-of-a-kind jewelry that must have surrounded him in his childhood. His parents, the legendary jeweler David Yurman and his inspired wife Sybil, founded their company in 1979, three years before Evan was born. In the following three decades, the Yurmans turned their name into a symbol of American elegance and one of the most powerful jewelry brands in the United States. You might recognize the twisted cable pieces that David introduced in 1986, or the company's sweeping black-and-white ads with Kate Moss, Natalia Vodianova, and Daria Werbowy shot by Peter Lindbergh. Growing up as a Yurman meant being totally immersed in the life creative. Although his parents would bring everything from sculpture to raw diamonds to their Tribeca home, Evan wasn't always so certain he would follow in his family's footsteps. In fact, he told me he mulled over a variety of vocations before deciding to become a jeweler. It wasn't until 2004 that he realized all his other passions—fossilized dinosaur bones, leathers, precious gems—could be incorporated into his own line of jewelry. I couldn't be happier with the choice he made.

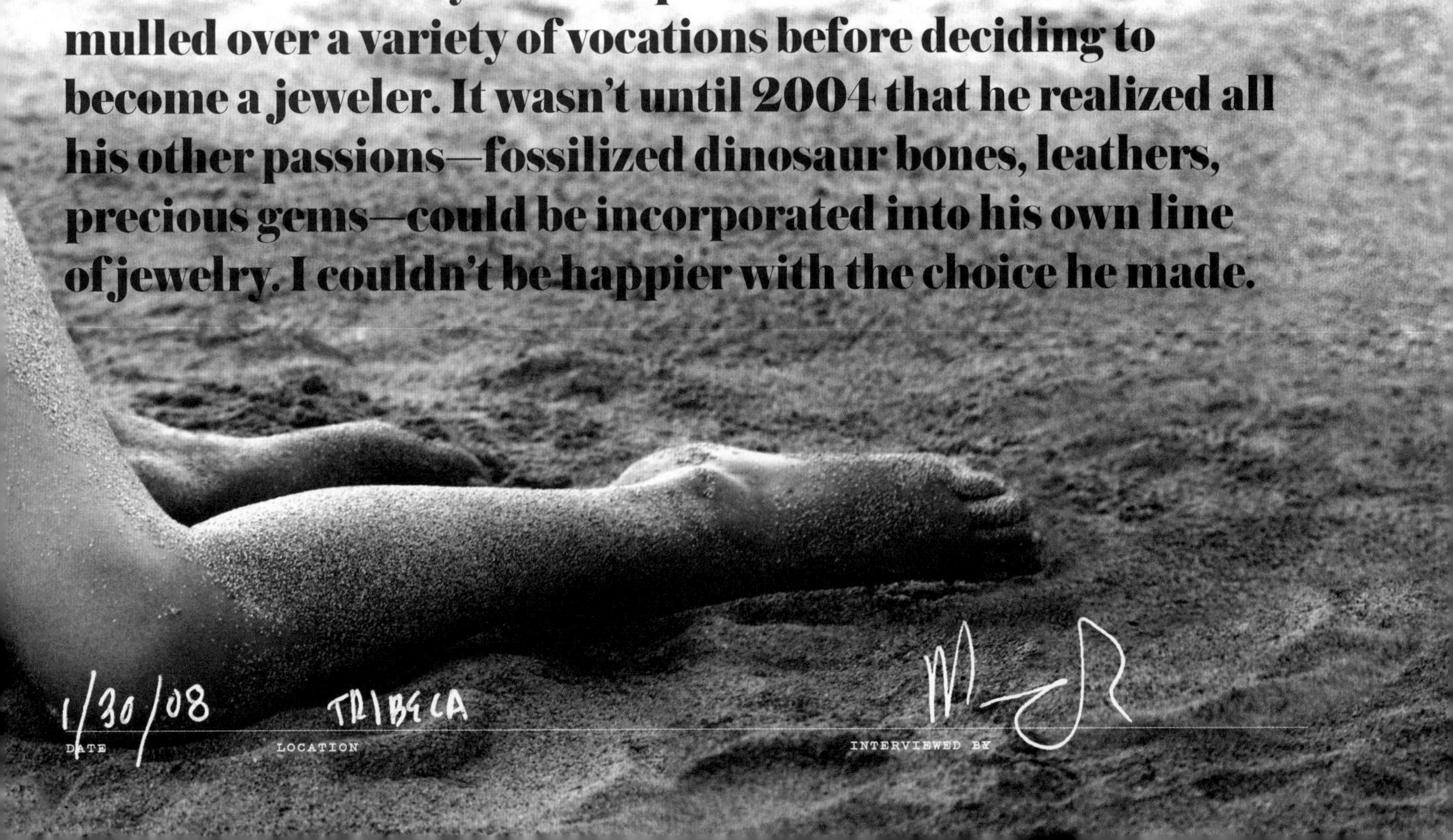

1/30/08

DATE

TRIBECA

LOCATION

INTERVIEWED BY

MKO: **Take me to the very beginning. Where did you grow up and what was your childhood like?**

EY: Right here in Tribeca. I had a New York City child-hood, which means you grow up really quickly. By the age of ten I was taking the subway by myself up to school, which was up on Seventy-something Street. Tribeca then was interesting because it was completely desolate. Nobody was around. Twenty-five years ago it was very much like a factory area. Someone dubbed us—the kids that grew up in that era—the "loading dock kids" because we would all play on loading docks since there weren't playgrounds.

MKO: **When did you first become interested in jewelry and gemstones? When did you realize that you were surrounded by, basically, a jewelry empire?**

EY: Jewelry was always something that my parents just kind of did. And I would always joke that the business was my stepsister or stepbrother, because it was a big part of my parents' lives. After school I would go to the studio to do my homework. We'd stay there until about eight or nine o'clock, we'd eat dinner there, and then we'd come home. At the time it wasn't something I looked at as an opportunity, or something I would ever go into, but looking back I can say it was all sinking in, and that it was a good thing.

MKO: **So it became your first passion?**

EY: Well, I've always collected things, like rocks from a driveway or stuff I'd gather in the woods. I think I had a passion for observation as a child. And I would spend a lot of time by myself because I was an only child, so I would create these worlds that were within myself that were very decadent and lavish, kind of an imaginary sort of situation.

MKO: **Evan's little dream world?**

EY: Yes, I grew up spending a lot of time in that world; I was pretty detached. People would talk to me, but sometimes I just wouldn't hear them. A lot of the time, actually. Ha. People would say that I had attention deficit or that I didn't pay attention, but I was just very content in my own world. I always collected little stones and rocks, and I always loved to draw and paint.

MKO: **How did you start learning about the stones? You probably know more about stones than anyone I've ever come across. Did you just do that through traveling and teaching yourself? When did you embrace that process?**

EY: I would meet these people who had an extensive knowledge of stones, and I'm really good at retaining information from people—on topics I care about. These were usually older, much older people. They'd take the time to explain things to me; once you have been doing something for so long, you want to share that knowledge with somebody, and it makes you feel good to share it. I've always acknowledged that and been a very good listener on these topics. I've had a lot of different teachers who have all been specialists and professionals within their industries, and I've traveled a lot and bought many

stones. A good stone can be the most beautiful thing that the earth can create—up there with sunsets.

MKO: **When did you start designing for men?**

EY: Actually, it was when I was on a nature hike—one of those walks when you're kind of searching for your-self—and I said to myself, "Stop all this bullshit; I want to contribute to something bigger." So I started designing for the men's line; that was about four years ago. That business already existed, but it was basically just cuff links. I felt there was a real market for men's jewelry, and after traveling around Europe and seeing all the guys wearing jewelry, I started brainstorming. The first thing I did was to take the designs that existed and put colored stones in them, and then I did different carvings and textures on the stones—that did well so they kept me.

MKO: **And reworked your father's signature and logo into the designs, right?**

EY: Yes, and that did very well too, and we continued: I did a collection with leather, silver leather, gold leather, and cognac diamonds, and then I did a sleeker collection, which has kind of morphed into what we have today. After that, things got a little wild in my life—trying to find my role in the company and the men's lines and my personal life—and I kind of lost it. So I headed upstate and was doing another one of my little nature walks. I was walking through the woods, and I came across this stone house. There was this guy in this ditch. He looked up at me and he was like, "Hi." He was just laying down some electric lines, so I asked to see his house, which was this really cool stone box. So I said, "Let me see your house—it's a stone box, it's really cool." He came out of the ditch and we talked for a bit. He had this amazing knife in his back pocket, which he made with his own two hands. Turned out he was a blacksmith; I said, "I want to make knives—cool!" So he told me to come by his studio on 128th Street. and Amsterdam. I got up there and he said first I had to learn how to make a hook. Well, first he couldn't believe I actually showed up. Anyway, after the hook he gradually led me to making knives, which was this technique that was almost therapeutic.
I spent, like, an entire year making knives.

MKO: **I want to learn how to make knives.**

EY: Turns out forging knives is fun, really fun. I just kept on making them, more and more knives. And I still go to the blacksmith's studio. It keeps me sane. I have lots of knives. It's my version of therapy. It was a great period of my life in which I learned a real trade, and I wasn't just drawing and designing and commanding a team of tons of people who were seasoned professionals. I created

Working as a forger in Harlem, first making hooks and later knives, were the first steps Evan made toward joining the family business. Here are some of his early wares.

CHEVRON CUFF BRACELET
IN STERLING SILVER.

PETRVS SHIELD
CUFF LINKS IN 22 KT.

SEA URCHIN NATURALS RING
WITH SUGAR LOAF GARNET.

PETRVS HORSE CUFF LINKS IN
STERLING SILVER AND 22 KT.

PETRVS SCARAB
CUFF LINKS IN 22 KT.

PETRVS LION AND OX RING IN
STERLING SILVER AND 22 KT.

PETRVS HORSE RING WITH TEXTURED
SHANK IN STERLING SILVER AND 22 KT.

BLACK DIAMOND ALBION CUFF LINKS
SET IN BLACK RHODIUM.

PETRVS WASP RING IN STERLING
SILVER AND 22 KT.

EXOTICS RING WITH BURMESE
JADE IN 18 KT.

NATURALS SEA URCHIN
CUFF LINKS WITH BLACK DIAMONDS.

something on my own. That was a huge turning point in my life. From there I said, "I think I'm ready to come back to work full-time for my father," and when I did I was very organized and methodical. I had a clear vision of what I wanted to do, and while I was doing all of this I developed this obsession with textures and organic patterns, which I started to incorporate into my designs.

MKO: But there must have been pressure. Did you feel timid or at all nervous about coming to work for your father's company?

EY: Sure, there was always this kind of pressure: Is the son going to fuck up the business? There is that pressure in a family business, and in a way I feel blessed to be going into a business that is doing well, that is successful, and that is also artistic at the same time. If you're a doctor you can't pass on being a doctor—you can only pressure a kid into being a doctor. It's not like a family business. So I'm very happy with what I do. It wakes me up in the morning.

MKO: Do you design for women?

EY: Privately I do, and a lot of my designs can cross over.

MKO: I love what you do for the men's line; in fact, that's what I'm most attracted to.

EY: That's why I interpret them into women's sizes or women's scale. The charms are kind of my art, my private jewelry. I'm not a men's designer—I'm a jewelry designer. But right now I've taken on the men's division in order to learn all the different aspects of the business.

MKO: Where do you see the men's brand going, or where would you like to see it? Or is it one day at a time, one step at a time?

EY: It's definitely not one step at a time.

MKO: So you have something similar to a three-year, five-year plan?

EY: There's gotta be. I gotta plan for it. Like, I have this watch here that I just designed, it's taken me six months to design, and it will be in stores in two years. And then I'm developing another watch the year after, and then five years from now.

MKO: It never ends. But you do personal projects, too. You and I talked about doing something together—how will it be working with me? Do you think we have a similar aesthetic?

EY: I would say absolutely. I think we share the same taste. Maybe not on everything, but aesthetically we both like the Old World, when things were made like they were supposed to [be made].

MKO: We came from that world.

EY: Exactly, exactly. And the rings that you're wearing could never be replicated for that. I love the value of antique jewelry. I get a lot of inspiration from antique pieces.

MKO: That's the core of this book: You're influenced by the Old World, the antiques. What else inspires you?

EY: I get a lot of inspiration from art nouveau, but not one person in particular. What I do love is the feminine and the—I know it sounds really weird—the bestiary (which is not bestiality) aspect of art nouveau. But it changes. In the past I was inspired by very clean, geometric shapes and very broad sweeping lines. Now I'm going more into organic things with animal textures and scarabs, mythological creatures—but that's just for my own stuff. Now for David Yurman I would tone it down just a bit.

MKO: In fashion you kind of have to change each season. For jewelry, do you have to keep a consistency?

EY: On the whole, jewelry does not need to sway with the seasons. That said, our jewelry has a quicker turnaround than most—that's what painted us into being a fashion jewelry company. We also drop our campaign at the same time other fashion houses do, and we follow the fashion seasons.

MKO: But in a way that's fun. [*Pauses*] Well, Evan, we might be done. . . .

EY: Wait, first you have to tell me about that ring.

MKO: It was a brooch that I found at Fred Leighton and turned into a ring. I thought it was so unique.

EY: It's a huge piece of garnet. Garnet doesn't usually come that big.

MKO: And the detailing on it is amazing.

EY: What are your other rings? Is that a new one?

MKO: No, this is a tiger I got for Christmas, but it's missing a little emerald as an eye. These are both David Webb.

EY: There's an antique jewelry show going on that I'm attending in Miami. Huge. It's the biggest one.

MKO: When?

EY: Like, Friday, Saturday, and Sunday. It's supposed to be massive. But the one to go to is the Palm Beach one. I can get you the dates.

MKO: Okay, then—let's go. I'm a sucker for a jewelry show.

CLOCKWISE FROM TOP LEFT: A young Evan with his father, David; a dog tag embellished with black diamonds that Evan designed; Evan with his mother, Sybil, and me; Evan with friends; horseback riding with his dad; a red coral bracelet; his parents; a Petrvs shield ring; with me at an event in LA; his favorite vintage picture of his mother; a chronograph watch; Evan Yurman: © JEFFREY PREHN 2008.

OPPOSITE: Natalia Vodianova in a Yurman campaign.

CONCLUSION

• • • • • • • • • • • • • • • •

Ralph Waldo Emerson once said, "It is not length of life, but depth of life." The past year of working on this book has been a fulfilling journey of being in the presence of admirable, passionate, and influential people—yet it is a relatively small chapter compared to all that has contributed to what I've endured in my twenty-two years. It's difficult to conclude any personal experience, and sum up this book in very few words, when every individual has a different perspective of life and what a definition of a well-lived life would be. But looking back at the numerous encounters and interviews on the previous pages, I can identify one concluding common thread: to encourage people to live life in the moment, which strikes a chord with Emerson's words.

Whether it be a tree in an open field, the color of one's childhood bedroom, the streets of New York City, a woman's physique, costumes of the theater, or an intriguing conversation—being present is imperative to not overlook the opportunities that lie in front of you and the inspiration that could potentially be the catalyst of a new adventure. John Galliano declared, "You only get a short life, so take chances." I'm aware that my most powerful memories are the moments I have fully embraced, whether they be a challenging obstacle or an achievement, a devastating moment or a celebration, laughter or tears. Without awareness, my life would lack depth and fulfillment. Young and perhaps naïve, what I do know, as this journey has come to an end, is that I still know nothing in perspective to the experiences and journeys life has to offer. This book is a testament to the endless opportunities and open doors that await.

—MARY-KATE OLSEN

"To be able to have
it all you have
to be able
to give back."
DVF

254

City Harvest

WHAT IT IS: Now serving New York City for twenty-five years, City Harvest is the world's first food rescue organization, dedicated to feeding the city's hungry. This year, City Harvest will collect twenty million pounds of excess food from all segments of the food industry, including restaurants, grocers, corporate cafeterias, manufacturers, and farms. This food is then delivered free of charge to more than 600 community food programs throughout New York City. Each week, City Harvest helps over 260,000 hungry New Yorkers find their next meal.

HOW TO HELP: Volunteer food, time, or money. Find out more at www.cityharvest.org.

The Scleroderma Research Foundation

WHAT IT IS: The Scleroderma Research Foundation is dedicated to finding a cure for scleroderma—a debilitating, chronic, and often deadly disease of the connective tissues—by financing cutting-edge scientific research into new methods of treatment and by drumming up public awareness of the disease. Over the past twenty years, the foundation has contributed over $23 million dollars to the cause.

HOW TO HELP: To make a donation, visit www.srfcure.org.

The Painted Turtle

WHAT IT IS: One of six in Paul Newman's family of Hole in the Wall Camps for seriously ill children, the Painted Turtle runs both summer-only and year-round camps for children with life-threatening diseases and their families, providing medical and emotional assistance and, of course, fun! Offering traditional recreational summer-camp activities—fishing, horseback riding, swimming—along with programs that encourage children to be self-reliant and self-confident, the Painted Turtle caters to the needs and desires of children who could not otherwise attend camp because of their medical needs and the financial constraints that accompany them.

HOW TO HELP: Volunteer as a Program Pal, a Family Pal, or a Cabin Counselor. Explore ways to give at www.thepaintedturtle.org.

The Kanye West Family Foundation

WHAT IT IS: Founded by Kanye West and his mother, Dr. Donda West, to combat the high dropout rate in high schools across America, the foundation's first initiative, called Loop Dreams, encourages students interested in hip-hop to learn more about its culture, history, and inception in order to help them develop creative and communicational skills.

HOW TO HELP: Visit www.kanyewestfoundation.org to make a donation.

The Nick Traina Foundation

WHAT IT IS: Founded in 1998 by author Danielle Steele after the loss of her son to manic depression, the organization aims to provide emotional and therapeutic assistance for the mentally ill and their family members; to prevent suicide, the second leading cause of death for people under the age of twenty-five; and to establish a network of support for people who are grieving the loss of friends or family members to mental illness or self-harm.

Vital Voices

WHAT IT IS: Vital Voices Global Partnership is an international agency devoted to empowering and educating emerging female leaders around the world, combating human trafficking and abuse against women and girls, providing support for female-owned businesses, and encouraging women to agitate for social change in their communities. With over 1,000 partners and a presence in 150 countries, the Vital Voices network is one of the most powerful agitators for women's rights in the world.

HOW TO HELP: Learn how to get involved at www.vitalvoices.org.

New Yorkers for Children

WHAT IT IS: Since its inception in 1996, New Yorkers for Children (NYFC) has made a difference in the lives of young people in foster care through college scholarships, tutoring programs, mentoring and networking opportunities. There are almost 17,000 children in foster care in New York City and NYFC is committed to providing these youth with the essential tools to help them become successful, self-sufficient adults.

HOW TO HELP: To learn more about New Yorkers for Children or to make a donation, please visit www.newyorkersforchildren.org.

Free Arts NYC

WHAT IT IS: The motto of Free Arts NYC—"Art Heals. Mentoring Works"—reveals the basic tenet of this volunteer-based nonprofit organization, which provides underserved children with arts instruction and mentoring support. The program mounts daylong art festivals, cultural field trips, weekly mentoring sessions, as well as communication workshops for the whole family.

HOW TO HELP: Visit www.freeartsnyc.org to donate or volunteer your time.

Darna

WHAT IT IS: Founded in 1995 as a response to the growing number of children living on the streets of Tangier, Darna (which means "our house") provides a network of safe, stable, temporary housing for women and children in need. Equipped with social workers, educators, and therapists, the houses encourage independence and self-direction by teaching street women and children about their civic rights and helping them reintegrate into Moroccan society.

HOW TO HELP: Visit www.darnamaroc.org to contribute.

Orangewood Children's Foundation's Guardian Scholars

WHAT IT IS: The Guardian Scholars Program is a partnership between Orangewood Children's Foundation and educational institutions that provides financial, job, housing, and academic assistance to youth exiting the foster care system and seeking a higher education at a college, university, or trade school. The program is currently represented on some twenty college campuses in Orange County, California, but interest in the initiative has spread throughout the state and nationwide.

HOW TO HELP: Make a donation, encourage your college or university to get involved, or mentor a youth. Learn more at www.guardianscholars.org.

Women's Campaign Forum

WHAT IT IS: WCF is an advocacy group dedicated to ensuring the growth and success of women in public life. WCF promotes the participation of women in the political sphere through a combination of educational programs and financial support.

HOW TO HELP: Volunteer your time, pledge to spread the word, or contribute financially to the cause, all on www.wcfonline.org.

AmFar

WHAT IT IS: Founded in 1985, AmFar is dedicated to fighting the global AIDS epidemic through its support of scientific and medical research. Since then the organization has donated over $260 million to over 2,000 medical research teams worldwide, helping to pioneer new breakthroughs in the treatment and prevention of the disease.

HOW TO HELP: Visit www.amfar.org for ways to lend your support.

The Prince's Trust

WHAT IT IS: The Prince's Trust is the UK's leading youth charity, committed to helping change young lives by providing support, training and mentoring to 14 to 30-year-olds, helping them to find work and discover their true potential, even when they can't see it themselves. Since the trust was set up in 1976 by HRH The Prince of Wales, it has helped more than 550,000 young people and helps hundreds more each day.

HOW TO HELP: Visit www.princes-trust.org.uk to donate or for more information.

Naked Heart Foundation:

WHAT IT IS: Founded by international fashion model Natalia Vodianova, the Naked Heart Foundation is dedicated to rejuvenating communities by providing clean, safe playgrounds for the estimated eight million Russian children living either on the street or below poverty level.

HOW TO HELP: Visit www.nakedheart.org to contribute.

VH1 Save the Music Foundation

WHAT IT IS: Since its foundation in 1997, VH1's Save the Music Foundation has raised over $40 million dollars to help restore instrumental musical education in public schools, and to raise awareness about the positive impact of musical education on childhood development.

HOW TO HELP: Visit www.vh1.com/partners/save_the_music to make a donation, help advocate, or plan a sponsorship event.

Surfrider Foundation

WHAT IT IS: The Surfrider Foundation is a nonprofit organization dedicated to protecting the quality and safety of the world's waterways and beaches, through conservation, activism, research, and education. Founded in 1984 by surfers in Malibu, the organization now has more than 50,000 members and eighty chapters worldwide.

HOW TO HELP: Visit www.surfrider.org for opportunities to speak out or take action, or to donate.

Second Harvest

WHAT IT IS: The largest hunger-relief organization in the United States, Second Harvest provides emergency food assistance to more than twenty-five million Americans every year through its expansive network of food banks and food rescue organizations.

HOW TO HELP: Find out how to donate time, food, or funds at www.secondharvest.org.

Crusaid

WHAT IT IS: Founded in 1986 in response to the growing AIDS epidemic, Crusaid originally worked to support hospital wards and subsidize the funeral expenses of AIDS victims. Twenty years later, Crusaid sponsors HIV-prevention and education efforts in the UK and Africa and supports continued cutting-edge research into new treatments for the disease. Crusaid also provides financial, social, and emotional support for people affected by HIV and AIDS.

HOW TO HELP: Sign up for an event, be a fund-raiser, or simply donate at www.crusaid.org.uk.

World Education

WHAT IT IS: Founded in 1951, World Education is dedicated to bettering the lives of disadvantaged and impoverished people around the world through literacy programs, HIV/AIDS education, community development, the expansion of health care resources, and small enterprise development. Since its inception it has worked in over sixty countries in all regions of the globe.

HOW TO HELP: Visit www.worlded.org to learn about career opportunities with the organization or to donate.

Art of Elysium

WHAT IT IS: Founded in 1997, the Art of Elysium is committed to a belief in the therapeutic effects of art education, providing free artistic workshops—in painting, theater, radio, comedy, songwriting, and creative writing—to children battling serious medical conditions. Widely supported by the celebrity community, the organization depends on established artists to run its various programs and to encourage artistic expression among its participants.

HOW TO HELP: Visit www.theartofelysium.org to donate.

 Ovarian Cancer Research Fund

The Ovarian Cancer Research Fund

WHAT IT IS: Founded in 1994, OCRF is committed to advancing research, generating awareness, and ultimately finding a cure for ovarian cancer. Since 1998 the organization has provided over $18 million in grants to some of the most promising cancer researchers in the nation.

HOW TO HELP: Visit www.ocrf.org to donate or commemorate loved ones who have succumbed to the disease. You can also shop a variety of products, a portion of whose proceeds will go to supporting the cause.

maggie's
cancer caring centres

Maggie's Cancer Caring Centers

WHAT IT IS: Maggie's Centers are part of an ever-growing network in Scotland, Wales, and the UK designed to provide emotional, social, and psychological support to anyone whose life has been touched by cancer, including cancer patients and their families, friends, and care-givers.

HOW TO HELP: Visit www.maggiescentres.org to attend a fund-raising event or to donate online.

NRDC
THE EARTH'S BEST DEFENSE

Natural Resources Defense Council

WHAT IT IS: One of the earth's most effective environmental protection agencies, NRDC uses law, science, and its expansive network of member support (over 1.2 million members and online activists!) to ensure the safety of the earth's living populations and the protection of its wildlife.

HOW TO HELP: Visit www.nrdc.org to take action and speak out.

MUSICARES®

MusiCares

WHAT IT IS: Established in 1989 by the Recording Academy, MusiCares is dedicated to a variety of programs designed to provide financial, psychological, and medical support to needy or troubled members of the music community, including addiction recovery services and financial assistance for struggling musicians.

HOW TO HELP: Visit www.grammy.com/MusiCares/Donate to make a donation.

OrphanAid Africa

WHAT IT IS: OrphanAid was founded in 2002 as a response to the abject poverty and multiple medical epidemics that each year cause thousands of African children to be orphaned. Originally dedicated to improving the medical, social, and educational conditions within African orphanages, the nonprofit has shifted its focus to finding families and helping orphaned and vulnerable children avoid institutional care.

HOW TO HELP: Donate or learn about volunteering opportunities at www.oafrica.org.

Protecting the World's Oceans

Oceana

WHAT IT IS: The largest marine protection advocacy group in the world, Oceana is dedicated to promoting the health of the world's oceans. With offices operating around the world and a global team that includes scientists, lawyers, and economists, the organization advocates for specific policy change that will reduce pollution and help bolster depleted marine life populations.

HOW TO HELP: Advocate for change or donate at www.oceana.org.

DISCONTINUED
2008

RIP

PETER BEARD
2/29/08

ALEXANDRE DE BETAK
3/1/08

2/3/08 Bob C.

BOB COLACELLO
2/3/08

DAVID COLLINS
3/2/08

frauület 2/15/8

GEORGE CONDO
10/29/07

FRANCISCO COSTA
2/15/08

Diane von Furstenberg

DIANE VON FURSTENBERG
4/17/08

JOHN GALLIANO
3/5/08

LAZARO HERNANDEZ & JACK MCCOLLOUGH
2/3/08

LAUREN HUTTON
11/2/07

KARL LAGERFELD
2/28/08

PETER LINDBERGH
3/11/08

CHRISTIAN LOUBOUTIN
2/7/08

January 25th 2008

MARGHERITA MISSONI
1/25/08

3/28/08

ROBERT LEE MORRIS
3/28/08

JACK PIERSON
10/29/07

RICHARD PRINCE
3/25/08

TERRY RICHARSON
1/29/08

GIAMBATTISTA VALLI
3/4/08

EVAN YURMAN
1/30/08

SPECIAL THANKS

Derek Blasberg
Editor

Rodrigo Corral
Art Director

Laura Schechter
Assistant Editor
Razorbill/Penguin

Ben Schrank
Publisher
Razorbill/Penguin

Jill Collage

Executive Vice President
Dualstar

Alex Hawgood

Contributing Editor

Kristen Walsh

Production Coordinator
Dualstar

Ben Wiseman

Designer

ACKNOWLEDGMENTS

Rankin, Daniela Jung, Dale Araten, Justo Artigas,
Courtney Applebaum, Nejma Beard, Betsy Biscone,
Sandrine Bizzaro, Christopher Bollen,
Heather Prizer, Jen Brill, Alisa Connan, Nicole Caruso,
Cassie Coane, Bill Collage, Matthew Compitello,
Shirley Cook, William Durney, Theresa Evangelista,
Robyn V. Fernandes, Lauren Flynn, Phoebe Gubelmann,
Linda Hay, Alexandra Taylor James Hamile, Rhalee Hughes,
Maggie Kayne, Lynette Layman, Carlos Lopez,
Magnolia Flowers, David Maloney, Lyle Maltz, Kevin Marks,
Tori Matt, Rebecca McCabe, Pamela McElroy,
Patrick McMullan, Kyle Miller, Tracy Morford,
Kristina Musailov, William Norwich, Mary-Clancey Page,
Kristen Pettit, Laina Reeves, Diane Reichenberger,
Elizabeth Richards, Alexis Roche, Mike Rosenthal,
Paul Rusconi, Elizabeth Saltzman Walker, Matthew Sandager,
Micah Schifman, Heidi Schuster, Hayden Slater,
Emese Szenasy, Clementine Tarnaud, Debra Trebitz,
Dean Walker, Nancy Walsh, Rachael Wang, Doug Whiteman,
David Wienir, Lianna Wingfield, and Annett Wolf.

Index

Abellán, Miguel, 78
airbrushing, 124
AmFar, 256
Anderson, Wes, 22
Arnold, Peter, 88
Art of Elysium, 257
art world, 34–35
Avedon, Dick, 99

Bacon, Francis, 16
Basquiat, 41
Beard, Peter, 14–19
Beard, Zara, 16
beauty, differing views of, 154
Beene, Geoffrey, 152
Berkeley Hotel, London, 47
bling jewelry, 154
Burton, Tim, 22

Calder, Alexander, 152, 154
Calvin Klein, 207
Calvin Klein Collection, 61, 66–67
Campbell, Naomi, 81
celebrity, 40, 230
Chalayan, Hussein, 25
Chanel, 107
chic, 240
Christian Dior, 84–85
City Harvest, 255
Colacello, Bob, 19, 30–41, 62, 73
collages, of Richard Prince, 210
Collins, David, 42–49
color, 46–47
compromise, 155, 229, 232
Condo, George, 13, 50–59
consistency in art, 152
Cook, Shirley, 88, 91
Cooper, Alice, 200
Costa, Francisco, 60–67
couture, 35, 84–85
creativity
    basics of, 66
    Bob Colacello's view of, 36
    inspiration for, 154
    as inspiration for more creativity, 134
    as natural sensation, 154
    original thinking in, 129
    spontaneity in, 230
culture
    fashion's place in, 84–85
    getting caught up in, 40
    popular, 35

Darna, 256
de Betak, Alex, 20–29
de la Renta, Oscar, 87, 94
Deutsch, Harry, 19
diet, 108
digital photography, 124, 229
Dior couture shows, 25
Doo.Ri, 152
Downey, Robert, Jr., 228
Duncan, Isadora, 108

Emerson, Ralph Waldo, 253
Emin, Tracey, 240
entertaining at home, 40–41
environmental issues, 26
Evangelista, Linda, 81

The Factory, 31, 32, 34, 52
fashion, 67
    art and, 34–35, 148
    couture, 35, 84–85
    cultural impact of, 84–85
    leaders in, 94
    personal style, 81
    style vs., 104
fashion design
    Francisco Costa, 60–67
    John Galliano, 76–85
    Hernandez and McCollough, 86–95
    Karl Lagerfeld, 106–119
    Giambattista Valli, 234–243
    Diane von Furstenberg, 68–75
fashion industry

changes in, 73–74
glamour of, 35
Margherita Missoni, 142–149
support for younger designers in, 94–95
fashion photography
    Peter Beard, 16
    Peter Lindbergh, 120–131
fashion shows
    of Louis Vuitton, 215
    producer Alexandre de Betak, 20–29
    theatrical aspects of, 78
fashion week, 144, 147
filmmaking, by Peter Lindbergh, 129
Forbes, Malcolm, 41
Foster, Jodie, 35
Free Arts NYC, 255

Galliano, John, 25, 76–85, 253
Garner, George, 154
Gilhart, Julie, 88
giving back, 73, 74, 254–257
Glamourcon, 215
Gone with the Wind, 46
Gunn, Tim, 88

Hadid, Zaha, 118
Hearn, Pat, 200
Hernandez, Lazaro, 86–95
Hilton, Paris, 41
Hopper, Dennis, 147
Huston, Anjelica, 222
Hutton, Lauren, 13, 96–105, 108

independence, 70
    and integrity, 94
    money vs., 138
inspiration, 154
    for Peter Beard, 16
    for David Collins, 46–48
    for George Condo, 52
    for Alexandre de Betak, 25
    for John Galliano, 78
    for Hernandez and McCollough, 91, 94
    for Karl Lagerfeld, 108
    for Peter Lindbergh, 129
    for Robert Lee Morris, 154
    for Jack Pierson, 200
    for Richard Prince, 210
    for Terry Richardson, 228
    for Giambattista Valli, 236
    for Diane von Furstenberg, 70
    for Evan Yurman, 250
interior architecture, of David Collins, 42–49
Interview magazine, 32, 34–36
intimacy, gender differences in, 100, 104

Jacobs, Marc, 209, 215
jewelry, 117–118
    of Margherita Missoni, 147
    of Robert Lee Morris, 150–157
    Evan Yurman, 244–251
Johns, Jasper, 34

The Kanye West Family Foundation, 255
Kent, Tony, 222
Klein, Calvin, 66
knives, 246, 250

Lagerfeld, Karl, 106–119, 129, 154
leaders in fashion, 94
Lebowitz, Fran, 41
life, well-lived, 253
Lindbergh, Peter, 120–131, 203, 245
Lindner, Richard, 16
Lomax, Jackie, 222
Louboutin, Christian, 13, 132–141
Louis Vuitton fashion show, 215

magazines
    airbrushing used in, 124
    Bob Colacello's work in, 30–41
    vintage reproductions of campaigns, 209
Maggie's Cancer Caring Centers, 257
Makos, Christopher, 34
Mankes, Suzy, 236
Mapplethorpe, Robert, 34
Marni, 240

McCartney, Stella, 16, 19
McCollough, Jack, 86–95
media industry. See also magazines
    and celebrity, 40
    changes in, 35–37
    paparazzi, 36, 40
    selling pictures/information to, 41
Missoni (company), 144
Missoni, Angela, 145
Missoni, Margherita, 142–149
Missoni, Rossita, 145
models
    castings for, 116
    Lauren Hutton, 96–105
Moreau, Jeanne, 124, 129
Morris, Robert Lee, 150–157
Morrisroe, Mark, 207
Morrissey, Paul, 32
Moss, Kate, 81, 129
MusiCares, 257

Nakata, Hide, 240
Naked Heart Foundation, 256
Natural Resources Defense Council, 257
New Yorkers for Children, 255
The Nick Traina Foundation, 255

Oceana, 256
Olsen, Ashley, 13, 158–177
    Peter Beard interview, 15–16, 19
    Bob Colacello interview, 31–32, 34–36, 40–41
    George Condo interview, 51–52, 57
    Francisco Costa interview, 61–62, 66–67
    John Galliano interview, 77–78, 81, 84–85
    Lauren Hutton interview, 97, 99–100, 104
    Karl Lagerfeld interview, 107–108, 116, 118
    Peter Lindbergh interview, 121, 124, 129
    Christian Louboutin interview, 133–134, 138
    on Mary-Kate, 179
    Robert Lee Morris interview, 151–152, 154–155
    Jack Pierson interview, 199–200, 203, 207
    Terry Richardson interview, 221–222, 225, 228–229, 232
    Diane von Furstenberg interview, 69–70, 73–74
Olsen, Mary-Kate, 178–197
    on Ashley, 159
    Bob Colacello interview, 31–32, 34–36, 40–41
    David Collins interview, 43, 46–48
    George Condo interview, 51–52, 57
    Alexandre de Betak interview, 21–22, 25–26
    John Galliano interview, 77–78, 81, 84–85
    Hernandez and McCollough interview, 87–88, 91, 94–95
    Lauren Hutton interview, 97, 99–100, 104
    Karl Lagerfeld interview, 107–108, 116, 118
    Margherita Missoni interview, 143–144, 147–148
    Jack Pierson interview, 199–200, 203, 207
    Richard Prince interview, 209–210, 215, 218
    Terry Richardson interview, 221–222, 225, 228–229, 232
    Giambattista Valli interview, 235–236, 240
    Diane von Furstenberg interview, 69–70, 73–74
    Evan Yurman interview, 245–246, 250
Oppenheim, Meret, 236
Orangewood Children's Foundation, 256
OrphanAid Africa, 255
The Ovarian Cancer Research Fund, 257

The Painted Turtle, 255
painting

George Condo, 50–59
    Jack Pierson, 198–207
    Richard Prince, 208–219
paparazzi, 36, 40, 118
personal style, 81
photography. See also fashion photography
    airbrushing, 124
    Peter Beard, 14–19
    digital, 124, 229
    Peter Lindbergh, 120–131
    Jack Pierson, 198–207
    Terry Richardson, 220–233
Picasso, Pablo, 129, 154
Pierson, Jack, 198–207
popular culture, 35
pottery, 207
Prada, Miuccia, 48, 240
Prince, Richard, 200, 208–219
The Prince's Trust, 256
Pugh, Gareth, 240

relationship, with yourself, 70
Richardson, Bob, 221, 222, 225
Richardson, Terry, 220–233
The Row, 154

Saint Laurent, Yves, 236, 240
Sarris, Andrew, 32
The Scleroderma Research Foundation, 255
sculpture
    George Condo, 57
    Jack Pierson, 198–207
Second Harvest, 257
Seidner, David, 34
sensationalism, 36
Shepard, Eugenia, 104
shoe design, by Christian Louboutin, 132–141
silhouette, 236, 240
Sprouse, Stephen, 215
storytelling, 129
Strassberg, Anna, 147
Studio 54, 40
style
    fashion vs., 104
    personal, 81
supermodel phenomenon, 121
Surfrider Foundation, 256

technology, 46
Tyrrell, Susan, 52

Vaernis, Alain, 207
Vallette, Amber, 129
Valli, Giambattista, 234–243
Vanity Fair, 218
VHI Save the Music Foundation, 256
vision, 154
Vital Voices Global Partnership, 255
Vivier, Roger, 134
von Furstenberg, Diane, 13, 68–75, 254
von Furstenberg, Egon, 70
Vreeland, Diana, 16, 36, 40, 99

Warhol, Andy, 32, 34–36, 40–41, 62, 73, 200
Weber, Bruce, 34
W magazine, 218
women
    as separate race, 104
    chic, 240
    empowering, 73
    relationships with men, 100, 104
Women's Campaign Forum, 256
Woodlawn, Holly, 32, 34
work
    attitudes toward, 62, 66
    giving back, 73
    pleasure of, 138
    value of, 41
World Education, 257

Yurman, David, 245
Yurman, Evan, 244–251
Yurman, Sybil, 245

Zara's Tales: Perilous Escapades in Equatorial Africa (Peter Beard), 16–18

Corral Design/Tracy Morford. 142: Photograph by Claudia Smith © Missoni. 143: Photograph by Oliviero Toscani © Missoni. 144: *Arianna* magazine, © Missoni—photograph © Missoni. 145: Photograph by Kim Andreolli, © Missoni. 146: Photograph © Mert Alas & Marcus Piggott. 148: Photograph © Missoni. 149: *Grazia* cover 1968, ph. Patrick Rouchon, © Missoni. 150: Photograph © Robert Lee Morris. 151: Sculpture by George Garner, photograph © Ashley Olsen. 153: "Kansai Duo" © Robert Lee Morris. 155: Photographs © Robert Lee Morris. 156: "Canoli Belt" © Robert Lee Morris. 157: "Desert Drums" © Robert Lee Morris. 158: Photograph © Rankin. 160–161: Photograph © Rankin, mask designed by Daniela Jung. 162: Photograph © Rankin, styling by Daniela Jung, kaftan by Michael Angel. 163: Photograph © Rodrigo Corral Design/Tracy Morford. 164–165: Photographs © Rankin, styling by Daniela Jung, blouse by Clu, hat by Stephen Jones for Giambattista Valli. 166: Photograph © Rodrigo Corral Design/Tracy Morford. 167: Photograph © Rankin, styling by Daniela Jung, dress by Sophia Kokosalaki, cuff bracelet by Chanel, lace-up heels by Guiseppe Zanotti, victorian capelet and belt courtesy of stylist. 168: Photograph © Rodrigo; Polaroid © Dualstar. 169: Photograph © Rankin, styling by Daniela Jung, jacket by Proenza Schouler, striped skirt by Jean Paul Gaultier. 170: (Clockwise from top left) all Polaroids © Dualstar; magazines, photography © Rodrigo Corral Design/Tracy Morford; Ashley, Patrick McMullan; scrapbooks © Dualstar, photography © Rodrigo Corral Design/Tracy Morford. 171: (Clockwise from top left) Polaroid © Dualstar; luggage, watches and bag, photography © Rodrigo Corral Design/Tracy Morford—*Tete et Profil*, Pablo Picasso, © 2008 Estate of Pablo Picasso/Artists Rights Society (ARS), New York; magazines, photography © Rodrigo Corral Design/Tracy Morford; jeans, photography © Rodrigo Corral Design/Tracy Morford; Ashley Olsen, Orlando Bloom, Snoop Dogg, and Johnny Depp, photograph © Frank Micelotta/Fox/Getty Images. 172–173: photograph © Dualstar. 174: Polaroid of Eddie Vedder and note, provided by Dualstar, photography © Rodrigo Corral Design/Tracy Morford; Ashley Olsen's apartment, photograph © Matthew Sandager—*Garden State* album cover, postcard and notes, provided by Dualstar, photography © Rodrigo Corral Design/Tracy Morford. 175: All photographs © Dualstar; all supplemental materials provided by Dualstar, photography © Rodrigo Corral Design/Tracy Morford. 176–177: Photography © Rodrigo Corral Design/Tracy Morford. 178: Photograph © Rankin. 180–181: Photograph © Rankin, styling by Daniela Jung, dress by John Galliano, necklace worn as headpiece by Erickson Beamon, vintage boots courtesy of Daniela Jung. 182–183: Photograph © Rankin, styling by Daniela Jung, lace corset and skirt by Chanel. 184: Photograph © Rodrigo Corral Design/Tracy Morford. 185: Photograph © Rankin, styling by Daniela Jung, feather and chain maille jacket by Balmain. 186: Photograph © Rodrigo Corral Design/Tracy Morford. 187: Photographs © Rankin, styling by Daniela Jung, blouse by Sophia Kokosalaki, sequin shorts by Chanel. 188: Photograph © Rankin, styling by Daniela Jung, glasses by Moss Lipow. 189: Photograph © Rankin, styling by Daniela Jung, headpiece by Moss Lipow. 190–191: Photograph © Rankin, styling by Daniela Jung, kimono by Jean-Paul Gaultier, metal and crystal suspenders by Erickson Beamon. 192: (Clockwise from top left) all photographs © Dualstar except Mary-Kate's bedroom, © Mike Rosenthal Photography; Mary-Kate's bubble-chair, © Mike Rosenthal Photography—Mary-Kate in white dress, © Patrick McMullan; ashtray, DVDs, clothes and books provided by Dualstar, photography © Rodrigo Corral Design/Tracy Morford. 193: All photographs © Dualstar; all supplemental materials provided by Dualstar, photography © Rodrigo Corral Design/Tracy Morford. 194: Andy Warhol, *Self-Portrait in Drag*, © 2008 Andy Warhol Foundation for the Visual Arts/ARS, New York. 195: Andy Warhol, *Truman Capote*, © 2008 Andy Warhol Foundation for the Visual Arts/ARS, New York. 196: Mary-Kate's vintage sunglasses, photograph © Rodrigo Corral Design/Tracy Morford. 197: (Clockwise from top left) Polaroid © Dualstar; Mary-Kate in black, Patrick McMullan; all photographs © Dualstar except for Mary-Kate and Richard Prince, © Derek Blasberg; all supplemental materials provided by Dualstar, photography © Rodrigo Corral Design/Tracy Morford. 198: *In Every Dreamhome A Heartache*, 1991 © Jack Pierson, courtesy Cheim Read Gallery, New York. 199: *On the Beach (Self-Portrait)*, © Jack Pierson, courtesy Cheim Read Gallery, New York. 201: *Silver Jackie with Pink Spotlight*, 1991 © Jack Pierson, Walker Arts Center, Minneapolis, photo by Tom Warren, courtesy Jack Pierson Studio, New York. 202: *Heaven*, 1991 © Jack Pierson, collection of Bill Block, Los Angeles, courtesy of Jack Pierson Studio, New York. 203: *Elvis*, 2008 © Jack Pierson, courtesy Cheim Read Gallery, New York. 204–205: *Stay*, 1991 © Jack Pierson, courtesy Cheim Read Gallery, New York. 206: *Pink Badlands*, 1992 © Jack Pierson, courtesy Cheim Read Gallery, New York. 208: Richard Prince, photograph © www.sebastianpiras.com. 209: Photograph © Derek Blasberg. 211: *Bitches and Bastards*, 1985–1986 © Richard Prince. 212–213: *Untitled (Living Rooms)*, 1977 © Richard Prince. 214: *Untitled (Kool-Aid)*, 1983 © Richard Prince. 216: *Untitled (Upstate)*, 1995–1999 © Richard Prince. 217: *Untitled (Upstate)*, 1995–1999 © Richard Prince. 218: (From top) Mary-Kate Olsen in front of *Las Vegas Nurse*, 2008 © Richard Prince, photograph by Derek Blasberg—all photography © Derek Blasberg. 219: *Danger Nurse at Work*, 2002 © Richard Prince. 220: Kate Moss 1996 © Terry Richardson. 223: Batman and Robin 1996 © Terry Richardson. 224: Bob Richardson 2003 © Terry Richardson. 226–227: Mary-Kate Olsen and Ashley Olsen 2008 © Terry Richardson. 229: Metalkids 1996 © Terry Richardson. 230: Ashley Olsen 2008 © Terry Richardson. 231: Mary-Kate Olsen 2008 © Terry Richardson. 233: Clown 1998 © Terry Richardson. 234: Giambattista Valli, photograph © Kate Barry. 235: Luigi Scialanga necklace for Giambattista Valli, photograph © Rodrigo Corral Design/Tracy Morford. 237: Dresses by Giambattista Valli, photography © Rodrigo Corral Design/Tracy Morford. 238: *Nostalgia*/Nostalgia/Getty Images. 239: Chris Moore/Catwalking/Getty Images. 240: Shoes by Giambattista Valli, photography © Rodrigo Corral Design/Tracy Morford. 241: Shoe by Giambattista Valli, photograph © Rodrigo Corral Design/Tracy Morford—David Bowie album cover, *Aladdin Sane* cover image courtesy of RZO Music, Inc. 242: Mary-Kate, Patrick McMullan; "Mary-Kate" sketch by Giambattista Valli. 243: "Ashley" sketch by Giambattista Valli; Ashley, Patrick McMullan. 244–245: Kate Moss, photograph © Peter Lindbergh, "David Yurman Lifestyle". 246: Knives by Evan Yurman, photograph © Rodrigo Corral Design/Tracy Morford. 248: Chevron Cuff Bracelet © David Yurman, photograph © Rodrigo Corral. 249: All jewelry © David Yurman, all photography © Rodrigo Corral Design/Tracy Morford. 250: Natalia Vadianova, photograph © Peter Lindbergh, "David Yurman Lifestyle". 251: (Clockwise from top left) Yurman Family Photo Archives; dog tag necklace by David Yurman, photograph © Rodrigo Corral Studio; Mary-Kate Olsen, Evan Yurman and Sybil Yurman, photograph © Derek Blasberg—photograph © Yurman Family Photo Archives—photograph © Yurman Family Archives—red coral bracelet by David Yurman, photography © Rodrigo Corral—Evan Yurman and Mary-Kate, Alexandra Wyman/Wire Image/Getty Images—Petrvs Shield Ring, David Yurman, photograph © Rodrigo Corral Design/Tracy Morford; Sybil Yurman, Yurman Family Photo Archives—Chronograph watch by David Yurman, photograph © Rodrigo Corral Design/Tracy Morford; Evan Yurman, © Jeffrey Prehn 2008 (center). 252: Photograph © Rankin, dress by Chanel, vintage fur shrug by Christian Dior, earrings by Erickson Beamon. 258: Photograph © Rodrigo Corral Design/Tracy Morford. 259: (Clockwise from top left) Peter Beard, photograph © Dualstar; Alex de Betak, photograph © Christophe Rihet—David Collins, photograph © Dualstar; Bob Colacello, photograph © Dualstar. 260–261: All photographs © Dualstar *except* John Galliano, photograph © Eric Ryan/Contributor/Getty. 262–263: All photographs © Dualstar. 264–265: All photographs © Dualstar. 266: Mary-Kate and Ashley Olsen 2008, photograph © Terry Richardson. Special thanks to Debra Trebitz for her photo research.

January 25th 2008

March 17 '08

Terry Richardson
1-29-08